From the Army to College

From the Army to College

Transitioning from the Service to Higher Education

Jillian Ventrone and Paul Karczewski

ROWMAN & LITTLEFIELD
Lanham • Boulder • New York • London

Published by Rowman & Littlefield
A wholly owned subsidiary of The Rowman & Littlefield Publishing Group, Inc.
4501 Forbes Boulevard, Suite 200, Lanham, Maryland 20706
www.rowman.com

Unit A, Whitacre Mews, 26-34 Stannary Street, London SE11 4AB

British Library Cataloguing in Publication Information Available

Library of Congress Cataloging-in-Publication Data

Ventrone, Jillian.
From the army to college: transitioning from the service to higher education / Jillian Ventrone and Paul Karczewski.
pages cm.
Includes bibliographical references and index.
ISBN 978-1-4422-4806-9 (cloth : alk. paper) -- ISBN 978-1-4422-4807-6 (electronic)
1. Veterans--Education, Higher--United States--Handbooks, manuials, etc. 2. College students--Services for--United States--Handbooks, manuals, etc. I. Karczewski, Paul, 1981- . II. Title.
UB357.V342 2015
378.1'9826970973--dc23
2015011842

Printed in the United States of America

Contents

Preface

Today's soldiers are highly motivated to serve, but face numerous challenges, especially considering the sacrifices they have made over the past decade of war. As the service branches face budget cuts and drawdowns, soldiers need to be aware of the resources and options available to help make them more competitive for promotion or more credible for potential civilian-sector employers. *From the Army to College: Transitioning from the Service to Higher Education* fulfills this need by serving as a long-term reference manual that will support soldiers throughout their higher education or vocational pursuits and assist with navigating the available funding resources. Aspiring civilians looking to join the Army, soldiers already on active duty, or those transitioning into the civilian sector will gain invaluable information to help them properly prepare, plan, and perform the tasks necessary for a successful transition into the world of education. If a soldier's goal is to expand his or her credentials through education or training, this book is the definitive field manual.

Introduction

The Army offers its soldiers many different opportunities for self-betterment, such as skills training, service to country, travel, active-duty educational benefits, and a solid career path. In this era of soaring higher education costs, many soldiers also join for the chance to earn the Post-9/11 GI Bill, an amazing benefit that helps students attain a quality education upon separation from the service without burdening themselves with debt.

From the Army to College: Transitioning from the Service to Higher Education is designed as a guide for soldiers who are preparing for their educational journeys. Soldiers have many education and career possibilities available to them because of their service, but they are often hard to find and navigate correctly. This book simplifies this process by disseminating necessary information and teaching readers how to pursue credible educational or career training while maximizing all available resources.

As the service branches face budget cuts and drawdowns, active-duty personnel are looking for ways to be more competitive for promotion or officer selections and more credible for potential civilian-sector employers. This book works as a long-term reference guide, assisting soldiers in creating educational and career-based goals and supporting them through their pursuit of success.

As academic counselors aboard federal installations, we have helped thousands of service members develop successful educational plans to achieve their goals. In this book we pass on what we have learned, equipping readers with the information they need to create a successful plan of attack and feel more confident about their decisions regarding their educational journeys.

Some of the information in this book is reprinted from the Marine Corps version, *From the Marine Corps to College: Transitioning from the Service to Higher Education*. Much of the information is applicable to service members from each of the different branches.

Chapter One

Get Going on Your Education

Higher education is a foreign environment for most service members, and getting started is the hardest part. Soldiers often put off school because they have received mixed advice, are confused by the process, or are nervous that they might make a mistake. This chapter helps soldiers prepare properly to take their first step with confidence.

GET STARTED

Getting started on higher education is usually the most difficult step a service member will take. Once that initial hurdle is overcome, the rest will begin to fall into place. That is not to say that it will be smooth sailing. But the fear factor will have dissipated, and you will learn to understand the rhythm of your classes. If you follow the directions outlined in this chapter and reference this book along the way, your trip down the higher education road should be much less stressful.

Returning to school after being in the military can seem like a daunting experience, but it will be worth your while. Many service members entered the military because they did not feel that college was the appropriate pathway for them. After serving in the Army for several years, achieving a college degree becomes an attainable goal. With the proper support, soldiers who were successful in the Army will be able to conquer an academic or vocational training objective. The skills acquired in the Army, along with the information offered in this book, can assist you in building and managing a plan of attack.

If you are still on active duty, Army Education Centers are available on most bases to assist in your decision-making process. After reading through this book, make an appointment with an academic counselor at the base where you are stationed. He or she will help guide you through the process of getting started. The counselor can also act as your guide along your educational pathway. If you ever feel that you are not progressing properly, the counselor should be your first go-to individual.

If still on active duty, there is a specific pathway to be eligible for Tuition Assistance (TA). The section on TA in chapter 6, Cost and Payment Resources, thoroughly covers the steps to receive funding through this program. If you are preparing to transition off active-duty service, make an appointment with a counselor to receive assistance in understanding your GI Bill benefits and how you can activate the benefit process. The counselors can also help you prepare for your new mission: higher education.

If you are a veteran and located close to a military base (any branch), contact the base education center for assistance. If you are not located near a military base, call the veterans' representative at the school you are thinking about attending. He or she should be your initial point-of-contact for everything at the school. These individuals are often veteran students at the school and have already been there and done that, so they know how to get you started along the proper pathway.

The following checklist will help you structure an educational plan. Take the time to write down your answers and review the information.

1. What do you want to be when you grow up? (This is still a difficult question for many of the career service members whom I counsel.)
2. What type of school should you attend—traditional or vocational?
3. Do you need a two-year or a four-year institution?
4. Have you picked a school already?
5. What are the institution's application requirements?
6. Have you collected your required documents?
7. Have you applied to the institution?
8. How will you pay for your schooling?

Let's sort through the list to help you start making decisions.

WHAT DO YOU WANT TO BE WHEN YOU GROW UP?

If you know which career you would like to pursue, you are already a few steps ahead. If not, try a self-discovery site such as CareerScope (http://benefits.va.gov/gibill/careerscope.asp), Kuder Journey (http://www.dantes.kuder.com/), or O*NET OnLine (http://www.onetonline.org/). The sites are free and might help narrow down possible career fields to fit your personality type, especially Kuder Journey, which offers three personality-based assessment tests and offers recommendations based upon the results. Researching different career possibilities including income levels, job openings, and required education levels usually helps soldiers begin to develop interest in a specific pathway. More information on these sites can be found in chapter 3.

If you have no idea which career pathway to take, starting at the local community college is often the best bet. Attending a community college may help you test the waters. Declare for an associate degree in general studies and use the elective credits to try different subjects. Elective credits are built into degree plans and offer you freedom to pursue topics outside your declared major. Many community colleges offer vocational classes; if you think that might be a viable pathway, you can add some of these classes as well. Academic counselors at community colleges can also help with career exploration.

Check out Army Credentialing Opportunities On-Line (COOL) (see chapter 3) if you are interested in reviewing civilian sector careers similar to your Military Occupational Specialty (MOS). Army COOL lets you track a pathway from your MOS to career selection and includes all relevant credentialing information, such as the type of credential, renewal information, potential apprenticeship possibilities, and costs. Sometimes researching MOS-related pathways in the civilian sector can help you develop ideas about potential career pathways. I have worked with service members in the past who used the COOL sites for research and found careers of interest that they had previously not been aware existed.

WHAT TYPE OF SCHOOL SHOULD YOU ATTEND: TRADITIONAL OR VOCATIONAL?

If you have chosen a specific career, you also need to decide upon the type of school necessary to achieve the appropriate degree or certification. Traditional majors such as criminal justice, engineering, or business will require a traditional degree path at a regionally accredited institution of higher learning. Traditional educational pathways typically require classroom-based learning. Online learning for traditional degrees is becoming more commonplace; however, strictly online learning while on the Post-9/11 GI Bill will result in a reduction of your housing stipend. The online-only housing stipend rate under the Post-9/11 GI Bill was $754.50 (http://www.benefits.va.gov/GIBILL/resources/benefits_resources/rates/ch33/ch33rates080114.asp#MHA) for the academic year 2014–2015. The difference between this amount and the full housing stipend will vary depending upon the location of the school. Veterans must take at least one class every semester through the face-to-face format in order to receive the full housing stipend under Post-9/11.

Vocational education might require a nationally accredited vocational school. Vocational training is more hands-on in nature and involves a more streamlined curriculum. Vocational pathways focus on the subject you choose to study and do not usually require a full round of general education classes.

The different types of schools you can select for your educational pursuits are discussed in chapter 4 of this book. Always check at your local community college to see if it offers the vocational education you are interested in pursuing. Often community colleges have apprenticeship or on-the-job training programs attached to their vocational training options. State community colleges hold regional accreditation, which enables students in many of the vocational programs to still be earning transferable college credit.

DO YOU NEED A TWO-YEAR OR FOUR-YEAR INSTITUTION?

Does your educational pathway require a two-year or four-year degree? If in doubt, check O*NET OnLine, or contact the schools in the area to inquire about the level of degree offered for that particular field of study. O*Net demonstrates the different educational levels along with corresponding wages nationally or for a selected state.

Most vocational pathways require either a one- or two-year certification, and often an associate degree is required. Typically, a two-year school is sufficient. Check the offerings at your local community college. Community colleges are in tune with the needs of the local community; if the local population has a great demand for welders, the school will most likely offer a welding pathway.

Most traditional career fields (think white-collar work) require a four-year bachelor's degree or a graduate-level degree. Often a quick search of the educational requirements on a job announcement will give you a good idea of the academic demands of that particular field. For example, if you are interested in becoming a computer engineer, job announcements might stipulate a bachelor's or master's degree in computer science or electrical engineering. Now you know what your minimum educational requirements will be if you decide to pursue a career in that field.

HAVE YOU PICKED A SCHOOL ALREADY?

If you have a school (or schools) that you are interested in attending, check to see that it is accredited and offers the degree you would like to attain. If so, the first phone call you make should be to the veterans' representatives. They should be able to answer all of your questions. If not, they will direct you to the appropriate individuals. Accreditation, which is covered in chapter 4, can be extremely important for career viability and should be given top priority in your school selection.

Here are a few questions to ask the veterans' representatives:

- What are the admissions requirements? Are they flexible for veterans? Do you need to take the SAT or ACT? What are the admissions deadlines?
- Will the school accept military transcripts (Joint Services Transcript)?
- Is the institution a member of Servicemembers Opportunity Colleges?
- Which GI Bill is best for the school: Montgomery GI Bill (MGIB) or Post-9/11?
- Will you have to pay out of pocket for tuition or fees above the amount the GI Bill will cover?
- Does the school approximate how much money books will cost yearly?
- Where are veterans buying their books? Through the bookstore or online? Is there a book exchange or rental program for veterans on campus?
- What veteran services are offered at the institution or nearby?
- How far away is the closest Veterans Administration center (http://www.va.gov)?
- How many veterans attend the school?
- Does the institution have a student veterans' organization?
- How can you find other veterans who need roommates (if applicable)?
- Does the school have a veterans' center, and what resources are available in the center?
- What helpful hints can they offer pertaining to your attendance at the school?

If you are trying to decide between two schools, hopefully the answers to these questions will offer more guidance.

If you do not know where to go to school, read on for more advice. College Navigator, which is discussed in chapter 3, can be incredibly helpful for conducting school searches. Remember: When in doubt, the local community college is a safe bet, and getting started should be the goal.

If you narrow your search to a few schools but are still unsure which one to choose, make a quick campus visit, check the application process, and review the timeline restrictions. Often settling on a school requires a leap of faith, but many small, often overlooked, factors can help guide your decision. For example, if you are about to deploy and are indecisive about choosing between two different schools, the school that offers the smoothest registration process or the most online support might be a better choice. Service members have to consider time spent and mission demands, because pursuing education while on active duty remains an off-duty benefit.

WHAT ARE THE INSTITUTION'S
APPLICATION REQUIREMENTS?

The school you choose might have stringent application requirements, or it might be quite lenient. Application requirements can help you eliminate schools if you missed deadlines or do not possess the materials required for submission—for example, an SAT or ACT score, or letters of recommendation.

If you choose a four-year university or college, most likely the institution will require SAT or ACT scores and a formal application process. You might also consider applying to more than one institution to increase your chances of being accepted by at least one. If you opt for community college, you can avoid a long application process and transfer to a university after acquiring a predetermined amount of college credit. The amount of credit you will be required to finish prior to being eligible for the transfer process will depend on the transfer requirements of the institution where you are trying to finish your bachelor's degree. If you are pursuing a vocational degree or certificate, these types of schools typically have open admissions similar to community colleges.

If your transition from active duty to veteran is quick, the open admissions process with a local community college can be a less stressful transition into higher education. As long as you follow an appropriate course of study, dictated by an academic counselor at your school, you should not need to worry about the transfer process until a later date. The counselors will tell you which classes you are required to take to be eligible for transfer, and they will be listed on your academic degree or transfer plan.

HAVE YOU COLLECTED ALL REQUIRED DOCUMENTS?

Prior to applying, verify with your school of choice which documents you will need to provide. If the ACT or SAT is required, have you tested? Do you have proof of residency? Have you applied for your GI Bill and received your Certificate of Eligibility (COE)? If you plan to attend a university, you might need a completed application, submitted test scores, letters of recommendation, an application fee (sometimes waived for veterans), and transcripts. Open admissions institutions such as community colleges and vocational schools usually require a completed online application and proof of payment such as the COE for GI Bill or a TA voucher for active-duty personnel. Visit chapter 6 to learn how to apply for your benefits.

HAVE YOU APPLIED TO THE INSTITUTION?

Complete the required application process using all applicable documents. This process is usually online and can take quite a bit of time. Most sites will save your information for a certain number of days if you are unable to finish in one sitting. Chapter 4 offers detailed guidance in this area. Many of the service members I (Jillian) counsel request help with this process, especially because a personal statement essay section often appears in one of the steps.

HOW WILL YOU PAY FOR YOUR SCHOOLING?

This is the time to pay good attention to your funding possibilities! When discussing funding options for education, GI Bills are best for veterans, TA is best for active-duty service members, and Federal Student Aid (FSA) is a possibility for both. The MGIB and the Post-9/11 GI Bill are not the same. Both help with academic funding, but the two bills work in sharply different ways. Veterans who use either bill will find that a great many expenses are still left uncovered.

Active-duty personnel and veterans can apply for FSA for extra help. Veterans also have unemployment as an option. Check out your state's Department of Labor for more information regarding unemployment eligibility and possibilities. Many of the active-duty service members I work with are awarded Pell Grant money through the Free Application for Federal Student Aid, and Pell Grants do not need to be repaid. Chapter 6 offers detailed information about funding your education.

To recap the checklist above in an abbreviated format:

- Choose a career.
- Find a school.
- Organize your finances.

If you are undecided on a career, get started on general education classes at the local community college. Exercising your brain is never a mistake.

Chapter Two

Educational Concerns for Active-Duty Personnel and Veterans

Service members' educational needs will vary depending upon their service status. Identifying an institution that fulfills an individual's specific needs is a high-priority task. If possible, soldiers should seek advice through counseling services at an education center on their base first. At minimum, they should consider what types of flexibility they are looking for in an institution and evaluate the possibilities using the resources offered in this book before making a final decision.

ACTIVE-DUTY PERSONNEL AND VETERANS' EDUCATIONAL NEEDS

In most cases, service members' needs vary greatly from the civilian population. Determining the types of needs you might have prior to settling on an institution will allow you to make a preemptive strike on any service-related issues that might occur upon your transition off active duty. Picking an institution that can cater to these needs or is located in an area where your needs can be met is imperative for creating a positive learning environment. For example, if you are a veteran with medical concerns, you might want to choose a school that is located near a Veterans Administration (VA) hospital or medical center.

If you are pursuing school while on active duty, considering your position, the amount of free time you have, location concerns, learning styles, Internet availability, and your personal needs before you begin searching will enable you to make a well-informed choice. While you can transfer schools if your initial choice is not a good fit, you always run the risk of losing credit in the transfer process and having to backtrack. Since you only have a limited amount of GI Bill benefits to use, this could set you back. The GI Bill may give you the ability to complete a debt-free education if you can plan your academic career accordingly. Use it wisely after educating yourself about higher education or vocational training and learning how your available veterans' benefits work.

Just as not all our personal needs are the same, not all schools are the same. School offerings will vary by the levels of education, resources, or support systems they can provide. Picking the right institution for you is a personal process and, in most cases, will require quite a bit of research. Understanding what your needs are prior to beginning will significantly reduce the amount of time you spend conducting your searches by streamlining the process.

Active-duty service members need great flexibility with their learning environment. Often, they require a school that offers a wealth of online courses and degree offerings, shorter or self-paced semesters, military familiarity, understanding professors, and an academic counselor who will always be available. Each of these items is necessary in order for the population to achieve academic success while still maintaining mission demands and promotion requirements.

Be careful opting for an online-only school if you are a hands-on learner. While this option might offer you more convenience, your grades could suffer, and you might create unneeded and unwanted stress for yourself. Distance learning is not an easier pathway. Online courses require the same amount of work as their face-to-face counterparts. Potential barriers include not having easy access to your professors and minimal class interaction. You need to have solid reading comprehension skills, the motivation to work independently, and the ability to organize on your own in order to process information and keep track of deadlines.

Most online courses also have mandatory check-in days and times. If you are considering online courses because you are in and out of the field frequently, make sure to determine how the online classroom environment at your chosen institution works. If the school requires mandatory check-in times and you cannot make them, you run the risk of either failing the class or receiving a reduction in your grades for failure to adhere to school or class policies.

If you are in the middle of work-ups for a deployment or already deployed, check to see if the institution offers classes that do not require any Internet connectivity. This is not a common pathway for schools to take for their course offerings, but sometimes it is possible. For example, Coastline Community College in California offers a program called Pocket Ed. Pocket Ed courses are strictly offered in entry-level general education subjects. Currently, nine different subjects are available: biology, personal financial planning, geology, US history, Western civilization, cinema, mass communication, psychology, and sociology. Courses begin at the start of each month and students have three months to complete the work. Proctors for exams can be other service members, officers, or certain enlisted personnel.

If you need to attend school in a face-to-face setting because it is better for your learning style, check to see that the school you choose maintains the flexible classroom offerings you need to be successful. Does the institution offer weekend, evening, or hybrid classes? Does it offer classes on your base? What are the professors' contact policies regarding their active-duty students? Lastly, what can the school offer in the way of support services?

Military students require high levels of flexibility by both the institution and its professors. Between deployments and permanent change of station moves, soldiers need to know that the school they have chosen will assist them at every turn no matter what type of situation arises. For example, what happens if you are deployed and lose your Internet connection for several days? Will the professor accept your assignment late without penalizing your grade?

Always try to discuss any concerns with the professor at the start of your class. Most will understand and try to make accommodations, but usually not if you approach them right before an assignment or right before the class ends. If that pathway does not work, try talking to your academic counselor. This is why it is imperative that schools with significant military populations maintain veteran-only academic counselors who understand service members' special needs and how to help in situations such as this one. Unfortunately, I often hear from service members that they cannot locate the academic counselor at their school. Some schools put people in these positions who are not trained, do not understand the special needs of the military population, or do not hold the proper level of education. At these schools, these positions tend to turn over often, and students might find themselves with a new counselor so often that the individual does not understand their concerns.

Always ask any school you are interested in attending if they have policies regarding deployments. Schools with clear policies will not require any guesswork on your part. For example, some institutions will allow students to finish courses remotely if an unforeseen deployment arises. During situations such as this, well-trained academic counselors can assist soldiers in finding options that might enable course completion to occur in a timely manner. At a minimum, they can give an active-duty service member a clear chain of command to contact when in need of assistance.

Service members' educational needs can vary greatly depending upon their long-term military goals. Soldiers who plan on staying in the military for long-term careers are usually aiming for degree completion. Soldiers completing only one enlistment are usually aiming for solid transfer credit to take with them and shorten the time they will need to spend in school upon their separation.

Degree requirements can be restrictive. Some degrees are difficult or impossible to find in an online format from a reputable institution, for example the engineering and science fields. If you are considering a degree that might limit how much of your education you can complete while on active duty, you might consider completing as much of the degree as possible in an online format, such as all of your general education classes or elective credit. Upon separation from the service, you can tackle the courses that must be completed in a classroom environment.

Be careful taking elective credits while still on active duty. Many schools will offer you elective credit based upon receipt of your DD 214 or your Joint Services Transcript. Why take credits that might be awarded to you at a later date? If you know the institution you want to attend prior to separation, contact the veterans' department and ask if the institution will confer credit in this manner. If so, stay away from the elective classes until a counselor tells you that you need them. More information on this topic can be found in chapter 7.

Credit transferability is a sticky topic. Several concerns should be considered before moving forward if you are pursuing transfer credit. Ultimately, credit acceptance is up to the final institution. Schools usually consider the accreditation of the prior institution and specific program requirements when reviewing credit brought in from other institutions. Some schools have pre-existing transfer agreements that will create a low-stress transfer pathway at a later date.

Some state schools have developed programs to show students how credits transfer between the institutions, such as ASSIST in California. ASSIST (http://www.assist.org) is a cooperative project between the University of California school system, the California State University system, and the state community colleges that allows students to compare class transferability by course of study, department, or general education/breadth agreements. These are commonly called articulation guides, and checking if the school is part of a particular system will allow you to choose intelligently when taking classes to transfer.

Classes do not always transfer for the credit they were originally intended to fill. You must also keep an eye on how many credits an institution will accept. For example, Arizona State University (ASU) will transfer a maximum of sixty-four lower-division semester hours (i.e., 100- and 200-level classes) from a regionally accredited community college (https://transfer.asu.edu/credits), although some exceptions apply for veterans. If you intend to transfer to ASU to complete a bachelor's degree, taking more than sixty-four lower-division credits from the school you are currently attending would be unproductive. Try your best not to find yourself in a situation where credits will not transfer or might need to be repeated.

Consider a few questions before moving forward in this situation:

- Always check the institution's accreditation. I cannot emphasize this point enough. Chapter 4 in this book reviews the different types of accreditation and concerns to be aware of prior to selecting an institution. If you make the wrong choice, you might have to backtrack later. This could cause you to run out of GI Bill benefits and have to find alternate funding for your schooling.
- Consider the state you come from or intend to move to before choosing a school to attend. Many schools have satellite locations in other states or at military installations. If you can find one from your state, in most cases it will be better for your needs.
- If you know which institution you would like to attend after separation from the military, check whether the school offers online classes. If feasible, it would be best to start while on active duty at the school where you intend to finish when you are a veteran. Many schools, including state-based two-year and four-year institutions, offer online classes and are approved for Tuition Assistance (TA). Marshall, Central Michigan, Penn State, and many other institutions offer strictly online master's degrees. Colorado State University, University of Massachusetts, and University of Maryland are a few of the big four-year universities with fully online bachelor's degrees that are TA approved. Many community colleges offer fully online associate degrees, such as Central Texas Community College, which is located at several military installations. Check the Department of Defense Memorandum of Understanding website (http://www.dodmou.com) to see if your school is approved for TA. Attending a school online that you can continue to attend once separated will make your transition much easier, and you will not run the risk of losing credits during the transfer process.
- If these options are not possible, contact the school you are interested in attending upon separation and ask if it has transfer agreements with any particular schools. Most big universities are fed by local community colleges, and most community colleges offer online classes. Usually, big state universities have transfer agreements with the local state community colleges.
- Check with the local education center to see which schools have a presence on the base.

Veterans' educational needs have been the topic of much discussion. The Post-9/11 GI Bill has allowed today's veterans more flexibility than ever before, and schools across the country have had significant increases in their veteran student populations. Unfortunately, veterans of the current conflicts face transition issues that pose many difficult challenges. Schools that recognize these challenges and tailor services on the campus to meet the special needs of their veteran populations should be recognized for their support.

Be careful when choosing a school that claims it is veteran friendly. A study conducted by the Center for American Progress determined that the criteria for listing schools as "veteran friendly" on some websites and media outlets is unclear. Schools should offer you a proper academic pathway as well as veteran-based support. Be leery of any institution that claims it is "veteran friendly" but cannot back it up with concrete proof.[1]

I (Paul) recently spoke to a soldier who was transitioning in one month and had already lined up an apartment in a city where he planned to attend a particular aviation maintenance program. The soldier even visited the school and the counselors told him face-to-face that they accepted the GI Bill. When we searched the VA website to verify this claim, we could not find this particular school on the list of VA-approved schools. After leaving my office he called the school to reconfirm and they admitted they were not VA-approved yet, but working on it. We had to find alternatives because it was very possible the soldier would have had to foot the bill himself if he started that school within the month. If possible, always check the available resources to verify information given by the school about external programs not specific to the school.

Ask about campus support services for veterans. You should look for veteran-only academic counselors, VA services on the campus or nearby, nonprofit veteran assistance such as American Veterans or Disabled American Veterans, student veteran organizations such as the Student Veterans of America (SVA), financial aid support, unemployment support, contact with off-campus services that specialize in veteran outreach, and a significant student veterans center that is consistently manned. The center should be prepared to handle, or refer to the appropriate agencies, any problem that comes its way.

Many academic institutions, including ASU, host the Veterans Upward Bound (VUB) program on their campuses (https://eoss.asu.edu/trio/vub). The VUB program is designed to encourage and assist veterans in their pursuit of higher education. The federally funded program aims to increase and improve qualified veterans' English, math, and computer skills to assist with literacy, laboratory science, foreign language, and college planning skills. All of the courses are free, and ASU offers courses daily on three of the school's campuses. One campus has classes offered at three different times during the day to better meet the schedule of the veteran population. Check the national VUB program website (http://www.navub.org/) to find out if your school offers the program. You can also find the specific VUB office for your particular state by finding your state on the dropdown menu toward the top left corner of their main website to inquire into the services they provide.

School location is important for veterans for many reasons other than the Monthly Housing Allowance (MHA) attached to Post-9/11. Usually, in a traditional higher education environment, we live where we go to school. This may not be the case for many veterans. Often, veterans are older and have families they must support while they pursue a higher education. Sometimes jobs dictate where we can live, and driving long distances to get to class may add unneeded stress to an already stressful transition. If you have already chosen the place where you would like to live, or are still on active duty, try to find a school within a decent driving distance. Check for veteran services offered around the school, because if you need help, you may not want to drive one hundred miles to get it.

The setting of the school's location is also important. If you need to be in a city for nightlife or a more fast-paced lifestyle, you should take that into consideration. If you prefer something without many distractions, consider a quieter institution in a small-town location. You can also check to see if the veterans' center at the school has a designated veteran-only study space allocated for quiet study time. Pay attention to the region as well. If you are a veteran exiting the service without any college credit, you will be spending four years at this institution. If you hate cold weather and snow, you might not want a school in a northern region of the country.

Class availability is imperative for veterans for reasons such as MHA amounts under the Post-9/11 GI Bill and socialization. Both of these subjects are extremely important to consider when thinking about your transition to school. Many schools offer veterans early-bird registration to assist them in achieving a full-time schedule of classes that are required for their degree plans. If a full-time schedule cannot be met, then veterans using their federal benefits will begin to see a reduction in the amount of money they receive. The MHA and degree plan requirements under Post-9/11 are addressed in chapter 6.

Isolation can become a concern for transitioning veterans who face an unknown civilian population that doesn't operate in the regimented fashion they are used to in the military. Soldiers who isolate themselves run a great risk of facing difficulty in the transition process. Making contact and developing relationships with other veterans at the school is a good way to combat this issue. According to a study conducted by the Defense Centers of Excellence:

> Peer supporters "speak the same language" as those they are helping as a result of shared experience(s), which fosters an environment of credibility and trust. Importantly, peers tend to interact more frequently with service members than

do chaplains or members of the medical community. As a result, peers are
most likely to notice changes in behavior and personality of an individual. [2]

Even if you do not believe that isolation will become a problem for you,
consider two reasons to pay attention to the situation anyway.

1. You should always have preemptive precautions set in place. Remember, prior, proper, planning.
2. You might be able to help another veteran who is not in a positive mental health frame of mind and needs assistance.

Soldiers should review the following checklist with a veterans' representative at the school they plan to attend:

- Make contact so you have a face to put with the name.
- Explain your situation and ask for helpful hints for anything you may need.
- Ask about housing and where you can find other veterans for roommates.
- Find out what services the school has set in place for its veteran population. Maybe the school has a veteran-only student body (president, vice president, secretary, etc.) that helps plan social events or promotes veteran well-being at the institution.
- Determine where the closest VA center is located.
- Ask about student veteran organizations (such as SVA) available on campus.
- Find out about the institution's veteran population. How many veteran students attend the school? Does the school/vet center host any veteran-only events?
- Ask whether veterans receive early admission.
- Ask whether there is a veterans' academic counselor.
- Ask whether the institution is a Servicemembers Opportunity College (SOC). Does it participate in the Degree Network System (DNS)? Be aware that SOC is in the midst of a change. The previous agreements offered to soldiers by the schools were referred to as the SOCAD (Servicemembers Opportunity Colleges Army Degrees). SOC is removing any service distinctions between the branches and will now label the agreement the DNS-2 for associate's degrees and DNS-4 for bachelor's degrees. More detailed information regarding the DNS can be found in chapter 7.

Veteran interaction on campus is important for veteran success. Many
veteran departments at schools actively participate in community events involving veterans or invite agencies such as the Veterans of Foreign Wars or

the American Legion to visit their campuses. This is a great way to meet new friends and help your peers. Interaction is not solely for you to create a school support web and make friends. Networking with other veterans is a great way to keep in touch with other people who have shared similar experiences. Sharing experiences with those who have "been there, done that" may help you reintegrate faster into civilian life. This network can also be an amazing tool later for job searches and entrepreneurship possibilities.

Most schools will have a Veterans' Services Office, which is often where you will find military-specific counselors and find peer groups made up of other veterans. For example, the University of Alabama has an office specifically for veterans entitled the Center for Veteran and Military Affairs. The school also offers a Career Transition Assistance Program specifically for veterans that focuses on job search skills and utilizing prior military experience to maximize success upon degree completion. The center features a Family Assistance Program that is meant to offer support for any aspect of a veteran's life, including spousal job searches, assistance in finding housing, day care, and navigating both the campus and local community in search of resources.[3]

Researching the topics mentioned above may help you understand the school's overall culture and attitude toward its veteran population. If the school does not seem to have many veteran services in place, you may want to consider other options. Schools should provide veterans a multitude of support services in case they face unforeseen issues while transitioning and need help.

The VA recognized the need for veterans to hear transition troubles and successes from peers and created a website to help. Make the Connection (http://maketheconnection.net/) helps veterans through shared experiences and support services. The site contains resources and videos from veterans who have faced issues you may be facing and offers advice based on personal experience. Local resources such as VA chaplains, veterans' centers, outpatient clinics, and PTSD programs can be found here as well.

Chapter Three

Academic and Career-Based Research Tools

Before you decide which school to attend or a specific career pathway, you need to complete an in-depth search of your available options. Using the free research tools outlined in this chapter will enable you to find a school that will meet your academic and career needs, as well as useful career-based information. These sites are not foolproof, but are a good start. Each tool offers invaluable information about planning your future, whether you opt for a long-term career in the Army or a civilian-sector route. Use all of these sites and cross-reference the information. If possible, always check with an academic counselor aboard the base where you are stationed for information relevant to your needs; for example, if you are a TA user, you will need to determine if the institution you have selected is approved for TA.

- College Navigator
- O*NET OnLine
- DANTES College & Career Planning Counseling Services, and Kuder Journey
- CareerScope/My Next Move for Veterans
- VA Education and Career Counseling Program (Chapter 36)
- Career One Stop
- Department of Labor
- Army Credentialing Opportunities Online
- Army Knowledge Online
- Counseling Services

COLLEGE NAVIGATOR (HTTP://NCES.ED.GOV/ COLLEGENAVIGATOR/)

College Navigator, offered by the National Center for Education Statistics, is a beneficial tool for both active-duty and transitioning soldiers. The free site enables users to search schools based upon very detailed criteria. Searches may be saved for future reference and dropped into the favorites' box for side-by-side comparison. Comparing schools side by side enables users to determine which school better suits their needs. For example, I (Jillian) searched Point Loma Nazarene (PLNU) and Loyola Marymount University (LMU) in California to determine which school would be less expensive. After dropping both schools into my favorites' box, I selected the compare option in that section. The side-by-side comparison tool lists PLNU's current tuition rate for a student that lives off campus at $36,341 and LMU's rate for the same student at $46,250. I still need to go directly to both schools' websites for more information, but my initial search shows the vast difference in yearly costs between the two institutions. I understand that the Post-9/11 GI Bill currently only will cover up to $20,235.02 (http:// www.benefits.va.gov/GIBILL/resources/benefits_resources/rates/ch33/ ch33rates080114.asp) per academic year for a private school, and I know further research would be required to determine whether LMU or PLNU are viable fiscal options for me as a veteran student. My next step would be to determine if either school is participating in the Yellow Ribbon Program (see chapter 6) through the VA.

College Navigator allows detailed searches in fields such as distance from zip codes, public and private school options, distance learning possibilities, school costs, percentage of applicants admitted, religious affiliations, specialized missions, and available athletic teams. This way, users can narrow down selections based upon specific needs. For example, if I were interested in attending a school with a Christian background as part of my learning, I could click on the religious affiliations tab at the bottom of the search section and add that criterion to my list.

Beginning each search within a certain number of miles from a zip code will enable users to narrow their search parameters from the start. If the selection is insufficient, try broadening the distance a bit prior to removing all of the other parameters you deem important. Many schools offer some degree of online schooling as part of the learning environment. If you are open to online learning, you may find that you can still attain all of your search parameters comfortably even if the school is a bit farther away.

A generic initial search on College Navigator might resemble this:

1. State—California
2. Zip code—90290, with a maximum distance parameter set at fifteen miles
3. Degree options—business
4. Level of degree awarded—associate
5. School type—public

Results demonstrate that four schools meet my (Jillian's) search criteria: Los Angeles Pierce College, Santa Monica College, Los Angeles Valley College, and West Los Angeles College. Because each of these institutions met my initial search criteria, I might want to narrow the mileage to a selection closer to my home base, or look for other, more particular areas that demonstrate the differences. These areas may include the student population, programs offered, and veterans' department structure. I may find that the veterans' department is nonexistent at one of the schools, which would not inspire my confidence in that institution's ability to take care of my unique needs.

Academic institutions' ballooning tuition costs and students' reliance on federal student aid to attend school raise concerns for students considering college. Beginning in 2009, schools have been required by the Department of Education to compile three pieces of data to allow students to better analyze the costs and value of attending a particular school. College Navigator provides graduation/retention rates, median borrowing rates, and the cohort loan default rates. Checking this information on College Navigator will give potential students better insight into an institution's value.

Graduation/retention rates track first-time and full-time students who graduate within six years for a four-year degree. This may only capture a very specific or small population at a particular school. If a student were to transfer in many credits and be classified as a transfer student, he would not be captured by this number. If a school you are considering attending has particularly low graduation/retention rates, it would be wise to contact the institution and inquire about this issue.

The median borrowing rates are the median amount of debt the student population is taking on to attend that institution. The cohort loan default rates are the number of students that attended the school and defaulted on their loans after leaving the institution. The assumption often made is that schools with high median borrowing rates and high cohort loan default rates along with low graduation/retention rates do not provide educational value to the student when he attempts to attain employment. In other words, students might not be able to afford their loans.

Unfortunately, these numbers are complex and only provide one small piece of the overall puzzle when assessing whether a particular institution is the right choice for a student. Talking to a counselor at the school and investigating the responses offered about these concerns can help a potential student better understand what the statistics may mean.

O*NET ONLINE (HTTP://WWW.ONETONLINE.ORG/)

O*Net OnLine is a career occupation website that enables users to complete detailed research on any careers they might be interested in pursuing. The career departments on the military bases use O*Net OnLine for résumé development. The site details areas such as career fields, needed skills, income possibilities, work contexts, and required education levels.

To research a potential career on O*Net OnLine, enter the name in the upper right-hand corner under the "Occupation Quick Search" tab. For example, I entered civil engineer. Upon clicking the link, I was taken to a page that listed civil engineering along with numerous other possibilities that are similar in nature: wind energy engineers, traffic technicians, construction and building inspectors, and civil drafters. This option enables users to research a broader base of potential career pathways prior to settling on one.

Occupations listed as "Bright Outlook" have growth rates that are faster than average in that field and are projected to have a large number of job openings during the decade from 2012 through 2022. These fields are also considered new and emerging, meaning they will see changes in areas such as technology over the upcoming years. Offering several different occupations under one particular search enables users to broaden their horizons and complete numerous more specific searches within a general career path.

Clicking on one particular career pathway will allow you to find the national and state-based median wages for the chosen occupation—for example, the search I conducted under civil engineer listed the national median wages at $39.45 hourly or $82,050 annually. The projected annual growth rate is between 15 percent and 21 percent, with 120,100 job openings during this time frame. Also listed are the majority of sectors where civil engineers are finding employment—in this case, professional, scientific, and technical services as well as the government.

Lastly, schools that offer the proper education pathways can be searched by state. Unfortunately, the school search cannot be narrowed down further by location, type of institution, or other minute detail. For more detailed searches, return to College Navigator.

DANTES COLLEGE & CAREER PLANNING COUNSELING SERVICES, AND KUDER JOURNEY (HTTP:// WWW.DANTES.KUDER.COM/)

DANTES College & Career Planning Counseling Services is available to service members for free, whether you are still on active duty or already separated from the service. Four main areas of education and career research and planning are available on the site—assessments section, occupations, education and financial aid, and job searches.

Soldiers can conduct inventory assessments that enable them to see their areas of strength and weakness. This gives test takers insight into career fields that match their personality types, thereby offering a broader base of potential careers to research. Background information on the careers can be researched to determine whether users are interested in pursuing the option further. Under the education section, users can match the requisite type of education to the chosen vocation as well as find schools that offer the desired degrees.

Résumé building and job searches can be conducted through the site as well. One interesting tool Kuder offers is the ability for users to build résumés and cover letters, attach other needed or pertinent information, and create a URL that hosts the information to submit to potential employers. This allows multiple pieces of information to be housed in one place in a professional manner for viewing by others.

CAREERSCOPE AND MY NEXT MOVE FOR VETERANS (HTTP:// WWW.GIBILL.VA.GOV/STUDENTTOOLS/CAREERSCOPE/ INDEX.HTML) (HTTP://WWW.MYNEXTMOVE.ORG/VETS/)

CareerScope hosts an interest and aptitude assessment tool similar in style to DANTES Kuder. CareerScope is hosted by the VA on the main GI Bill webpage. The free site assists service members in finding and planning the best pathways for those transitioning off active duty and into higher education. Assessments are conducted directly through the site, and a corresponding report interpretation document demonstrates how to interpret assessment results. The easy-to-understand site is a valuable research tool both for those who have already identified which career pathway they want to take and for those who are still undecided.

VA EDUCATION AND CAREER COUNSELING PROGRAM (CHAPTER 36) (HTTP://WWW.BENEFITS.VA.GOV/VOCREHAB/EDU_VOC_COUNSELING.ASP) (HTTP://WWW.VBA.VA.GOV/PUBS/FORMS/VBA-28-8832-ARE.PDF)

Although it is not widely known, the VA offers free education and career counseling advice. The counseling services are designed to help service members choose careers, detail the required educational pathway, and assist in working through any concerns that arise that might deter success. Veterans should refer to the website for eligibility, but the main determining factors are that the veteran must:

• Be eligible for VA education benefits (or dependents using transferred benefits) through one of the following chapters: 30, 31, 32, 33, 35, 1606, or 1607;
• Have received an honorable discharge not longer than one year earlier; or
• Have no more than six months remaining on active duty.

Fill out an application on the second website listed above and return it to get the ball rolling. Soldiers who have already separated from active service and are not located near an Army base will find this to be a solid outlet for assistance.

CAREER ONE STOP (HTTP://WWW.CAREERONESTOP.ORG/)

Career One Stop is one of my (Jillian) go-to sites for career exploration, and is the first site I visit when I work with military students who are interested in apprenticeship programs. The site holds valuable information regarding topics other than apprenticeships as well. It is a comprehensive career exploration site. Career One Stop has six main sections for exploration:

• Explore careers—learn about career fields, explore different industries, take self-assessments, and research different job skills.
• Salary and benefits—information on relocating, wages and salaries, benefits, unemployment insurance, and paying for education or training.
• Education and training—information on traditional education and apprenticeship programs, conduct a search for community colleges, find credentials, and research employment trends.
• Job search—learn how to network, interview, and negotiate, and find special tips on veterans' reemployment.
• Résumés and interviews—samples and formats, create a cover letter and thank you note, and find out how to get ready for an interview.

- People and places to help—workforce services in different locations.

If searching for information regarding apprenticeship programs, click on the "Education and Training" tab, then under the "Find" section click "Apprenticeship." This page hosts links that cover the following:

- Apprenticeship videos
- A state-based search site
- Information from the Department of Labor
- American Job Center information

Use the state-based search option to find a program in the state and county of your choosing. For example, Sergeant Bowen is from Maryland. He would like to participate in an electrician Registered Apprenticeship program. He clicks on the "Find registered apprenticeship programs" tab, then selects his state. Each state has designed its own website, so the directions will vary, but you need to find the link to search for apprenticeship programs. For Sergeant Bowen, he clicks on "Find an Apprenticeship" at the top of the page, then "View Links to Program Websites." On this page, he can search for the appropriate link for an electrical program and the contact information. He can also click the "Veterans ReEmployment" link at the very top of the main page to input his particular Military Occupational Speciality (MOS) and find occupations he may be qualified, or nearly qualified, for based on the specific military training he received in the Army.

DEPARTMENT OF LABOR (DOL) (HTTP://WWW.DOL.GOV/)

The DOL is the one-stop shopping place for many topics, but I use the site for information regarding unemployment, Registered Apprenticeships, and career exploration. On the main DOL page, under the "Popular Topics" tab, I use the "Unemployment," "Training," and "Veterans' Employment" tabs the most.

Most of the service members I (Jillian) work with are eligible for unemployment upon separation from the service. The DOL website is a good place to start looking for initial information regarding the benefit. On the corresponding page the "Unemployment Compensation for Ex-Servicemembers" tab has eligibility information regarding the benefit, a fact sheet, and a link that allows users to search for specific State Workforce Agencies.

The "Training" section has a tab on the right-hand side of the page for information on apprenticeship programs and the process for participating. The DOL is a good place to begin a search for a specific program in a specific location. Read the Fact Sheet before clicking on the "Office of

Apprenticeship" tab, which will take users to the main page regarding Registered Apprenticeships. Anything you need to know about an apprenticeship program can be found here: http://www.doleta.gov/oa/.

The "Veterans' Employment" section has a wealth of information that is relevant to most veterans. Topics such as apprenticeship information, veterans' preference, and employment assistance are covered. Information on the Uniformed Services Employment and Reemployment Rights Act (USER-RA) can be found here as well.

Bureau of Labor Statistics Occupational Outlook Handbook (http://www.bls.gov/ooh/)

The Bureau of Labor Statistics Occupational Outlook Handbook is a useful tool for career exploration. Conducting career research before starting school will assist you in making a more knowledgeable decision regarding your education. Search career fields by pay levels, educational requirements, training requirements, projected job openings, and projected job-growth rates. You can research various career sectors or find out what the current fastest-growing job fields are. If I wanted to find out the level of education required to be a petroleum engineer and how much money they make, click on the "Architecture and Engineering" tab and scroll down (the options are in alphabetical order). Here you can view a short job summary, see that the field requires a bachelor's degree, and learn that the median pay in 2012 was $130,280. Clicking on the link takes you to more in-depth information regarding the career field. Lately, many of the service members I counsel are asking about petroleum engineering education pathways. While you can see on this page that petroleum engineering has a faster than average growth rate (26 percent), I think the pay scale is what attracted them!

ARMY CREDENTIALING OPPORTUNITIES ON-LINE (COOL) (WWW.COOL.ARMY.MIL)

The Army Credentialing Opportunities On-Line program (COOL) enables soldiers to find certifications and licenses associated with their MOSs. If used properly, COOL may help some service members attain the civilian requirements related to their military specialty, thereby fast-tracking their pathway into a future career. Each MOS is listed on the Army COOL website, making it easy for soldiers to find their specialties. Broad civilian career fields can be searched as well to find pertinent certifications and licenses even if you are not interested in what you have done, or are doing, for the military. Many civilian websites attempt to keep track of the vast list of certifications and licenses across the United States, but struggle with keeping it updated. This makes the Army COOL website a unique tool across the Internet.

The COOL websites allow users to search their military specialties for the civilian requirements, obtain information on licensure and certification including test locations and payment possibilities, and find resources to help prepare for exams. Sometimes, exams are approved for GI Bill funding. If so, the website will indicate if this is possible once an MOS has been selected and credentials are listed. The site will also cover the program's accreditation, potential for college credit, and potential for promotion bonus points.

Review the list of icons found on the "Resource Icon Overview" tab located under the "COOL Overview" tab before researching your MOS. That way you will have a better understanding of the resources available to you under your specialty. While your training in the military has undoubtedly given you a leg up with the knowledge required to pass these exams, it is strongly suggested that you self-study or find a preparation program to maximize your chances of passing.

On the main page of the Army COOL site select either enlisted or warrant officer search, and find your specialty. For example, select the Warrant Officer MOS of 890A Ammunition Technician, and then select 89D-Explosive Ordnance Disposal Specialist. The search results demonstrate numerous certification and licensing options related to the selected MOS. Options that lead to promotions points are also listed here with a staff sergeant rank icon. According to Army Regulation 600-8-19 paragraph 3-45, up to five certifications or licenses for ten promotion points each can be obtained for a total of fifty. For the purposes of transitioning to the civilian workforce, a careful review of each selection will help you determine which choices are most viable for personal career needs.

Choosing the "State Licenses" tab outlines the credentials a service member would need based upon state requirements. The "Apprenticeships" tab gives the user information pertaining to overall understanding of apprenticeships, links to state specific programs, and a master list of current occupations that have apprenticeship training available.

If you are following along on the sites, you will notice that the "Related Occupational Opportunities" and "Continuing Education" options are listed at the bottom of the page. Searching under "Related Occupational Opportunities" lists civilian and federal job titles, salaries, and a job search link. Links for the career possibilities take users to O*NET Online's My Next Move for Veterans, where service members can conduct career exploration. Lastly, searching under the "Continuing Education" link details further career enhancement prospects, often in higher education.

Further career credentialing research can be conducted on the following websites:

Career One Stop:

> http://www.careeronestop.org/EducationTraining/KeepLearning/GetCre-
> dentials.aspx
> Bureau of Labor Statistics: http://www.bls.gov/ooh/

ARMY KNOWLEDGE ONLINE (AKO) (HTTPS:// WWW.US.ARMY.MIL)

The Army Knowledge Online (AKO) system is the premier Army online portal for access to updated Army news and information, email access, and a gateway to a variety of different systems that are important to a soldier's career. Access is no longer granted to those that have separated from the military, but those still in the military can use it to prepare for leaving the Army and assisting with educational goals. Of particular relevance are three programs that may be needed for your own military career goals, but can also be used to potentially further civilian education: the Army Career Tracker (ACT), the Army Correspondence Course Program (ACCP), and the e-Learning Skillport program. The Army also provides access to a host of information for future college students to explore as potential avenues of interest.

The Army Career Tracker is an Army leadership development tool that can be accessed through AKO. Every soldier early in their career should jump into ACT to get a head start on career progression and potentially earning college credit. ACT provides a soldier with a list of tasks that should be completed for their rank in order to achieve the next rank. Often these categories are broken down into tasks for the E1-E4, low-level NCOs, and senior NCOs. The ACT system will provide a specific list of tasks that typically directs you to different systems depending on the task.

Two other programs that are important to note are the Army Correspondence Course Program and the e-Learning Skillport program, because it might be possible for you to be awarded college credit for completing them. The Structured Self-Development (SSD) module series (which every soldier should become familiar with) may also be worth credit, and there is a record of it in your Joint Services Transcript. There are five modules within SSD labeled I–V and each is completed based on your progression through the noncommissioned officer ranks. When in doubt, check your Army Training Requirements and Resources System transcript, which should have a record of all trainings completed here: https://www.atrrs.army.mil/studentsup.aspx.

Providing this transcript to a school will allow them to tell you if you will receive credit. The ACT does attempt to match the training completed with specific schools and degrees that are part of the College of the American

Soldier program, which makes researching potential schools easier if you want to maximize military credit.

ACCP modules must be completed by soldiers in specific MOSs, although some may be completed by all soldiers. You will receive one promotion point per five hours of training on your ACCP list of modules. The modules include various videos and interactive software followed by tests of knowledge. When viewing the courses in the ACCP website (found outside of AKO here: http://www.atsc.army.mil/tadlp/accp/index.asp) it will display the American Council on Education (ACE) recommended number of credits per course, whether the course is lower or upper level, the ACE ID number, and the subject area the course may apply toward in a degree. Whether the goal is promotion points or college credits, any soldier serious about their professional or academic career should try to complete as many modules as possible in the ACCP system.

Along with the ACCP program, the Army e-Learning program is a module-based system that allows a soldier to seek knowledge in a broad range of different subjects. Similar to ACCP, some of the modules will be important to a soldier's job and MOS, and others will simply give a soldier a firmer grasp of knowledge he or she thinks is important. One module assists soldiers in learning the finer points of using Excel, while others prepare them to pass certifications such as Security+ and Project Management Professional. Many of the modules are based on information in the areas of information technology, business leadership, and personal development and link directly to certifications that can be found for an MOS in the Army COOL website. The breadth and scope of the information in the modules is such that Tuition Assistance through GoArmyEd cannot be used for any certificate that specifically targets information already found in the e-Learning program.

Many of the modules in e-Learning Skillport are ACE recommended for credit. These modules require that you use the ACE Tracking Form found in e-Learning for the module you have studied, then typically you must visit the testing center in your education center to take a proctored test called a Course Test Prep Exam or Final Exam. After the proctor notates the completion date of the test and your score on your ACE Tracking Form, you will email the form to the Army e-Learning Program Office at army.elearning@us.army.mil. ACE will provide information for the $40 application fee and you can send the transcript to any school that you wish. A full list of e-Learning Skillport modules can be found here: https://www.atrrs.army.mil/selfdevctr/. Also, keep in mind that these modules are accessible to any soldier, regardless of MOS, so take a look at the catalog and fire up a module if you believe you might be at all interested in the topic. Exposing yourself to the material for free may give you an idea of interests you did not even know you had.

While these programs can lead to a specific number of promotion points, if you receive college credit, you can technically "double dip" and receive promotion points for these credits on your transcripts as well. You should take any transcripts you have to an education counselor who can write a memo to give to your S1 (Personnel Office). Currently, there are up to seventy-five civilian education credits worth seventy-five promotion points per Army Regulation 600-8-19 paragraph 3-45. Obtaining a degree while in the military also nets you ten extra promotion points.

AKO also houses a link to the language-learning program that is available to soldiers and their dependents. When the military's contract with Rosetta Stone expired in 2011, a new language program was instituted entitled Transparent Language, which can be found outside of AKO here: http://www.transparent.com/libraries/military/. Promotion points can also be earned by completing the language modules here: http://hs2.lingnet.org/, though you must be logged in through the Joint Knowledge Online portal, which can also be accessed by way of AKO.

COUNSELING SERVICES

The Army Education Center is a unique institution on a military installation and would be unique even if found in the civilian world of adult education. I (Paul) would speculate that if the average American had access to the services found in an education center, it is possible Americans would not currently be $1.3 trillion in student debt. The personnel that work in education centers are there to serve as your advocate and to keep your best interests in mind. They do not work for schools who will inevitably answer to the school itself, lenders who may be seeking student loans to make a profit, or the countless random services that have sprung up attempting to profit off of the growth of veteran college attendance.

One of the primary services an Army Education Center provides is access to education counselors that can help you disentangle the variety of career and academic funding questions and concerns you will have both during and after your military career. Education counselors are subject matter experts in navigating the college world and providing customized solutions to your college needs. Often, they will begin by using many of the tools presented in this chapter, along with others found in this book, to help figure out which occupations may interest you the most after the military.

Upon nailing down a potential job field and the corresponding required education, an education counselor can help sift through potential schools for you to investigate to see whether they meet your needs. Not all schools are created equal, and many have more value than others for the different types of students pursuing higher education. I (Paul) often have service members ask me what I think is the "best" school, but the "best" school varies greatly depending on the person, and the only reply I have is asking what they mean by "best." Every student will evaluate a school differently based on location, reputation, services, cost, and most importantly what the service member wishes to gain from attending that school.

An education counselor can help you figure out your priorities and help find the school that is the best fit based on those criteria. Once you have chosen a direction, counselors will help with the application process for the different funding options you may have available. Often they will have learned valuable tidbits of information that might benefit you since they have already helped numerous other service members.

One specific service that may be of particular interest to transitioning soldiers is commonly referred to as the "School-Out Option." According to Army Regulation 635-200 paragraph 5-16, a soldier can request up to ninety days for an early separation to attend school. This program is used to ensure soldiers can begin their education without missing start dates and without potentially long delays. Command support is mandatory for this pathway, so seek their counsel.

A current schedule of courses or an acceptance letter from a school for a firm term start date that begins before you separate is necessary. Commands must consider the amount of terminal leave soldiers have available, and soldiers need to show that they have the ability to pay for school, which typically requires a memo from an education counselor verifying that the school accepts the GI Bill. Be aware that this program does change an individual's date of separation to ninety days prior to the current date of separation, so soldiers must verify that this pathway will not decrease overall GI Bill worth.

Veterans are a population that education centers serve, so feel free to go to https://www.goarmyed.com/public/public_goarmyed-education_centers. aspx and search by zip code for the nearest location. Clicking each education center will pull up its unique GoArmyEd homepage with a list of services and contact information. If you are a soldier who will transition soon to the civilian world, reach out to the education center in the state you will eventually end up in to attend school. Often these counselors have been working in that location for a while and are familiar with all of the state-based benefits and school systems.

Chapter Four

What Should I Look For in a School?

Schools are not all the same, and neither are soldiers. Your best possible choice for an institution might be the worst possible choice for another service member. This chapter outlines important institutional factors that will assist you in making an educated decision. The following topics are discussed:

1. Types of schools
2. Reserve Officer Training Corps
3. School accreditation
4. Admissions requirements
5. Admissions process including essays
6. Standardized admissions tests

TYPES OF SCHOOLS

You have learned about the tools available to help assist in your research; now you need to know what to look for during the search. Different types of schools serve different purposes. Understanding the differences will help you make a more educated and empowered decision.

In most cases, career choices determine the type of institution you should attend. For example, are you taking a vocational or traditional pathway? Do you need a two-year degree or a four-year degree? If two years are sufficient, then you can eliminate most four-year universities from your search. Narrowing your search by a few key factors will help in the selection process.

Technical schools, community colleges, universities, public and private, not-for-profit and for-profit schools have different guiding factors and structures. This section offers brief explanations of the types of schools and how to choose the one that best suits your needs.

Two-Year Schools

Two-year schools are community colleges (CCs) or technical schools. Most are state based, but not always. CCs offer the following:

* Associate degrees
* Transfer pathways to universities and colleges
* Certificate programs
* Vocational programs which might include apprenticeship opportunities
* Open enrollment, which is especially good if you had trouble with your high school GPA
* No SAT, ACT, or essay required
* Significantly cheaper tuition and fees than universities and colleges
* More available locations

Two-year CCs can help students save money and lessen the financial burden college can place on a veteran. Students can spend up to two years at a CC before a transfer to a more expensive four-year institution becomes necessary. Many CCs offer specific transfer pathways into the four-year schools located in the state and sometimes for institutions located across the country as well.

Because CCs are usually found in numerous locations throughout each state, they are easy to find and often convenient to your home, which is helpful because most do not offer on-campus housing. The open-enrollment policy makes for a stress-free transition from active duty and is the fastest way to start school. Most of the service members I (Jillian) assist opt for a CC when they are on a time crunch because of deployments or training. Sometimes it is the only pathway, especially if university admission deadlines have passed.

Most CCs offer vocational programs that require an associate degree or a certification process. Many of the vocational pathways also have available significant hands-on learning options, such as apprenticeship programs or on-the-job training options. Attending a vocational program at a state CC gives you a safe, regionally accredited option to transfer credit if you decide later to pursue a bachelor's degree at another regionally accredited school.

Always check with the specific school about the program you would like to attend. Some programs, such as nursing and radiologic technologist, are overenrolled. This means there are more students than spots available, so acceptance may be delayed. A nearby for-profit school may offer more than enough seats for their students in these types of programs, but you are usually paying a higher premium in tuition for this luxury. Therefore, knowing the differences between the types of schools out there allows you to make the best decision possible.

CCs frequently offer internships and apprenticeships within the surrounding community. These programs may help you gain employment at a faster rate, generate work experience for a résumé, or credential you for a specific career. Often these pathways are attached to an associate of applied science (AAS) degree. AAS degrees do not require students to take a full course of general education subjects. Typically, they will only require basic freshman-level math and English courses. This can mean faster program completion and a quicker route into the workforce. AAS degrees are not designed as transfer pathways to four-year institutions. Skills development for entry-level employment or advancement in an existing position are the two main purposes of the AAS degree, although some classes may still be transferable.

Four-Year Schools

Colleges and universities are four-year schools. Each state has a state university system, but not all colleges and universities are state based, as you will read about in the next few paragraphs. Four-year schools can offer the following:

* Bachelor's degrees
* Research institutions, centers, and programs
* May specialize in different fields, for example liberal arts or technology
* Financial aid—four-year colleges can be very expensive
* On- and off-campus enrichment opportunities, such as study abroad and guest lecture series
* Various fields of study that offer a wide range of job opportunities
* Broader range of course selection than CCs
* Large, diverse campuses and populations at some of the bigger universities and state schools; smaller campuses and smaller, more familiar class sizes at smaller liberal arts colleges
* Competitive admissions process
* On-campus housing possibilities

Many universities also have graduate schools, where students can continue their studies to obtain advanced degrees such as an MA, PhD, MD, or JD. Before going to graduate school, however, students must finish their undergraduate coursework, and another admissions process is necessary for acceptance.

Attending a university can sometimes be overwhelming. Classes can be so large that you never have a one-on-one conversation with your professor, which sometimes makes students feel anonymous. Finding your niche might take some time in a large population, but it will afford you more opportunities to interact. Large institutions usually offer numerous degrees and classes to choose from; smaller liberal arts colleges may be a bit more specialized.

If you feel that a four-year institution might be too much, too soon or simply do not have the time to organize all of the required admissions documents, starting at the local CC might be the best option. Many civilian students take this path for the same reason. CCs are also beneficial for students who might need more one-on-one attention during their studies, or simply have not been to school in a long time and feel safer in a smaller, less competitive environment. Whatever the case, arm yourself with information before making a decision. Sometimes, a visit to the campus will settle the issue. The school should be a comfortable fit because you will be spending a significant amount of time there.

Study abroad can be a fun option. Students may diversify their résumés by demonstrating global understanding of their subject of study. Learning new cultural perspectives through interactions in a foreign environment enhances your education and broadens your community reach. Some students who opt for study abroad are also able to become proficient in a foreign language, which can help widen their potential options for employment.

Many service members choose this option; some are interested in cultural exploration, and others are married to foreigners and intend to live in their spouse's home countries. Whatever the reason, preparing correctly for study abroad takes some time. Participating in a study abroad program offered through your institution in the United States is a safe option. Attending a foreign institution for your entire degree will require a bit of research first. Most foreign schools do not abide by the regional accreditation that is preferred for traditional education in the United States. This can cause future problems. Make sure to find out if the degree can be translated in the United States prior to committing.

Information on foreign degree or credit evaluation can be found on the National Association of Credential Evaluation Services website (http://www.naces.org/). If the degree from the foreign institution you are considering attending cannot be evaluated by US standards, you may have difficulty later. You run the risk that a potential employer may not value your degree or that an advanced degree program may not recognize the level of education you have achieved.

Public Schools (Universities and Community Colleges)

Public schools, often referred to as "state schools," are typically funded by state and local governments. In-state residents pay lower tuition charges than out-of-state students. Some schools' out-of-state tuition charges can total an extra $10,000 or more per academic year. Sometimes state schools have reciprocal agreements with schools in other states that allow for reduced out-of-state tuition charges—for example, the Midwest Student Exchange Program (MSEP; http://msep.mhec.org/). MSEP has nine participating states with public schools that charge undergraduate students a maximum of 150 percent of the in-state tuition charges and private schools that offer a 10 percent reduction in tuition.

State schools offer a wide range of classes, degree options, and degree levels, and often state residents get priority admissions. Class size at state schools can be a concern. Sometimes, more than 250 students may be enrolled in a lecture. This can make it difficult to interact with professors or staff.

Most states have a flagship university with smaller locations available throughout the state for easier access. In some instances, students attending state universities cannot graduate in the standard four-year time frame because mandatory classes are often full, although many institutions now offer priority registration to veterans and active-duty personnel. This enables veterans to maintain full-time status while using their GI Bills, so that they also qualify for full-time benefits.

Also keep in mind that public schools are not specifically profit-driven and can therefore fall prey to many of the ills that affect any state-administered institution, such as a large amount of bureaucracy and poor customer service. This of course does not mean you should avoid public institutions. Just be prepared to research as much as possible and be your own best advocate when seeking assistance and help. If you have sent an email or called an advisor at the school and have not received a response, ask to speak to a supervisor and let it be known that you are not receiving the assistance you require.

Private Schools

Private schools do not receive funding from state or local government. They are financially supported by tuition costs, donations, and endowments. They may be nonprofit or for-profit in nature, traditional or nontraditional. Private schools usually charge students the same price whether they are in-state or out-of-state residents. The cost of private school tuition is often more than resident tuition at a state school, but not always. Many private schools offer scholarships and grants to greatly reduce the tuition costs. Usually, private schools have smaller class sizes than public schools, which can mean greater access to your professor. Private-school acceptance may be less competitive than state acceptance, but not in top-tier or Ivy League institutions. Some private schools have religious affiliations, are historically black or Hispanic-serving institutions, or are single-sex institutions.

Think about the tuition costs of a private university similarly to the sticker price when buying a car. Unlike public schools, which are required by the state government to charge a specific price, high prices at private schools can sometimes be overcome. If the institution really wants to have you as a student they may reduce the amount of tuition by offering "scholarships." Typically, these are not traditional scholarships, but instead they allow private schools to reduce the amount of tuition at a school through in-house benefits. The amount of tuition paid by a student can vary greatly.

I (Paul) was recently speaking at a prestigious private institution in Southern California. The admission counselor stated that if the school wants you, and you can afford to pay half of the tuition yourself, then they will waive the remaining cost of tuition. Be up front with the institution if you are not able to cover all of the tuition and fees. You might still be able to attend depending upon the interest level of the school and the type of student they are looking to add to their classrooms. The cost of college is exploding, so talk to the counselors and the financial aid department during the process; it may save you thousands of dollars in the long run.

Be informed when choosing your school. The College Board reported average costs of published state-school tuition and fees for the 2014 to 2015 school year at $9,139, and average private-school tuition and fees at $31,231.[1]

Veterans should be concerned about private-school cost because the average cost for 2013 was significantly higher than the current Post-9/11 payout of $20,235.02 for academic year 2014–2015. If you decide on a private school that charges tuition and fees above and beyond the Post-9/11 payout amount, check to see if the school is participating in the Yellow Ribbon Program (YRP). The YRP, which is explained in depth in chapter 6 may help you close the tuition gap.

For-Profit Institutions

The difference between for-profit and not-for-profit basically is in the title. For-profit schools are operated by businesses, are revenue-based, and have to account for profits and losses. According to a recent government report on for-profit schools, the "financial performance of these companies is closely tracked by analysts and by investors"; this means that the bottom line is always revenue.[2] For-profit schools typically have open enrollment. Open enrollment can be helpful when you are transitioning from the military and have many other urgent needs at the same time. Open enrollment means that everyone gains entry to the school. That may prove disastrous for an individual who is not ready for the demands of higher education, but if the student is well prepared, it might provide a good pathway.

If you are looking for ease in the transition process and flexible class start dates, for-profit schools can offer you that benefit. Usually, they have classes starting every eight weeks, or the first Monday of every month, with rolling start dates.

For-profit institutions are inherently private, so cost concerns are similar to those described in the private institutions section. They have come under fire recently by Congress for several different concerns, including their intake of Federal Student Aid (FSA) and GI Bill money. If you would like more information on these concerns, see http://www.help.senate.gov/imo/media/for_profit_report/PartI.pdf or http://www.sandiego.edu/veteransclinic/news_research.php.

Not-for-Profit Institutions

According to the National Association of Independent Colleges and Universities, "private, not-for-profit higher education institutions' purposes are to offer diverse, affordable, personal, involved, flexible, and successful educations to their students.[3]

Not-for-profit private schools sometimes offer flexible admissions for veterans that many state institutions cannot. Offering flexible admissions to veterans is a school-specific benefit, and veterans should address that option with their preferred institution.

Some private, not-for-profit schools like Harvard and Yale can have tremendous name recognition. On a smaller scale, many private, not-for-profit colleges and universities are well known within local communities. For example, in my (Jillian's) hometown of Chicago, three well-known private, not-for-profit schools are DePaul University, Loyola University, and Columbia College. Each of these schools enjoys an excellent reputation, has a comprehensive veterans' department, and is well known throughout the Midwest.

Attending this type of school is typically a safe pathway, especially when listing your school on a résumé. Be aware that private schools can be very expensive, and the cost can sometimes be prohibitive. For example, DePaul is roughly $34,500 per academic year.

The good news is that many private schools also participate in the YRP. For example, DePaul participates with unlimited spots and $12,500. As you will read in chapter 6, this means the VA matches that amount, and you end up with an extra $25,000 on top of your private school maximum of $20,235.02. Basically, your tuition is covered. Make sure to determine whether the school is participating in the YRP and in what manner before committing to attend.

Vocational-Technical and Career Colleges

Vocational-technical (votech) schools and career colleges prepare students for skill-based careers in technical fields. Many technical schools are state run, subsidized, and regionally accredited. Credits from these schools are generally accepted elsewhere. Career colleges are private, usually for-profit institutions, and they mostly hold national accreditation. Credits from these schools may not be widely transferable.

Programs at these schools can run anywhere from ten months to four years, depending on the skills required to finish training. Many have rolling admissions. Programs often run year-round, including the summers, in order to get students into the workforce faster.

Typically, in a votech-based program, general education classes such as English and math are not necessary. Program completion results in a certificate of completion or an associate degree in applied science. The associate degree in applied science will require entry-level math and English classes. Votech schools focus directly on the task at hand, meaning training for an industry that is skills-based and preparing students for a career.

If you have decided to take a votech pathway, research the school's cost, credentials, faculty, program requirements, and student body prior to committing to a specific institution. Cost is important: the GI Bill has a set maximum amount it will pay for private school. Find out whether you will also be eligible to apply for FSA, but remember: you are mainly interested in the Pell Grant. You can find more information regarding student aid in chapter 6.

Determine whether the school is licensed by the state and which accreditation it holds. If the program requires licensing by the state, but the school does not have the proper licensing agreement, you might not be able to sit for the state exam. Why go through a program that does not allow you full completion and credentialing? That could translate to a lower-paying job, or the inability to get hired in your field.

Ask about the professors' backgrounds and qualifications. Find out if you will be able to apply any military credit toward the program and if the program includes on-the-job training or internship possibilities. Visit the campus to determine what type of equipment you will be trained on and review the faculty setting. Check the school's completion rates, meaning how many students graduate and whether they graduate on time. Last, verify that the school offers job placement services. Find out the following:

- What is its rate of placement?
- Where are students being placed?
- What positions are they getting right out of school?
- How much money are they earning?

Usually, a phone call and follow-up school visit are required to fully understand the program benefits. Remember that vocational fields prepare students for specific career pathways, so transitioning later to a different pathway will require retraining.

Votech schools usually hold national accreditation. Make sure to review the accreditation section later in this chapter, which explains the difference between regional and national accreditation. Nationally accredited programs' credits frequently cannot transfer into a regionally accredited school, although some exceptions exist at schools that hold dual accreditation. For this reason, always check the local CC for similar programs. Many CCs offer vocational programs that can be converted later to transferable college credit.

RESERVE OFFICER TRAINING CORPS (ROTC)

The Department of the Army has a variety of different options for soldiers who are interested in becoming officers by earning their second lieutenant gold bars. Reserve Officer Training Corps (ROTC) programs that use the Green to Gold (G2G) program as an entry point are similar in design and format. However, ROTC programs for civilians without prior service, or those veterans not entering ROTC while on a current military contract, will use a different process and are held to different eligibility requirements.

Similar to the G2G program described in chapter 5, scholarships are available for two-, three-, and four-year periods which pay full tuition, provide funds to pay for books, and a monthly stipend not to exceed $5,000 a year. These future officers will incur a four-year obligation with four more years in the Individual Ready Reserves (IRR). There are also nonscholarship options that require a three-year obligation and five years in the IRR. Earning a commission in the National Guard or Reserves is also an option.

Attending the first two years of college does not obligate you to join the Army unless you received a paid scholarship for this period of schooling time. For more information, speak to the ROTC recruiter at the schools you are interested in attending. To find a list of all ROTC programs nationwide, or participating institutions nearby, go to http://www.goarmy.com/rotc/find-schools.html.

While conducting your research, remember that schools with an ROTC program can be either public or private universities, and offerings at the institutions can vary greatly. Check in to all aspects of the institutions, not just the ROTC program. Think about the options that might be important to you. Maybe you are interested in academic assistance programs, sports programs, or social outlets. You need to make the best possible choice for your academic pathway and doing so requires you to gather information first.

All potential candidates must be US citizens between the ages of seventeen and twenty-six, so don't think that just because you missed your chance right out of high school that this pathway is not an option for you. You must have a minimum GPA of 2.5 on your high school or college transcript, depending on where you are in your academic career. Ensure that you have the highest GPA possible, because acceptance into the ROTC program is typically competitive. You could be accepted to your school of choice but not accepted into the ROTC program!

An applicant of any age must meet the Army Physical Fitness Test minimum requirements with a score of 60 in each push-up, sit-up, and two-mile run event. Four-year applicants must have a minimum SAT score of 920 or a minimum ACT score of 19 (scores on the written portion are excluded). Experience with the Junior Reserve Officer Training Corps (JROTC) in high school may boost the viability of your application and a letter of recommendation from the JROTC instructor (who is certified by the United States Army Cadet Command) may also be an advantage.

Once you have begun attending your institution, you will experience life as a college student similarly to life as a noncadet student. However, you will report for formation and physical fitness training some mornings before your classes.

During all four years of your college experience, you will also attend elective military science courses that will teach you the basics of military traditions, operations and tactics, and leadership. The first two years are part of a Basic Course, and during your junior and senior year you will attend the Advanced Course, which consists of advanced training in these topics.

If you have applied for less than a four-year scholarship, you must attend the Leader's Training Course, which is a condensed version of the Basic Course to bring you up to speed with your class. This course consists of an intense, fast-paced classroom and field training experience for four weeks at Fort Knox, Kentucky.

Outside of these requirements, all cadets must attend the Leader Development and Assessment Course during the summer after their junior year. It is a five-week course, also at Fort Knox, that is meant to imitate deployment-ready preparation. Topics include field training, squad and platoon tactics, equipment maintenance, and Situation Training Exercises. Your performance during this last piece of training is heavily based on instructor and peer evaluations of your capabilities as an officer. Your score on the Order of Merit List will determine whether you will get your first preference for a military branch and occupation as an officer.

Think carefully about the commitment required of the Army ROTC program. Speak to your family and make sure you make the best decision possible. Whether you are applying right out of high school or at the maximum age of twenty-six, you may very likely be committing the next twelve years of your life to the Army—four years of schooling and a potential eight-year service requirement.

If you decide this is the right move for your future career, go to http://www.goarmy.com/rotc/high-school-students/four-year-scholarship.html and create an account to access the application. You may also want to contact the specific ROTC recruiter or Professor of Military Science at your school if you have questions or concerns about the process. Also contact the ROTC recruiter at your school to apply for the nonscholarship option and the two- and three-year scholarship options.

ACCREDITATION

Accreditation is an often overlooked topic that service members need to consider prior to making a final selection on an institution of higher learning. Most service members that I counsel are not aware of the different types of accreditation that schools may hold, but should take the time to research the topic. Selecting a school with the wrong type may cause a soldier significant backtracking at a later date.

The United States does not have a formal federal authority that oversees higher education. Each individual state exercises some level of regulation, but generally speaking, colleges and universities have the ability to self-govern. Accrediting organizations were born to supervise and guide institutions of higher learning to assure students that they are receiving valuable educations. The organizations develop and maintain specific standards for participating schools that hold the institutions accountable for the quality of education they are delivering. The standards "address key areas such as faculty, student support services, finance and facilities, curricula and student learning outcomes."[4]

Accredited schools adhere to the accrediting bodies' standards. Having accreditation is like having quality control for higher education, and when searching for schools, it should be an important factor to consider. Students who attend accredited universities and colleges have a greater chance of receiving a quality education and benefiting from their degrees.

If a school does not hold accreditation, you will most likely not be able to apply for federal or state-based financial aid. Credit hours earned from non-accredited schools will not usually transfer into accredited institutions and will not be recognized for entrance into most master's degree programs. Ultimately, attending an accredited institution means that "a student can have confidence that a degree or credential has value."[5]

Typically, students need to look for institutional accreditation and possibly programmatic accreditation. Institutional accreditation means that the college or university as a whole is accredited. This enables the entire school to maintain credibility as a higher learning institution. Only regional or national accrediting agencies can give institutional accreditation.

The degree you chose will dictate the type of accreditation you will need. Traditional degrees in areas such as education, engineering, business, anthropology, and criminal justice require regional accreditation. Nontraditional degrees might, but might not, require national accreditation. Nontraditional education encompasses subjects that are more vocational in nature, such as welding and electrical work.

Every single state school (state CCs, state colleges, and state universities) in this country hold regional accreditation. The Post-9/11 GI Bill is used most effectively at a state school in the state the veteran holds residency. For example, if Sergeant Smith enlisted in Wisconsin, maintained his residency, returns to the state upon separation from the Army, enrolls in a Wisconsin state school, and finishes his degree in the allotted thirty-six months (nine months per year x four years), he will not pay a dime for his tuition. Free school—what's better than that? Do not panic if you are intending to pursue a private school; other options do exist.

Regional accreditation is the most widely recognized and transferable (credit hours) accreditation in this country. There are six regional accrediting bodies in the United States. The accrediting bodies are based on the region of the country:

- Middle States Association of Colleges and Schools: http://www.msche.org/
- New England Association of School and Colleges: http://cihe.neasc.org/
- North Central Association of Colleges and Schools: http://www.ncahlc.org/
- Northwest Commission on Colleges and Universities: http://www.nwccu.org/
- Southern Association of Colleges and Schools: http://www.sacscoc.org/
- WASC Senior College and University Commission: http://www.wascweb.org/

Regional accrediting organizations review schools in their entirety. Both public and private and two- and four-year schools can be reviewed. Holding regional accreditation should allow credits to transfer smoothly between different member schools depending upon the established transfer criteria at the receiving institution. Remember: Ultimately, the college or university you are trying to transfer into has final say on credit transferability.

Schools that hold national accreditation typically offer educational pathways that are more vocational (nontraditional) in nature. This type of education might lead to a completed apprenticeship program or certification. Vocational education is a means of training future workers with skills more directly relevant to the evolving needs of the workforce. These types of career fields are more hands-on and technical in nature. Many nationally accredited schools can offer students successful pathways to promising careers. The programs are designed to get students into the workforce as soon as possible, and can usually be completed in two years or less, significantly faster than a four-year bachelor's degree.

Students do not need to attend a nationally accredited institution to receive vocational training. Many local state CCs offer nontraditional education and often have apprenticeship or on-the-job training programs offered in addition to the educational classes. This might be a better pathway if you are unsure of your future career demands. Credits from a state CC are more widely transferable than credits from a nationally accredited institution because they hold regional accreditation.

I worked with a service member who wanted to be a welder, but did not want to pursue a full degree or apprenticeship program at that time. Attending a state CC for the program would enable him to have more flexibility at a later date if he decided to pursue further education. For example, if he completed a certificate program in welding at a state CC, he would retain a greater chance of transferring those credits toward an associate degree in welding at a later date.

Sometimes, institutional accreditation is insufficient and programmatic accreditation is also necessary. Programmatic accreditation is specific to a department within an institution, and is often needed for certain degrees above and beyond the institutional accreditation, such as nursing, business, and engineering. Programmatic accrediting organizations focus on specific courses of study offered at a college or university. Attending a program that maintains programmatic accreditation can help your degree be more effective (as in getting you a job!) or make earned credit hours more transferable. If you are not sure whether your degree requires programmatic accreditation, search the Council for Higher Education Accreditation's website (http://www.chea.org/Directories/special.asp) for further information.

Choosing a school with the right type of accreditation is important. Credits from a regionally accredited institution usually transfer into a nationally accredited institution, but credits from a nationally accredited institution almost never transfer into a regionally accredited institution. The exception would be if a student was transferring into an institution with dual accreditation, but there are very few in the country. This means that a rigorous search for qualifying information must be made in order to determine the proper academic pathway for a soldier's selected career.

In these cases, looking at programmatic or specialized accreditation may be more important than institutional accreditation, or in other words, regional or national accreditation. For example, Platt College is nationally accredited, but holds the diagnostic sonography accreditation from the Commission on

Accreditation of Allied Health Education Programs. This is the premier accreditation for sonography programs. Therefore, these credits may not transfer to a regional institution, but since the program holds the proper accreditation for sonography, you are generally safe in your ability to find a job in sonography after finishing the degree. You should always do the research to see if your particular industry requires specialized accreditation, and sometimes this will outweigh its "institutional" accreditation (regional versus national) in an academic sense. Be aware that if you choose this option your credits will most likely not transfer at a later date.

To search for a specific school's accreditation or a particular program of interest, go online (at http://www.chea.org/search/default.asp) and agree to the search terms. You can also complete a search of the national accrediting agencies that the US Department of Education considers reliable (go to http://ope.ed.gov/accreditation/) or on College Navigator (http://nces.ed.gov/collegenavigator/).

ADMISSIONS REQUIREMENTS

Admissions requirements at each school will vary depending upon the type of school, specific degree requirements, and the school's ability to offer flexibility to service members. Some, such as CCs and many vocational schools, maintain open admissions. Others, mainly four-year institutions of higher learning (universities), have a predetermined set of admissions qualifications that can be quite rigorous. This section will discuss the possible requirements for admission into colleges and vocational schools.

State-Based Community and Technical Schools

Entrance into a local community or technical college is typically much less stressful than entrance into a four-year university. Attending CC is a great way to get started with school for those who have little or no time to prepare the required documents or manage application deadlines. This is a beneficial option for service members who often have little time between returning from deployments and transitioning off active-duty status. CCs also do not have the same rigorous admissions requirements that universities demand from potential students. This allows students who lost time to prepare due to mission demands to still get going on their educations without a delay.

State-based community and technical colleges may offer or require the following:

- Open admissions
- Acceptance, in most cases with or without a high school diploma or GED
- Early registration for soldiers on active duty and veterans

- An application fee
- Registration deadlines
- Special entrance criteria (prerequisite classes), and a waiting list for start times in specific, high-demand programs (too many applicants and not enough available open spots)
- English and math placement tests, typically, to determine proper level placement
- Admissions application, typically online, that only takes a few minutes
- Supporting documents—for example, high school transcripts, military transcripts, and residency proof
- Proof of immunizations

Four-Year Colleges and Universities

Four-year institutions of higher learning usually have selective admissions with application requirements and deadlines. Some may offer veterans flexible admissions, but, in most cases, veterans will follow the same pathway as civilians. A written timetable of deadlines for all materials can be obtained by contacting the school and checking the admissions sections of the website. Be prepared to spend a fair amount of time preparing.

College and university admissions may require the following:

- An application (in most cases, this can be done online)
- Application fees
- ACT and SAT test scores (see the "Standardization and Admissions Tests" section in chapter 4)
- Essays
- Letters of recommendation
- A college pathway in high school, meeting minimum subject requirements
- High school and college transcripts
- Minimum high school GPA
- Minimum high school class rank
- Demonstration of community service; military service may fulfill this requirement
- Proof of immunizations

Vocational-Technical and Career Colleges

Depending upon the program to which a student is applying within the school, admission requirements may vary. In certain fields, such as nursing, entrance exams may be mandatory. Exams can include physical fitness tests, basic skills exams, and Health Education Systems, Inc. entrance exams.

Always research carefully the career you are choosing to determine whether your certification or license from a career college is valid. Often, states have mandatory requirements pertaining to the fields of education taught at a technical school, and students need to verify that the school meets these standards. Always check the state government website; many list the state-approved programs.

Typically, admissions are open with a few minimum requirements, such as the following:

- High school transcript and diploma or GED
- Completed admissions forms
- An interview
- Statement of general health
- Any mandatory subject-specific exams

THE ADMISSIONS PROCESS (INCLUDING ESSAYS)

Most schools generally follow the same admissions process, even though the requirements can differ drastically from school to school. Whether a student is an incoming freshman, a transfer student, or an applicant to a vocational school, the pathway to gain admittance will follow the same route, but it may vary in difficulty. Prospective students at schools with an open-enrollment policy will normally have a less intensive pathway to admittance. Students pursuing schools with selective admissions will spend more time preparing.

On a typical pathway, you

1. pick a school or schools, call the veterans' representatives, discuss admissions requirements, and decide on an institution;
2. apply (usually online);
3. receive acceptance;
4. apply for Tuition Assistance (TA), the GI Bill, or FSA; and register for classes (choose classes based on a degree plan).

Pick a School

Contacting the veterans' representatives should initially give you a good feel of a school's perspective toward its veteran students. The vet reps have been there, done that already. If there are any tricks to gaining admission, they will know. Also, it enables you to identify yourself as a veteran, active-duty personnel, or military spouse. Your pathway, cost, and required documents may be different from those for the civilian population, and the vet reps will be able to guide you in your quest for the appropriate resources.

Do the appropriate amount of research and request pertinent information, whether it's on paper or online. You will need to know all relevant information, including application and registration deadlines, financial aid timelines, class start dates, dorm-based information (if applicable) or in-town housing options, and who will be your point-of-contact for GI Bill concerns and Certificate of Eligibility. This topic is covered in depth in chapter 6.

Contacting the veterans' department of your school of choice should be a top priority. Difficulty in reaching representatives at your chosen location is not a good sign. The veterans' department at the school is your support system. If you cannot find anyone prior to attending the institution, how hard will it be to find a rep when you are in residence? If you check the Comparison Tool on the VA website, it will tell you how many individuals have used GI Bill benefits at that school. A high number may be either a good or a bad sign. Schools with high numbers demonstrate that they are familiar with the process, but may be overworked. Consider your own goals and your immediate need to receive answers. Again, be your own best advocate and weigh whether this institution will be able to fulfill your needs and provide for a smooth transition. I (Paul) would never rely only on customer service as a reason not to attend a particular school, but if you are not receiving the answers you need, you may need to consider a different school.

Apply

You have finished your research and settled on a particular school or schools. Now it is time to apply. Make sure you verify with the vet reps whether you need to pay the application fee; many schools waive the fee for active-duty personnel and veterans.

Check the school's website prior to applying. In most cases, schools have an application checklist on their admissions page. This should help you prepare all relevant documents such as your Joint Services Transcript (JST), DD 214, personal statement, SAT scores, and immunization records in advance.

Often the application checklist for a four-year college or university does not list a personal statement, but after you begin, the process will surprise you by requiring it. Personal statement length requirements range from 350 to 3,000 words. Some institutions list very specific essay prompts they want you to follow instead of writing a generic personal statement.

Writing a personal statement should not be nerve racking, although many service members feel tremendous stress during the experience, most just trying to find a starting point. Once you get going, you will find the experience to be a good precursor to your new college life. College does require a fair amount of writing.

Here are a few steps to guide you through your personal statement. Remember that you have unique experiences the typical applicant will not have.

Try to impress on the school how these unique experiences will help you make the school a better place if you attend. Most schools would be lucky to have you as a student with a real working knowledge of what it is like to be an adult who has lived past the age of eighteen *and* endured the rigorous demands placed upon soldiers.

Step 1

If you are having trouble starting, try brainstorming. I recommend sticking to topics related to your military experience. Think about your time in the service and the accomplishments you achieved. Consider the following topics:

- Why did you join the Army?
- What do you do in the Army?
- Did it require specialized training, such as Advanced Individual Training school, or even something like recruiter school?
- Were you assigned anywhere to put that training to use? Did you go anywhere interesting to conduct that training such as an overseas deployment?
- Have you visited interesting cities for training or deployment? Where? What did you do while deployed?
- Did you deploy to a war zone? How did it make you feel?
- Did you meet people from other countries on deployment or overseas assignment? What were the cultural differences?
- Did you deploy with other branches? What was that experience like?
- Did your deployments or combat experiences help shape the decisions you are making now? Is that why you are pursuing higher education?

Keep in mind that you are communicating to a board of civilians who may not share the same experiences as the typical service member or veteran. Ask yourself what it meant to be a squad leader. What did it mean to be a platoon sergeant? What did it mean to lead or follow soldiers in life and death situations and live with the consequences? Relate to your experiences as a human being tasked with these responsibilities. Do not underestimate your life as a soldier.

Step 2

Next, typically you can pick a subject and narrow the talking points. Sometimes it helps to brainstorm topics on paper that interest you to see if subjects overlap. Many soldiers feel that they do not do anything exciting in the military, which is definitely not true. Everything service members do is exciting to civilians. Where else can you see these types of activities? Maybe it is all in a day's work for you, but civilians find it fascinating.

Step 3

Once you settle on a topic, write it down on a piece of paper. Think about the topic, and write brief statements about everything that comes to your mind surrounding it. For example:

I joined the military after I graduated high school because I come from a military family.

Topics can include:

- Work
- Training
- Adventure
- Education
- Patriotism
- Security
- The war

Once you have drawn up a list, you need to add more layers to discuss. Here is an example:

- Work: productive suffering, meaningful work equals personal satisfaction, physical work, community environment
- Timing: graduated high school or college, came of age, rite of passage
- Patriotism: American flags, pledge of allegiance, 9/11 firefighters, serve my country, family military history, higher calling
- Security: airports, military bases, national events, worldwide, job security, pay, career
- The war: participate, serve my country, combat veteran, benefits, test of strength and willpower, face the unknown, perseverance

Step 4

Think about the notes you have written. Narrow your subject or topic by eliminating areas that don't seem to fit. For example, I (Jillian) don't think the section on security follows the theme of the other topics in the example above. When I review each section, it seems that I joined the military after high school graduation because it is a rite of passage that occurs in my family. The military taught me good work values and community involvement. I was able to participate in the defense of my country, which bolstered my perseverance to succeed. Somehow, the security section does not seem to fit with the rest, so I am eliminating it.

Step 5

- Organize your thoughts, and start to think about expanding the topics into a paper format.
- Patriotism: American flags, pledge of allegiance, 9/11 firefighters, serve my country, family military history, higher calling
- Timing: graduated high school or college, came of age, rite of passage
- Work: productive suffering, meaningful work equals personal satisfaction, physical work, community environment for the greater good
- The war: participate, serve my country, benefits, test of strength and will-power, face the unknown, perseverance

Now you need to determine why this experience shaped your current perspectives on education and organize the thoughts you listed in a logical written order. You should also start thinking about your career goals, your character strengths, and why you have chosen this particular institution. Below, I have numbered each group in the order I feel it belongs to be able to write an effective personal statement.

- Patriotism: American flags, pledge of allegiance, 9/11 firefighters, serve my country, family military history, higher calling (2)
- Timing: graduated high school or college, came of age, rite of passage (1)
- Work: productive suffering, meaningful work equals personal satisfaction, physical work, community environment for the greater good (3)
- The war: participate, serve my country, benefits, test of strength and will-power, face the unknown, perseverance (4)

Before you begin to write your statement, you need to consider your audience.

Here are a few questions to consider while writing:

- Who will read this essay?
- What does the reader already know about this subject, and why is it important?
- What do I want the reader to know about this subject?
- What part of my topic is the most interesting?

Your reader could be a dean at the school, an academic counselor, or a professor. Most likely, this individual has no knowledge of your topic if you write about a particular military experience, but do not discount the fact that she could also be a veteran. You need to explain why this experience shaped your decisions moving forward. You want her to see you in a different light than other applicants. You want your essay to stand apart and be more memorable than all of the others. Make sure to pick a topic that you can write about easily and that will attract interest.

Essay Example

After graduating high school in June of 2004, I enlisted in the United States Army. After watching the terrorist attacks on New York on September 11, 2001, I knew I could not ignore the pull I felt to participate in the effort my country was making. I also come from a long line of service members, and following in their footsteps seemed a natural thing to do.

Upon completion of my military occupational specialty of aviation mechanic, I was assigned to Joint Base Lewis–McChord to work on helicopters. Working under soldiers that were considered masters in their field, I learned to work in a team environment, be detail oriented, and be highly efficient with the time allotted to me. Within this training environment, I learned how to respond during high-stress situations and mastered my responsibilities.

Both Iraq and Afghanistan were combat-laden hotspots at this time, and I was soon sent to Iraq to assist with the mission. The year-long deployment to Iraq shaped my perspective on hard work and productive suffering. I knew that if I did not fulfill my responsibilities my fellow soldiers might be killed in action. The preparation and training we went through as a group prior to deploying paid off when we needed it most.

Iraq was a meaningful experience for me. It taught me to consider my actions as an integral player in the overall mission, regardless of my own personal considerations, because I had signed my name on the dotted line and had agreed to this position. Although I love the Army, I am ready to pursue the second chapter of my life, a bachelor's degree in mechanical engineering. Using the hands-on skills I learned repairing and rebuilding Army helicopters will enhance my education and diversify the classroom learning environment. My time in the service taught me what it takes to succeed, teamwork and willpower, and I am willing to share my work ethics with those around me.

I chose to attend XYZ University because of its reputation as a leader in the field of community involvement and its excellent mechanical engineering program. The university offers a holistic approach to the education of its students, and I feel my background will be respected and put to use to increase the effort and learning of my peers. The university's Veterans' Center offers numerous services to assist me should I need anything and offers many opportunities for veteran interaction. I hope that XYZ University will take the time to consider me as a prospective freshman student. If selected for admission, I know that working together with my professors, we can make the classroom a more productive and challenging place for learning.

Now you need to create your JST account (see chapter 7) and be prepared to send your official transcripts to the school immediately. Although many schools will take these at a later date, the earlier you submit them, the faster your application process can be completed. You will also need to apply for your Federal Student Aid (FSA) (see chapter 6). If you are applying to multiple schools, you can list up to ten on the federal aid application. This might lead to federal money for education expenses that does not need to be paid back!

Receive Acceptance

Most open enrollment schools quickly offer official acceptance. Schools with selective admissions often send official acceptance after many months. Check the school's website for reporting dates, or ask the veteran representatives. I have found a few schools with selective admissions that are able to give almost immediate acceptance or denial to veterans—for example, DePaul University in Chicago and Robert Morris University in Pittsburgh.

In most cases, your acceptance letter or your student account website will tell you the next steps you must take. These steps may include payment of fees to hold your spot in the school or for on-campus housing. This is typical for face-to-face schooling. Most active-duty service members pursuing school will not face these extra fees. Determine the final date for reimbursement of these fees in case you decide to attend another school at the last minute. That way you will not lose that money!

Apply for Tuition Assistance, GI Bill, or Federal Student Aid

You have received your school acceptance letters and decided upon an institution. Now it is time to activate your GI Bill or apply for TA to pay for your schooling. If you are still on active duty, you should contact the local Army Education Center to inquire about TA. If you are separated already, or soon will be, it is time to activate your GI Bill. If you rate both MGIB and Post-9/11, chapter 6 will help you decipher which one to choose. The veterans' representatives at your school of choice should be able to help as well, but many schools will naturally prefer the Post-9/11 because the school is paid directly. Be sure to consider the cost-benefit analysis of attending any particular school, since the Post-9/11 is not always the best entitlement to use. The section in chapter 6 titled "GI Bill Application and Conversion Process" will explain how to get your benefit started.

If you have a state-based benefit that pertains to your situation, you may need a bit more one-on-one help to determine your best pathway. Review carefully the explanation in chapter 6 of the benefits available to you before committing to either federal GI Bill. In some states, veterans can bring in more money by double-dipping on state-based educational benefits and MGIB than those strictly under Post-9/11. Again, if you cannot decipher the best pathway on your own, contact the veteran representatives at your school for advice on what other veterans have chosen. Never guess about the benefits: you could miss out on hundreds of dollars every month.

Now is also the time to apply for your FSA. Remember, TA and the GI Bill only go so far. TA does not cover books, computers, or tools, and it is capped at $250 per semester credit hour. FSA money can help bridge any gaps.

Register for Classes

You will need to meet with an academic counselor in order to choose the appropriate classes for your degree. If attending school online, often your academic counselor will email you a degree plan. The degree plan lists every class you need to take to attain your declared degree or certification.

Typically, degree plans will also reflect any free military credits the school awards you based on the information provided in your JST. Most schools will not inform you of the evaluation outcome until you have committed to a schedule of classes, so more guidance may be needed from an academic counselor prior to class selection for the first term. Starting with general education subjects is a safe route. Most of the time military credits only knock out elective credits, and general education subjects in a traditional degree pathway are always necessary.

If you need help registering for classes, you may want to visit the registrar's office of your school. In most cases, face-to-face registration will still be possible. You may also need to check to determine if a "hold" has been placed on your GoArmyEd account. Sometimes, if the TA process has not processed correctly because documents are missing, your account may be on hold. The registrar can tell you why.

Always be aware of the registration deadlines. Check with your school to see if the institution offers early registration for active-duty service members or veterans. This is an especially crucial step for veterans using their GI Bills. The VA will only cover classes listed on your degree plan (just like TA). Early registration allows veterans to pick classes before the civilian population. Basically, every class you want should be open. If you miss these deadlines, you may have trouble getting into the classes you need to maintain full-time status according to the VA (full-time status = full-time housing allowance on Post-9/11). If you miss the final deadline, you also may lose your spot at the school. This is important if you have not been a full-time student and you are taking classes as they become available or because you have a full-time job.

Veterans will most likely need to produce a copy of their DD 214 for the veterans' department at the school to prove benefit eligibility. It is a good idea always to keep a copy on hand along with your student identification number. Active-duty personnel may need a copy of their orders to be on the base where they are currently stationed. Often the local community college will want to see a copy of these orders in order to grant the service member in-state tuition. Spouses may need a copy of the orders as well as their dependent identification card in order to receive the in-state tuition rate for some states. Make sure your spouse has access to a copy of your orders just in case you deploy. Spouses using transferred Post-9/11 benefits should keep a copy of their service member's DD 214 if he or she has already separated.

If you previously attended other schools, you will need to have those transcripts sent to the new institution for evaluation. In most cases, the transcripts will need to go from the old school directly to the new one in order to remain official. It is usually a smart idea to have a couple of spare sets of transcripts on hand. Once a transcript is opened, it is no longer considered official, so order an extra one for yourself. You should take a copy of the transcript with you to meet with your academic counselor to help guide your class selections prior to evaluation of your official transcripts. No point in taking a class you have already taken!

You are most likely ready to matriculate at this point. At a CC, you will need to take math and English placement tests to determine your starting point for these two classes. If you test below college freshman level, the school will place you in remedial classes. This is not a big deal, but it can slow your progress. These classes will help boost your baseline skill level and make you more successful in your future classes. If you would like to boost your math and English skills prior to taking the placement test, see http://www.petersons.com/DOD and click on the "Online Academic Skills Course" link. The same Peterson's website also hosts the College Placement Skills Testing program, which was designed to help students score better on college placement tests. Testing into freshman-level math and English helps you avoid remedial coursework.

Matriculation usually requires an orientation session. Some schools offer the orientation in an online format; others require you physically to attend. Your academic counselor should inform you when your paperwork has been processed and your official degree plan is on file. Then you have matriculated!

All of the initial hard work to start school is done at this point. Now you need to prepare for everything else. If you are a veteran, you may need housing. Again, check with the vet reps for recommendations. Some service members find roommates through the vet reps, the Facebook page for veterans attending the school, or the student veterans' associations.

Start checking out all of the veteran services offered on the school campus or in the surrounding areas. Knowing where the services are located may save you heartache and time later on. Some of the services offer outreach; some might be strictly for socialization or networking. Take advantage of both.

If you have served in a combat zone, find your closest VA Vet Center at http://www.va.gov/directory/guide/vetcenter_flsh.asp. The Vet Centers may offer eligible veterans counseling, outreach, and referral services to help with postwar readjustment to civilian life. Research the VA service at http://www.vetcenter.va.gov/index.asp.

Student veterans' organizations that are school specific operate on many campuses. Usually, you can find their information on the school's website. Student Veterans of America (SVA: http://www.studentveterans.org/) connects veterans through social media outlets to offer support and promote student vet success. Participating in an organization can help veterans integrate into their local veteran community. Veterans who seek out other veterans typically have higher success rates. Veterans who isolate themselves may have difficulty transitioning.

STANDARDIZED ADMISSIONS TESTS

SAT and ACT

Depending upon the school you select to attend, an ACT (www.act.org) or SAT (www.collegeboard.org) score may be necessary for acceptance. Many schools offer veterans flexible admissions by bypassing these exams and accepting writing samples and/or placement tests instead. To determine individual requirements, call the veterans' representatives at the school. Typically, a quick call can help you learn about all of the required application materials.

If the school requires an ACT or SAT score, you need to develop a plan of attack. You will need to research application deadline dates and test dates and locate study resources. To find the required application dates, check the school's website and contact the vet reps. In some cases, schools can accept scores for veterans at a later date. Many institutions are aware that often soldiers return from deployment and transition shortly thereafter, leaving little time for test preparation and test taking.

Test dates can be tricky. ACT and SAT tests are only offered on specific dates on Army bases. Soldiers need to book an appointment through their education centers and clear the time with command. Make sure to leave plenty of time to prepare appropriately. If possible, SAT and ACT exams should not be taken at a moment's notice.

Always check with a school to determine which test the institution accepts, then focus on that particular test for preparation. Some schools will take either; in that case, students may want to take both and submit their best score.

When testing at a base, you can list your school's name or leave it blank. If you decide to take both the SAT and the ACT and submit your top score, do not list the school's name on the test application. If you list the school's name, your scores will go directly to the institution. If you *do not* list the school's name, later you can request that your scores be sent from either organization. Scores are always kept by the individual organization that administered that test, such as the College Board for the SAT scores. These can be found and sent to your future school by using the military score request form. This specific form is necessary because tests taken in the military are funded by the DANTES program and scores are retrieved differently. It may require an additional fee.

If you opt to send your scores to a school or schools during test registration either on the base or off-base, you will receive four free score reports for the ACT and SAT. If you decide to wait and send your scores after determining the results, each SAT request will cost $11.25 (http://sat.collegeboard.org/register/us-services-fees#), and each ACT request will cost $12 (http://www.actstudent.org/scores/send/costs.html). To put your best foot forward, I recommend that you take both tests, wait until your scores are posted, and then pay to send whichever test produces the most competitive results.

If soldiers are not satisfied with their score, they may retest the ACT and SAT off-base during the next test date with no waiting period. On base, a six-month waiting period applies. Soldiers receive one free test on the base. Currently, the SAT runs $49 and the ACT $39 at the education center on most military installations.

SAT and ACT scores are not returned immediately. Typically, when testing on a base, test scores take approximately ten weeks to be delivered. However, scores can be viewed earlier on the SAT and ACT websites. ACT multiple-choice scores are typically reported within eight weeks (http://www.actstudent.org/scores/viewing-scores.html); essay scores, roughly two weeks later. SAT scores (http://sat.collegeboard.org/scores/availability) take approximately three weeks to be posted online.

The SAT and ACT are completely different tests. Table 4.1 demonstrates some of the differences. For more detailed explanations of the tests, visit the SAT and ACT websites. The biggest difference is that the SAT tests your ability to apply knowledge while the ACT tests your current level of knowledge on subjects.

You will notice when looking at Table 4.1 that the SAT does not test science, but the ACT does. You will not need to know incredibly specific science information for the ACT; rather, it tests your reading and reasoning skills. The SAT has a stronger emphasis on vocabulary, and the ACT tests higher-level math concepts than the SAT (trigonometry).

The optional essay on the ACT is not factored into your composite score. If you take it, the essay is scored separately. The SAT essay is required and factored into the writing score.

The ACT keeps each subject area separate, whereas the SAT subject areas move back and forth. This may be difficult for some test takers.

Free test preparation for military and dependents for both SAT and ACT can be found at http://www.eknowledge.com/Affiliate_Welcome.asp?coupon=3A8E9CEFCE. Khan Academy (http://www.khanacademy.org) has free test preparation help for the SAT math section. Both the SAT and ACT websites have free test questions available for you to use for test preparation as well. Check YouTube for SAT and ACT videos, but always consider the source of the videos before deciding whether to use the information.

Numerous test preparation companies offer classes, but no reimbursement is available for these options. These programs offer structured classroom environments and curriculum that may help some service members, but classes do not emphasize an individual's strengths and weaknesses as a self-paced program would. Just remember that "self-paced" means "self-motivated." You have to organize your time and effort on your own.

Table 4.1. SAT ACT

SAT	ACT
Test covers: reading, vocabulary, grammar and usage, writing, and math (includes essay) 3 main components: critical reasoning, mathematics, an essay.	Test covers: grammar and usage, math, reading, science reasoning, and an optional writing section (check with school) 5 main components: English, math, reading, science, and an optional essay (check if school demands essay)
Test timeframe: 3 hours 45 minutes	Test timeframe: 3 hours 30 minutes (4 hours with essay)
Format: multiple choice and grid-in	Format: all multiple choice
Guessing penalty of a quarter-point	No guessing penalty
Measures student's ability to: draw inferences, synthesize information, understand the difference between main and supporting ideas, vocabulary in context, apply mathematical concepts, problem solve, interpret charts, communicate ideas, revise and edit, understand grammatical structure.	Measures student's: written and rhetorical English, mathematical skills, reading comprehension, interpretation, analysis, reasoning, problem solving, writing skills stressed in high school and entry-level college classes
Scoring: Penalty for guessing. Maximum score 2400, each section is worth 800. Average score in 2012 was 1498, critical reading 496, mathematics 514, writing 488.	Scoring: ACT assessment only counts correct answers. Composite scores range from 1 to 36, sub scores from 1 to 18. The composite score is an average of the four sub scores. National average in 2012 was 21.1.

Graduate Record Examination (GRE)/Graduate Management Admission Test (GMAT)

If you are planning to attend graduate school, you may find that your institution of choice requires a GRE or GMAT score. Always check with the school to determine which standardized admissions test is required for your graduate school program. Traditionally, the GRE is taken for most graduate degrees outside of business, and the GMAT is taken for business school. Only the university and college can tell you exactly which test the institution will demand, but taking the GRE might open more options.

Currently, the GRE costs $195 and the GMAT is $250. You can receive reimbursement for taking these tests, as well as for professional tests such as the LSAT, which is required for law school. You can receive reimbursement through your GI Bill, but it will reduce your remaining benefits. If you are still on active duty, it is best to go through DANTES and save all of your education benefits.

In the past few years, the GRE has become more widely accepted for admissions to business schools, and many top-tier universities, including Yale, Harvard, and Georgetown, have jumped on board. Princeton Review has a link that lists more than seven hundred schools currently accepting the GRE for business school (http://www.princetonreview.com/uploadedFiles/ Sitemap/Home_Page/Business_Hub/Opinions_and_Advice/MBAAccepting-GRE.pdf). Try an initial search, and then cross-reference with the institutions that interest you. If your institution of choice accepts either, try taking a practice exam for each test first (check both websites). You might find that you have an aptitude for one more than the other.

Free GRE/GMAT Test Preparation

- GRE: http://www.ets.org/s/gre/pdf/practice_book_GRE_pb_revised_ general_test.pdf
- GMAT: http://www.mba.com/us/the-gmat-exam/prepare-for-the-gmat-exam/test-prep-materials/free-gmat-prep-software
- Georgetown University: http://www.youtube.com/watch?v=xFyqJSucqSo
- Khan Academy: http://www.khanacademy.org/ (GMAT math)

Reimbursement while on Active Duty

To receive reimbursement through DANTES for either the GRE or the GMAT, visit your local education center for the correct forms, or follow these steps.

1. Visit the following link to download the appropriate reimbursement forms for the GRE and the GMAT: http://www.dantes.doded.mil/_content/exams_reimbursement_form.pdf#zoom=100
2. Sign up to take the GRE or GMAT. The applicant is responsible for all testing fees up front.
3. Receive official GRE or GMAT scores (about three weeks).
4. Fill out the appropriate forms, and return them to the education center's Test Control officer within ninety days of testing.

Veterans' Reimbursement for Testing Costs

In many cases, you can be reimbursed the costs of standardized tests through the GI Bill by filling out the 22-0810 through the Veteran's Online Application (VONAPP). VONAPP is also used to activate your benefit, and details of this process can be found in chapter 6. The calculation of benefits also differs for each GI Bill. Under the MGIB the cost of each test will be deducted from the overall worth of your MGIB, which currently stands at $61,812 if you have never used the benefit before. Therefore, if your test costs $250, only $250 will be deducted from this amount. If you are working with the Post-9/11, the benefit is slightly less generous. For every test paid that you elect to have the GI Bill cover you will lose one month of the benefit, even if the test only costs $50. Visit http://www.benefits.va.gov/gibill/national_testing.asp for more information.

Chapter Five

Unique Army-Based Programs

The Army provides soldiers many diverse pathways to advance and excel within its ranks. Civilian education is frequently promoted as a recruiting tool, and most soldiers, sooner or later, know they must plan for life after the military. In many cases, starting life in the Army on the right educational foot can maximize the amount of benefits and opportunities you will have available later. Take advantage of starting or continuing your education while in the Army to improve promotion potential while in the service and to assist in the transition process to civilian life after the Army.

Chapter 5 describes the programs and benefits that are unique to the Army, with a focus on commissioning programs and educational opportunities in general, regardless of rank. The programs and opportunities provided by the Army to pursue an academic credential are diverse, but typically hard to find and navigate. Counselors at the local education center can assist in finding you a program that fits your needs, and help you review your potential options to advance your education for the betterment of both the Army and your future endeavors as a civilian.

COMMISSIONING IN THE ARMY THROUGH EDUCATION

Some Army commissioning programs are ideal for teens and young adults who want to enter the Army as officers, such as the United States Military Academy or the Uniform Services University of Health Science. Though some of these programs are available to civilians, many specifically target current enlisted personnel hoping to become officers. Almost all of the programs have equivalent pathways for National Guardsmen and reservists.

The following is a list of available programs:

- United States Military Academy
- Direct Commission Officers

- Uniform Services University of Health Science
- Army Medical Department
- Officer Candidate School
- Green to Gold

United States Military Academy

Founded in 1802, the United States Military Academy (USMA) is the oldest military academy in the United States. Located in West Point, New York, it is not only dedicated to molding exceptional future officers, but does so as one of the most elite academic universities in the nation. According to the *U.S. News and World Report*, the institution is ranked twenty-fourth among all national liberal arts colleges[1] and has a selective acceptance rate, currently 8.96 percent. This is only a few percentage points higher than prestigious universities such as Harvard and Yale. Many of the degrees are science-oriented and include engineering, mathematics, and physics, but the school also offers degrees in humanities and social sciences.

A full scholarship paying tuition and room and board is awarded to each student; it requires that future officers serve a five-year active-duty service obligation in the Army. Candidates for admission must be between the ages of seventeen and twenty-two, not be married, not be pregnant, and not be legally responsible for any children. Review the components of the USMA admissions package to learn more information (http://www.usma.edu/admissions/SitePages/Steps.aspx). All potential candidates must submit a questionnaire (https://candidate.usma.edu/guest/cq/dad_pcq_part1.cfm?field1=BW) to determine eligibility.

You must be nominated in order to apply to the USMA. You can be nominated by a member of Congress, the president or vice president of the United States, or the secretary of the army. Most US representatives and senators—as well as the president and vice president—will have a link directly to the form you need to fill out to seek their nomination on their respective websites. You may also be able to obtain a service-connected nomination if you are the son or daughter of a current military service member with at least eight years of service, a dependent child of a service member who has been killed in action, currently in the National Guard or Reserves, or if you are a student currently in a junior or senior ROTC program in high school. Service-connected nominations are technically self-nominations due to either merit or a relationship with a current service member, and each requires a different type of documentation detailed on the nominations page found here: http://www.usma.edu/admissions/SitePages/Apply_Nominations .aspx.

To be competitive for admission to the USMA, you will want to pursue a challenging high school curriculum by completing as many Advanced Placement courses as possible, as well as at least two years of a foreign language. You will also need to demonstrate leadership abilities during high school. Join clubs and seek positions within the student government or the community that show your leadership potential. Either the ACT plus the writing test or the SAT is mandatory.

You should be able to pass a Candidate Fitness Assessment that includes a run, sit-ups, and push-ups (similar to the standard Army Physical Fitness Test [APFT]), as well as some unique tests such as a timed shuttle run and throwing a basketball from the kneeling position. You will also need to undergo a full medical exam to ensure that you are physically and mentally fit.

Find the "Prospectus" link on the USMA website for more on the admissions process, as well as what daily life is like for those who are accepted into the academy. If you have great aspirations for yourself and are determined to join the military as an officer, then West Point may be for you. While your character and integrity will always shape your worth as an officer, not many Army officers have the distinction of wearing a West Point class ring.

Direct Commission Officers

The Army's direct commissioning program, referred to as Direct Commission Officers (DCO), allow those with the necessary training, education, and licenses to become commissioned officers in the Army in the quickest way possible. Lawyers, chaplains, and civilians in medical fields—such as doctors, dentists, veterinarians, and clinical psychologists are eligible for this program. However, professionals in the medical field become officers as DCOs through the Army Medical Department, which is discussed later in this chapter.

Judge Advocates General's Corps (JAG)

Judge Advocates General's Corps (JAG) attorneys commonly represent soldiers who are defendants brought up on criminal charges under the Uniform Code of Military Justice, but may also represent the Army in such cases as a prosecutor. They also provide legal advice to commanders, soldiers, and family members outside of the courtroom. Their expertise can include legal reviews or advice in civil matters, and laws dealing with employment, international law, intelligence, and contract laws.

Being selected to direct commission as a JAG attorney requires that eligible candidates have successfully obtained a Juris Doctorate (JD) and have passed the bar in any state or the District of Columbia. They must also be US citizens and be under the age of forty-two at the time of entry into active duty.

Second-year law students pursuing their JD may apply for the Army Summer Intern program where they will serve under current JAG attorneys and are assessed on their legal capabilities. If it is determined that a candidate possesses the required legal skills, he may be offered a commission in the Army as an officer. Currently, the program accepts seventy-five interns annually. The JAG lawyer pathway is also open for reservists, and many of the standards are the same as for active-duty JAG officers. Although it is common for officers to begin their careers as first lieutenants directly out of law school, prior military service may count toward starting at a higher rank.

Packets must be compiled and submitted by a recruiter, and locations can be found here: http://www.goarmy.com/locate-a-recruiter.html. Select "Army Law" under "Area of Interest." Paralegal specialist is under this program, but does not result in commissioning as an officer.

If selected, JAG candidates attend the Direct Commissioning Course (DCC) that consists of six weeks of field and classroom training. The course will review the basic necessities of leadership principles and military tactics. More information on what to expect can be found here: http://www.benning.army.mil/infantry/199th/dcc/. After general officer training at DCC, JAG attorneys will attend a ten and a half week course in Charlottesville, Virginia, which covers the specifics of Army legal matters.

Current soldiers might be able to have the Army pay for law school under the Funded Legal Education Program, also resulting in a commission; however, only fifteen scholarships are awarded per year for this highly competitive program. Speak to a military career counselor or the Retention Office for more information on how to apply for this program.

Army Chaplain Corps

Those who wish to tend to the spiritual health of the Army community may commission as an officer through the Army Chaplain Corps. Eligibility requirements dictate that potential applicants hold a baccalaureate degree as well as a graduate degree in theological or religious studies. The graduate degree must include at least seventy-two semester hours. This abnormally large number of semester hours is required because these programs typically include additional coursework in a certificate or certification preparation program leading to some form of pastoral counseling. Potential applicants must also already be serving as certified clergy in their chosen faith and have done so for no less than two years. Active-duty chaplains must not be older than forty-two and commit to serve three years. This program is available for reservists as well, and the Reserve pathway does not require two years of prior professional experience. Reserve officer chaplains must commission before the age of forty-five.

Similarly to JAG candidates, your packet must be organized and submitted by a recruiter. Find your closest location here: http://www.goarmy.com/locate-a-recruiter.html. Select "Chaplain" under "Area of Interest." Soldiers considering a chaplain assistant's option also should contact a recruiter; however, it does not result in commissioning as an officer.

Selected candidates will attend the USA Chaplains Center and School at Fort Jackson, South Carolina, which is conducted in four stages. The first is the Chaplain Initial Military Training, which teaches common Army skills such as military traditions and customs, field operations, and combat survival. Phase I focuses on Army writing and correspondence and Phases II and III train chaplains on how to apply their spiritual duties in the hierarchical Army environment.

Under the Chaplain Candidate Scholarship Partnership, it may also be possible for current theological graduate students to receive tuition waivers for their program at select schools and gain entry into the Army Chaplaincy as officers. The eligible graduate programs can be found at http://www.goarmy.com/chaplain/candidate-program/candidate-scholarship-program.html, but require the assistance of a chaplain recruiter to apply.

Uniform Services University of Health Science

The Uniform Services University of Health Science (USUHS) is available to both military and civilians, but according to the USUHS website, 30 to 40 percent of the incoming student body has prior military experience.[2]

USUHS is open to any branch of the military and assists service members in obtaining MDs, and a master's- or doctoral-level credential in many health-related fields, including dentistry, public health, nursing, health administration, and psychiatric care.

As with most medical schools, a baccalaureate degree and a competitive Medical College Admissions Test score are required. Applications for each school are submitted separately and can be found at https://www.usuhs.edu/apply. Prior to selection, each applicant must state which branch of the military they wish to join after graduation. Those selected will receive full pay and benefits of an O1, and all tuition and fees are covered. Prior to attendance at the university, all accepted students must attend a four-to-six-week officer training course that covers military customs, traditions, and officer responsibilities. Upon graduation students will be commissioned as an O3. Service obligations can vary depending on the type of credential received.

A new program has been established recently entitled Enlisted to Medical Degree Preparatory Program, which allows currently enlisted personnel who hold a bachelor's degree to complete the necessary prerequisites to apply to either a postgraduate program within USUHS or the Army's Health Professional Scholarship Program, which leads to a medical degree from a civilian school. Service members wishing to apply must have a minimum of a 3.2 GPA and one year of college algebra and one year of college English. They must also not be older than thirty-one and have achieved at least a 600 on all categories of the SAT or a minimum of a 28 on the ACT. Application packets must be submitted to usarmy.jbsa.medcom.mbx.medcom-emdp2@mail.mil no later than January 23 before the following academic year. Instructions for the application packet can be found here: https://www.usuhs.edu/emdp2, but access to MILPER message 14-326 requires Army Knowledge Online (AKO) access.

Army Medical Department

The US Army Medical Department (AMEDD) is a broad organization that administers the training and recruiting of the physical and mental health job specialties for the Army. These occupations range from radiologist to clinical social worker, and everything in between. There are a total of eighty-five occupations and the entire list can be found here: http://www.goarmy.com/amedd/medical-specialties.html.

Based at Fort Sam Houston in San Antonio, Texas, it has medical training facilities all over the United States and each specialty encounters a different path for training and education. Currently, all specialties, except the IPAP (Interservice Physician Assistant Program), require a recruiter to determine your eligibility and assist in the organization of your packet for selection. A full list of AMEDD recruiters can be found here: http://www.goarmy.com/locate-a-recruiter.html. Select "Medical (AMEDD)" from the dropdown menu and search by desired zip code.

Doctors of multiple specialties, dentists, and veterinarians can often join the Army with a current board-certified license from any state. Most highly skilled medical professionals become officers through the DCO pathway of the AMEDD program. Contact an AMEDD recruiter to review your options if you currently hold a license for a particular state and you do not require further education. Typically, the only additional training required after being recruited as a DCO is a two-week officer course describing basic rank structure, customs, and traditions of the Army. There are a few available programs that will pay for advanced schooling in a medical field if an eligible soldier needs it, such as the Health Professional Scholarship Program (HPSP). This program will pay for full tuition, a generous monthly stipend (currently slightly above $2,000), and the pay of a second lieutenant for six weeks a year. Regardless of the method of entry, most officers will commission directly as a captain.

One recruiter I (Paul) spoke with told me the story of a student who was being considered for entry into a particular medical school. Medical programs are increasingly concerned with the student's ability to pay because many medical professionals exit school with hundreds of thousands of dollars in debt. When the board learned the student was awarded an HPSP scholarship, the student felt that they regarded his application as more competitive because of his ability to pay the full tuition. If you have the academic skills and ambitions of becoming a medical professional for the Army, contact a recruiter to look into the variety of entry points offered, including those offered to become an Army Reserve officer.

The three most common programs are: the AMEDD Enlisted Commissioning Program, the Interservice Physician Assistant Program (IPAP), and the Master of Social Work (MSW) Program.

AMEDD Enlisted Commissioning Program (AECP)

The AECP program pays for the bachelor's degree of science in nursing (BSN) and leads to commissioning as a second lieutenant. Candidates must be a US citizen between the ages of twenty-one and forty-two, be in the grade of E4 or higher, and be able to extend their current contract up to seventy-two months prior to selection to the program. You may select the school you wish to attend as long as it is accredited by the Commission on Collegiate Nursing Education or the National League for Nursing Accreditation Commission.

AECP will pay up to $9,000 a year in tuition for up to twenty-four months along with a book stipend and current full pay and benefits. Most soldiers I (Paul) encounter are working on the prerequisites commonly required by schools for entry into BSN programs. AECP maintains a list of common requirements (http://www.usarec.army.mil/downloads/mrb/AECP/Application_Process/FY_14_AECP_Guidelines.pdf), which includes:

- 6 semester hours (SH) in math/statistics
- 23 SH in natural sciences (anatomy and physiology, chemistry with a lab, microbiology with a lab, etc.)
- 9 SH of social sciences (psychology/sociology/growth and development)
- 6 SH of English (must include English composition)
- 3 SH of humanities (literature/philosophy)
- 6 SH of history

Tuition Assistance (TA) can be used to fund these courses if you either temporarily select to pursue a degree that contains these courses or obtain a memo from the school you are electing to obtain your BSN from stating that you still require these courses for entry in their program.

Interservice Physician Assistant Program (IPAP)

What exactly is a physician's assistant (PA)? PAs are health care professionals certified to practice medicine under the supervision of a physician. PAs often diagnose common illnesses and prescribe some forms of medication. While PAs are not medical doctors, it is common for military PAs to be referred to as "docs" because they serve many of the lower-tiered functions of a doctor.

All selected candidates are released from their current duty stations to attend the PA program at the University of Nebraska Medical Center to receive both a bachelor's and master's, which is common for most PA programs. A common misconception with the IPAP program is that candidates must have an associate's degree in order to apply, but this is false. Candidates must have sixty transferrable credits at the University of Nebraska. If you do have an associate's degree, the University of Nebraska will simply carve up your degree, take the credits they like, and reject those they do not. These credits must specifically include:

- 6 SH in English (3 SH must be composition) and CLEPs are authorized
- 6 SH of humanities to include government, history, foreign language, art, social science, or religion
- 3 SH of psychology
- 6 SH of chemistry (general or higher, not introductory)
- 3 SH of anatomy and 3 SH of physiology, though taking anatomy and physiology I and II can be used to fulfill this requirement
- 3 SH of college algebra or higher
- A medical terminology course

You can use TA for these prerequisites, even if you already hold a bachelor's degree; however, you must obtain a memo from the IPAP program manager stating which prerequisites you need and TA will only be eligible for these specific courses. TA can also be used for any science courses that you previously completed that are older than five years. An SAT score of 1,000 between the reading and math section is required, with neither section's score below a 450. You must have a minimum of a 2.75 GPA, but having the highest possible GPA will increase the chances of selection. The remaining sixty SHs can be a combination of general education courses, electives, or credit awarded from your military training.

If you currently work in the health care field for the military, your training may be able to cover some of the natural science requirements. The Academic Delay option might also be a possibility if you are still working toward a maximum of fifteen SHs, but these courses must be completed before December 31 of the current year. A slot will be reserved for you if you are selected. You will be paid as an E5 during the twenty-nine-month program, be commissioned as a first lieutenant, and be eligible for the rank of captain within thirty months, or become a commissioned Reserve officer.

Master of Social Work (MSW) Program

The MSW program for the Army is administered at the Fayetteville State University (FSU) campus near Fort Bragg, North Carolina. Unlike the AECP and IPAP programs, the MSW program requires that you have already obtained a bachelor's degree. While a bachelor's degree in social work is not specifically required, the prerequisites for entry into this program do target many of the classes that are found in most social science degrees and include:

- 3 SH of human biology, though anatomy and physiology I and II or the psychology course of human growth and development also suffice
- 3 SH of humanities
- 18 SH in social or behavioral sciences

While you can use TA for any of the prerequisites that you have not completed, you will need a memo from the FSU MSW program stating that the courses are required. An overall undergraduate GPA of 3.0 and a minimum combined score of 290 on the Graduate Record Exam are necessary, as well as the FSU program application for admittance.

Civilians are also eligible to apply to become commissioned officers. If selected, you will be sent to the Basic Officer Leader's Course before attending the thirty-eight-month course to complete the MSW. The last two years of the MSW program consists of twenty-four months working at an internship site, which is a common requirement of any MSW program. After graduation from the program, students are commissioned as officers and incur a five year and two month service obligation. The program is also open to the Army Reserves.

This section is intended to provide a brief guide, introducing those who are interested to the possible options within the Army medical fields. With eighty-five separate programs, and most of the legwork completed by an AMEDD recruiter, this information is only an overview of the potential options. Contact your nearest AMEDD recruiter to review all possible options, determine eligibility, and investigate the gaps that currently exist in your potential application. The counselors at your local education center can also assist in determining any further education you may need to become eligible.

Officer Candidate School

Like West Point, and the countless ROTC programs found on college campuses across the United States, Officer Candidate School (OCS) allows both civilian and enlisted personnel to fill the ranks of future Army officers without specialized industry training. In the past, it was possible to attend OCS with 90+ semester hours toward a specific bachelor's degree with the understanding that the degree would be completed within a specified amount of time after commissioning. Now all OCS applicants must already possess a degree. I (Paul) suggest that you speak with a counselor at your education center to discuss options for finishing a degree and create a timeline for the OCS application. Depending upon your progression toward the degree and the total amount of credits you may have from one or more schools, it is possible that your counselor could suggest a specific school that may either accommodate more of your credits or have an accelerated program that can be finished quickly.

The primary Army regulation that outlines OCS policy is the 350-51. Every year new Military Personnel (MILPER) messages are issued to modify current policies and eligibility requirements. Since one of the roles of OCS is to fill the gaps in the number of officers commissioned every year, it is important that you find the latest MILPER message to ensure you are aware of the most current considerations. The latest MILPER message, numbered 14-219 and dated 7 August, 2014, will dictate policy until it is amended at some point in the future. The eligibility requirements are:

- Be a US citizen, age thirty-three or younger
- Have a bachelor's degree
- Possess an APFT score of 240 with a minimum of 80 in all three events
- Have a General Technical Score of 110 or higher
- Not have over five years of service
- Must hold the rank of E1–E7 (E8, E9, and warrant officer ranks are not eligible)
- Must not be on a medical profile

Waivers cannot currently be obtained for the above requirements. However, waivers can be obtained for legal/moral/civil issues, soldiers with less than six months on their current tour or less than twelve months in their current Military Occupational Speciality (MOS), soldiers on Permanent Change of Station (PCS) orders, soldiers slotted to attend a training school, and soldiers that have between five and six years of service. Waivers must be submitted at least forty-five days prior to the submission deadline of packets to usarmy.knox.hrc.mbx.opmd-ocs-acc-br@mail.mil, and must include a 4187 signed by the Company Commander, a 4187-1-R signed by the battalion commanding officer, the most updated Enlisted Record Brief, all college transcripts, and the most current APFT scores.

If interested in pursuing this pathway, your very first move is to speak with your company's commanding officer. His or her guidance and assistance will be required throughout the process. Not only will the company commander need to sign your 4187s if you require any waivers, but they will be filling out the DA Form 5339, which is an endorsement of your skills as an officer. He or she will grade your verbal and written skills, your leadership skills, and problem-solving skills. In other words, if your company commander does not believe that you are officer material, your packet will be doomed from the start. The personnel office, or unit-level S1, will advise you about the necessary steps prior to submitting your packet. They are required, per the AR 350-51, to provide the best assistance and guidance possible; however, as a potential officer, you must take the initiative and gather all of the documentation on your own. If your S1 is not providing adequate guidance, you may also need your company commander to help you follow through with all appropriate documentation. Human Resource Command (HRC) also holds periodic Defense Connect Online webinars regarding the instructions about the proper process in assembling and submitting an OCS application. Email usarmy.knox.hrc.mbx.opmd-ocs-acc-br@mail.mil to obtain an invite and push your S1 and command to attend.

To obtain a complete list of all required documents visit https://www.hrc. army.mil/LoginRedirect.aspx?redirect=https%3a%2f%2fwww.hrc.army.mil %2fOfficer%2fOfficer%20Candidate%20School. You will need a Common Access Card (CAC) or an Army Knowledge Online (AKO) username and password to access this site. The first document you should review is the OCS Checklist. The most important documents include:

- Essay: A one-page handwritten essay with the title of "Why I Want to Be an Army Officer." Be honest, selfless, and humble in your statement. You should also have someone review your essay for grammatical mistakes prior to admission.
- DA Form 61: This is your Application for Appointment and will require you to input personal information as well as obtain two recommendations from your immediate and second immediate commanders.
- Transcript Assessment Memo: This is obtained from a counselor at your local education center. The memo will state the date you obtained your degree, total number of credits, and your total GPA. Any course listed on any transcripts you may have will be part of your GPA calculation, not only those grades on the transcripts from the school you obtained your degree from. You want to ensure you have the highest GPA possible.
- DA Form 5339: Company commander's evaluation sheet.
- DA Form 705: Most current APFT scores. The latest scores must not be older than sixty days from the date of the submission of your packet.
- DA 5500/5501: If you exceed the height and weight standards, males must obtain the 5500 and females must obtain the 5501 for tape measurement.
- Letters of Recommendation: It is highly suggested you obtain three of the four maximum allowed. Aim to obtain letters from the highest ranks possible, but it will help if you have at least one letter from a sergeant major.

As the right-hand personnel of commanders at every level of the Army, they are usually the best unbiased judges of an officer's character.
• Commander's Tattoo and Branding Certification Memo: Army regulations concerning tattoos changed just recently, so it would be wise to review the AR 670-1. Tattoos can no longer be visible on the neck.

One of the first tasks that the S1 will help you with is to ensure all of the information in your iPERMs and ERB are up to date. Once most of your packet is complete, your unit S1 will submit it to the battalion S1 for review, who will then submit it to the brigade S1. It is the brigade S1's responsibility to organize your structured interview, which is not to be conducted below the O6 level. While it may be organized by an O6, it is possible your interview will be conducted by one O4 and two O3s, but the exact makeup of the board may vary across brigades. Your answers will be ranked according to many of the same personal dimensions that your company commander used to rank you on the DA Form 5339. Common questions of enlisted soldiers include:

• Why you initially joined the Army.
• Specific events in your Army career that provided the most satisfaction and the most frustration.
• Examples of how you accomplished a task with little to no guidance.
• Examples of leadership experience and how you handled the situation.
• Long-term goals in the military.

After the structured interview, which is recorded on the DA Form 6285, your packet is submitted by the brigade S1 through AKO. You can expect an answer within eight to ten weeks by email. You can also check with your S1 because they will also be notified of HRC's decision. I (Paul) suggest you visit http://www.benning.army.mil/infantry/199th/ocs/ to get an idea of what to expect during OCS after being accepted.

The eligibility requirements to become a Reserve officer are identical, but assistance and packet submission is organized by your Army Reserves Career Division, who can be reached at usarmy.usarc.arcd.mbx.hq-ops-spcmsn-organizational-mailbox2@mail.mil.

Green to Gold

Soldiers commonly attend a wide range of different colleges throughout their military careers. Constant PCS and deployments mean soldiers may have taken classes from a variety of schools that happen to be present on military installations. One of the more difficult aspects of being a soldier student is nailing down one college to finish a degree with. Green to Gold (G2G) solves this problem because the Army releases you from either your current contract, or normal duties, to finish your degree with the end goal of commissioning as an Army officer. There are four different programs under G2G, and choosing the correct one will depend on where you are in your academic career, as well as your financial situation. All of the programs share similar eligibility requirements and application details, but they can vary widely in terms of the process and benefits. The four programs include the two-year active-duty option, the two-year non-scholarship option, the two-/three-/four-year scholarship option, and the Commander's Hip Pocket Scholarship.

The first step is finding the right school, along with the right ROTC program, to finish your degree. A full list can be found at http://www.goarmy.com/rotc/find-schools.html. The school you attend as a student does not necessarily have to be where you complete your ROTC requirements, so feel free to choose the best school for you as long as it has a partnership with a nearby ROTC program. Your application is submitted online by creating an account at www.goarmy.com/rotc/enlisted-soldiers.html. It is your responsibility to gather all of the appropriate documents and submit the completed application sometime between August 1st of the previous year and February 1 of the award year. This should be the February immediately before the fall semester that you wish to attend.

The first document you want to review is Appendix A, which lists the required documents for a complete packet. The application begins with the CC Form 174-R, which asks for personal information, as well as recommendations by your immediate commander and field grade commander (O5). You will also need separate favorable letters of recommendations from these individuals.

Waivers can be acquired for many eligibility requirements, and are submitted with your packet using the DA Form 4187. Waivers will be forwarded automatically to Headquarters Cadet Command (HQCC) after you have been selected for the program. Waivers are not granted for the following eligibility and document requirements for all programs:

- General Technical score of 110
- Having less than ten years of Active Federal Service
- APFT of 180, with a minimum of 60 in each event. Soldiers on profile are not accepted.
- An acceptance letter from the school you wish to attend.
- An acceptance letter from the ROTC program issued by the Professor of Military Science.
- An official evaluation of credits by the school (except four-year scholarship option).
- CC Form 104-R worksheet to be complete by school (except four-year scholarship option).

• Have forty-eight months remaining on current contract. This may require that you reenlist before applying.
• Soldiers married to another soldier who is seeking to apply to ROTC at the same time.
• Soldiers in the rank of sergeant or higher must submit last two Non-Commissioned Officer Evaluation Reports.

The following are also eligibility requirements, but waivers are authorized:

• Have completed two years of active-duty service.
• GPA of a 2.5 for previous coursework.
• Soldier has two dependents or less, including spouse.
• Single soldier with no dependents.
• Married to another soldier with no dependents.
• Divorced soldiers whose child dependents are in the custody of another legal guardian if the soldier is paying child support.
• Civil conviction, as long as court documents and personal statement are submitted with packet.

You will be removed from the program if you:

• Fail to maintain a GPA of 2.0.
• Do not maintain APFT and Height/Weight standards.
• Do not complete the degree within twenty-one months (except three- and four-year scholarship options).

Regardless of which program you use, you should apply for grants through the Free Application for Federal Student Aid. This may allow you to cover your tuition or allow you to pocket money to assist with school and living expenses.

Two-Year Active-Duty Option

This is one of the more popular options for enlisted soldiers because it allows you to keep your pay and benefits while attending school. The HQCC only slots two hundred selections per year for this option. Your tuition will not be paid and TA is not authorized; however, you may activate your Montgomery or Post-9/11 GI Bill to pay tuition. Keep in mind that you are still on active duty, so both benefits will not be calculated to your advantage and will only pay the cost of tuition (though the Post-9/11 will still provide the book stipend).

The acceptance letter from the school must also reflect your admittance as a junior-standing student if you are pursuing a bachelor's degree. Many soldiers interpret this as meaning they must have an associate's degree prior to selection. Similar to IPAP, soldiers do not need an associate degree, but must have at least sixty transferrable credits that are accepted by the college. Due to the large discrepancy in transfer credit acceptance by different institutions, you may be a junior at one school, but only a sophomore at another depending upon how your credits are evaluated.

I (Paul) began working with a soldier who was toward the end of obtaining these sixty credits. In order to speed up the process she shopped around for a school that gave her a generous amount of credit for her military training. Unfortunately, the handful of schools she was looking at attending for G2G were not nearly as generous, so she did not have the sixty transferable credits at her universities of choice and was ultimately not classified as a junior, which made her ineligible for this particular option. Compare your current credits with the degree plan at your school of choice and try to obtain an idea from the school how they may regard the credits on your Joint Service Transcript (JST). If you already have a bachelor's degree, an acceptance letter from a master's degree–awarding program will be necessary to receive approval for the two-year active-duty option.

Your degree and commissioning as an officer must be completed by the age of thirty-five. You will be agreeing to eight more years of service, a minimum of three on active duty with the remaining amount served in the National Guard, Reserves, or Individual Ready Reserves.

Two-Year Non-Scholarship Option

The Two-Year Non-Scholarship Option is the most common option soldiers apply for because it is not competitive, primarily because participants are released from active duty and receive no pay or benefits. The program also does not pay for tuition, though participants will receive a $350 monthly stipend. MGIB or Post-9/11 can be used, since soldiers accepted into this pathway are no longer on active duty. This makes using federal benefits more cost-effective as the full amount of the benefit (such as the housing stipend) will be received.

Soldiers can also participate in the Simultaneous Membership Program, which allows eligible participants to be members of a drilling National Guard or Reserve unit and receive reserve component pay of E5, potentially making you eligible to receive state National Guard or Reserve Tuition Assistance. You must not be older than thirty years of age on June 30 at the time of commission; although, your PMS in your ROTC program can apply for a waiver to increase this age to thirty-two. Unlike the other G2G programs, you must contact the recruiting officer at the school you wish to attend to apply for this option, but most of the documents and eligibility requirements are identical. Soldiers can also use this option to attend a master's degree program.

Two-/Three-/Four-Year Scholarship Option

Similar to the two-year nonscholarship option, pay and benefits are suspended upon entry into this program; however, soldiers may elect for the Army to pay either the tuition at the school, or the room and board. If you plan to live on campus, I (Paul) suggest that you elect for the Army to pay the higher cost of the two.

Under this option you can also use either the Montgomery GI Bill (MGIB) or Post-9/11 GI Bills. If you elect to have the Army pay tuition, do not activate the Post-9/11 because you are being redundant with your benefits. In this case, it may be wiser to have the Army pay your tuition and pocket the $1,717 that the MGIB is currently worth per month. Or, if the Monthly Housing Allowance (MHA) is particularly high for your school, you may want to have the Army pay your room and board, have the Post-9/11 cover your tuition, *and* pocket the MHA. Make sure to run the numbers for your institution of choice and its specific costs before deciding upon the best combination of benefits. The Army will also provide a flat rate stipend per year for books and supplies.

Under this program, you must be under thirty-one years of age by December 31 on the last day of the year in which you earn your degree . Waivers are not granted for this requirement. Be careful in your calculations, otherwise you will be dropped from the program and placed back as enlisted personnel into an MOS determined by the needs of the Army. There is also no guarantee that you will be commissioned as an active-duty officer. The Army has free reign to commission you as a National Guard or Reserve officer instead, giving you no choice in the matter. You will incur an eight-year service obligation between the National Guard, Reserves, or IRR, with a minimum of four years of active duty if you are accepted as an active-duty officer.

Three-year option applicants do not need to submit SAT or ACT scores with the G2G packet, but your school may still require them for admission. Three-year option applicants will also have to obtain an acceptance letter showing they are sophomore-standing students with their schools.

A few differences exist for soldiers who wish to pursue the four-year option. Soldiers must take either an SAT or ACT exam and submit the score with their applications. The minimum score requirements are set at 920 for the SAT or 19 for the ACT. Be aware that these scores are not particularly competitive, and your school may have higher score requirements in order to gain acceptance. Four-year option applicants are not required to submit the CC Form 104-R or the official evaluation of credits by the school, but will need at least a 2.5 GPA on their high school transcripts.

Commander's Hip Pocket Scholarship

This program allows the commander general (CG) of a military installation to handpick a set amount of enlisted soldiers he or she deems officer-worthy to attend G2G. This pathway is not a guarantee, but is as close to one as a soldier can get. A general's recommendation can certainly go a long way. I (Paul) would suggest you pursue this path right from the start, if possible.

The letter of recommendation you are required to submit must be written by the CG as well as your immediate commander. The installation where you are stationed may have a specific process in place to select applicants, and very often the process requires an interview.

The Commander's Hip Pocket Scholarship will pay full tuition, $1,200 a year for books and supplies, and a $500 monthly stipend.

Scholar-Athlete-Leader

The most important aspect of any G2G application is the Scholar-Athlete-Leader (S-A-L) standards the Army is looking for in its future officers. Your application will contain an S-A-L checklist that your commander must use to list your qualifications. Your letters of recommendation should also contain these standards. Years ago it was possible to be competitive by meeting at least one of the S-A-L areas, but with the intense competition for the G2G program and the slimming down of the Army, you will want to demonstrate excellence in all three. Below are common examples of merit that used to be listed on older versions of the G2G application.

Scholar:

- Honor Graduate/Commandant's List of noncommissioned officer education system schools
- For two-year scholarship applicants, either (1) cumulative GPA over 3.0 on all college level courses or, (2) if 25 percent of the course work is in math, science, engineering, or technical courses, cumulative GPA over 2.7
- For four- or three-year scholarship applicants, cumulative high school GPA over 3.0 *and* four-year scholarship applicants must also have an SAT/ACT over 1100/21
- For four- or three-year scholarship applicants, top one-third of class and either: (1) cumulative GPA over 3.0 or (2) SAT/ACT over 1100/21.

Athlete:

- Score 270 on APFT with a minimum 90 points in each event
- Active competitive involvement on post level or higher sports team
- Placement in top three of individual athletic competition (triathlon, mountain biking, running, martial arts, etc.)

Leader:

- Selected as Soldier/NCO of the quarter/year at battalion level or higher board
- Served in team leader/squad leader position for minimum six months with favorable endorsement from company commander
- Inducted into the Sergeant Audie Murphy/Sergeant Morales Club
- For four- or three-year scholarship applicants, any of the following: (1) elected member of student government class, activity; (2) captain of athletic or academic team; (3) EagleScout/Gold Award.

EDUCATIONAL OPPORTUNITIES WITHIN THE ARMY

These programs are available to enlisted and commissioned personnel to increase the chances of advancement, but simultaneously improve a variety of different skills or boost civilian education credentials for success after transitioning from the military.

- Functional Academic Skills Training
- Advanced Education Program
- Soldier for Life: Transition Assistance Program

Functional Academic Skills Training

Many soldiers entering the fighting ranks of the Army may need a review of their academic skills to boost their critical thinking and analytical skills to increase mission readiness. These types of programs fall under the Functional Academic Skills Training (FAST) program administered for free by many education centers. They may focus on reading, mathematics, writing, speaking, and/or computer skills and may include General Education Development (GED) test preparation, reading skills development, and preparation for college.

FAST includes two programs that have slowly merged into one, the Basic Skills Education Program (BSEP) and the General Technical (GT) Improvement classes. BSEP originally provided classes to soldiers that scored below a 10.2 grade level on the TABE (Test for Adult Basic Education) with the goal of reaching the twelfth grade level in mathematics, reading, and language skills. This course was solely meant to improve soldier mission readiness. The classes served to assist soldiers in improving the GT score they initially received when taking the original Armed Services Vocational Aptitude Battery (ASVAB) at a Military Entrance Processing Station before enlistment.

Most education centers now have one class, commonly referred to as either a FAST, BSEP, or GT Improvement class, which serves both of these purposes. GT score improvement has largely taken over the FAST program as its primary goal, but you should always check with the local education center for additional programs that may fall under the broad FAST program objectives that improve a wide range of academic and professional skill sets.

Within the Army community it is widely understood that FAST classes are a means of increasing the original GT score for the practical purpose of career advancement. For example, a GT score of 107 is needed for entry into Special Forces, and to become an officer or warrant officer a score of 110 is required. While the test can have a maximum score of 145 (depending on the version taken), anything over 110 is merely for bragging rights and has no official benefit.

To improve upon his GT score, a soldier must take the Armed Forces Classification Test (AFCT), the in-service version of the original ASVAB. It is identical to the ASVAB and any study material currently in print or online for the ASVAB will work equally well for the AFCT. Like the ASVAB, the AFCT is made up of the same nine subjects: arithmetic reasoning (AR), auto/shop information (AS), electronic information (EI), general science (GS), mechanical comprehension (MC), mathematics knowledge (MK), paragraph comprehension (PC), word knowledge (WK), and assembling objects (AO). The GT score is made up of only the AR, PC, and WK sections of the ASVAB and AFCT; therefore, these are the sections emphasized during the FAST class.

The Army does not currently conduct any programs with the sole purpose of improving scores for the other tests. All nine tests must be taken at once, and all scores from the AFCT will replace existing scores from the ASVAB or a previously taken AFCT. Soldiers must understand that certain scores must be maintained for certain military MOSs, because a decrease in scores may mean that the individual can be forcibly re-classed to a new MOS.

Many soldiers need their mathematics skills strengthened in order to produce better test scores, so the FAST class will concentrate on the types of problems that are encountered on the AR portion of the AFCT. These include basic mathematics such as division, but also decimals, fractions, and calculating weights, distances, and volumes within word problems. This is typically the easiest section of the GT score to improve because methods and strategies can be taught through repetition. The AR section is weighted more heavily than either of the other two sections, so great strides can be made in increasing the GT score by concentrating on mathematical skills.

Paragraph Comprehension (PC) is the second most difficult section to study. The test will feature a paragraph, or paragraphs, that give some general knowledge about a subject. The multiple-choice answers will include one statement that is true, based on the knowledge presented. The answer will be based on your power of deduction and not simply a rewording of some sentence already in the paragraph. Studying for this section can be difficult because it is based on the ability of an individual to comprehend the content that he is reading. Reading, like any skill, only comes with practice. It can be challenging to improve this skill in the forty to sixty hours it takes to complete a FAST class. Although some techniques can be taught, I highly suggest that you begin reading now and often, because that is the best way to increase reading comprehension.

Scores on the final section, or Word Knowledge (WK), are the hardest to improve in a short FAST class that takes a maximum of sixty hours. During the test a word will be presented and its synonym, or word most similar in meaning to the original word, must be selected from the multiple-choice selection. The Oxford English Dictionary claims there are around 250,000 words in the English language. There are common "word lists" that your FAST instructor may cover and the meanings of some words can be deduced from their prefixes, suffixes, and root words. This section is difficult to study for, and like the PC section, only by reading more and exposing yourself to more words will your knowledge of words and their meanings increase. Study guides for the ASVAB can provide strategies and techniques to increase both paragraph comprehension and word knowledge. The military provides a study guide for free at www.petersons.com/dod.

So what can you expect in the FAST class? FAST is an on-duty class that can be all day, or only a few hours a day, for the duration of the course. This means that your company commander must release you from normal duties in order for you to attend. You will report to the FAST classroom in uniform. The class comes in a forty- or sixty-hour format, so it could be as long as three weeks depending on location. Various tests will be administered throughout the class to test soldiers' progress, but the first is the TABE test. The scores from the TABE test will give the instructor an idea of your strengths and weaknesses so this period of time can be used more effectively.

The Online Academic Skills Program is used to enhance the FAST class. This online program is free for service members and registration can be completed at www.petersons.com/dantes. The initial test results will allow the program to customize the modules throughout the program based on the user's weaknesses. These modules will instruct the user on how to correctly solve problems commonly found on the AFCT. One feature of this program is that your instructor can log in as an administrator, monitor your progress, and modify the material you will use in the face-to-face class.

At the end of the class a different version of the TABE is given to see what new grade level you have achieved. A GT predictor, or a test identical to the AR, PC, and WK sections of the AFCT, is also given to test speed in completing each section and give a general prediction of the GT score you may receive when you officially test. You should speak to a counselor to discuss your scores and your readiness to take the test. Be honest and do not feel embarrassed in your discussions about your capabilities. Remember that taking the AFCT at the end of the FAST class is ultimately up to you, and you should never feel compelled or coerced by either your command or the education center to take the test if you do not feel that you are ready.

Other programs under the umbrella of the FAST program can vary widely across installations, because each military population has different needs and each education center has different resources available. The High School Completion Program for eligible soldiers and their family members was originally part of the FAST program. The need for this program slowly declined as military standards for recruitment began to tighten and required those entering the military to already have a high school diploma or GED; however, options still exist. Army education centers may be aware of high schools or community colleges that offer high school diploma programs for adults in the local community. A list of programs can also be found on the DANTES website here: http://www.dantes.doded.mil/service-members/prep-for-college/high-school-diploma-programs/index.html. Luckily, it is possible to obtain TA for these types of programs, but only if they are public institutions. For similar reasons, GED preparation programs have also become harder to come by on military installations, but they can also be found in the local community. While costs of the test can vary by state, sometimes as high as $100, the Testing Center in the education center often offers the test for free through the DANTES program.

English as a Second Language (ESL) programs may be available through your education center, but availability depends on the priorities of that particular military installation. For example, one Army installation in California petitioned the state for funding to conduct ESL classes through a local community college, and now offers two basic ESL courses for free to soldiers and their families and two advanced courses worth college credit that require external funding. Regardless of what may be available on your installation, the local education center should be able to help you review any potential options in the local community.

The Headstart and Gateway programs are only available through education centers located outside of the continental United States. These programs are usually two to three weeks long and instruct soldiers and family members on the local culture and rudimentary language skills of the country where that installation is located. Sometimes these classes are mandatory for newly arrived soldiers overseas. In many cases, small field trips or other cultural events might be part of the class. TA is also authorized for up to fifteen SH worth of college courses in the host-nation language. Don't forget that languages are considered humanities courses, which are part of every degree's general education requirement, regardless of the school.

Remember, the services available through your education center can vary greatly. Other programs may also be administered to improve basic skills alongside programs that fall under the FAST program directive. For example, Central Texas College (CTC), which has a presence on many military installations, offers a free on-duty program entitled the Leadership Skills Enhancement Instruction (LSEI) program. LSEI is composed of twenty-five separate courses meant to strengthen the leadership skills of aspiring NCOs and includes twenty hours of instruction in topics such as effective military writing, conducting briefings, career management, and managerial planning. The courses are taught by a senior NCO and each class is also worth one SH of college credit with CTC. So stop by your education center to discover what unique programs are out there for you.

Advanced Education

The premier program for obtaining advanced civilian education in the Army is the broadly termed Advanced Education Program (AEP). The programs supported by this initiative are diverse and flexible by design because one of its goals is to provide the most cutting-edge civilian education in emerging occupational fields or knowledge bases. Though the AEP mostly targets officers who may require a master's degree to fully function in their branch, some of the educational opportunities may target enlisted personnel seeking an associate degree or warrant officers seeking a bachelor's degree.

The Advanced Education Requirements System (AERS) is administered and maintained by Human Resource Command (HRC) and dictates what civilian education opportunities are available. These opportunities are highly dependent on the occupational requirements for a soldier's job in the Army. One of the best ways to stay informed of the needs of the Army and what requirements are part of the AERS system is to keep your ear to the ground within your own command as well as talking to those who may share your occupation. Commands are frequently the first to know of standardized advanced educational needs of the Army or hear of potential new ones on the horizon. HRC, in maintaining the catalog of required appropriate civilian education, continually elicits input from the field, including from commands, subject matter experts (SME) who currently operate in this capacity, and the Career Division or Functional Area Manager offices.

Currently, the AEP program funds the tuition for up to 1,400 students a year. PhDs might also be possible under these programs. CAC or AKO username and password are required for access, and more specific information for each program and how to apply can be found here: https://www.hrc.army.mil/Default.aspx?ID=5566. You will typically retain pay and benefits of your current rank while attending school and must usually report at least once a month to "participate" with an ROTC program or U.S. Army

Recruiting Command battalion nearby. The nature of this participation may vary.

The Advanced Civil Schooling (ACS) program is one of the more popular programs under AEP. ACS is only open to active-duty officers with less than seventeen years of time in service, though waivers can be requested. Only 412 slots were available for the current FY15. Your undergraduate degree must correspond to the master's degree you are seeking and prerequisites will not be funded by ACS, though it may be possible to justify the use of TA under the broad description of "career advancement programs" mentioned in previous Information Papers issued by HRC. Visit your education center to inquire into their current interpretation and implementation of seeking TA for prerequisites under this description.

A minimum GRE score of 153 in Verbal Reasoning, 144 in Quantitative Reasoning, and 4.0 in Analytical are required, even if the graduate program has no such requirement. For management-related, comptroller, acquisition management graduate programs and MBAs, a GMAT score of 500 is required. The cost of the graduate program you choose will be determined by your functional area managers and classified as either low cost—less than $26,000 a year, medium cost—less than $43,000 a year, or high cost—less than $55,000 a year, and capped at this amount. An active duty service obligation (ADSO) of three days for each day of schooling is required upon completion of the program, which is a six-year commitment for a typical two-year graduate program.

The Expanded Graduate School Program (EGSP) under AEP includes two programs, the Menu of Incentives (MOI) program and the Graduate School Option (GRADSO) program. The MOI program is a commander's program meant to target outstanding junior officers to increase the intellectual capital of the Army as a Joint and Expeditionary Force. In other words, as more and more joint operations alongside foreign armies are conducted, particularly across the globe, this program attempts to increase the intellectual horizons of officers serving in these capacities. To fulfill this purpose these graduate programs often focus on cultural awareness, diplomacy, foreign language, and geographical knowledge. Under the MOI program tuition and fees cannot exceed $26,000 a year.

The Graduate School Option under the Career Satisfaction Program function of EGSP, termed GRADSO due to the concurrent ADSO of three years incurred for taking advantage of this program, is only available to seniors who are on the verge of commissioning through ROTC or USMA. About six hundred of these opportunities are offered each year and you have the choice of studying up to 210 Army-approved disciplines including everything from psychology to civil engineering.

Most officers exercise the ability to take advantage of their GRADSO option between their sixth and eleventh year of service after attaining the rank of captain. Unlike ACS, there is no cap on the amount of tuition covered, so it is possible to attend almost any graduate program in the United States, regardless of cost. For both the MOI and GRADSO programs, participants incur a service obligation of three days for each day of schooling paid, for a typical maximum of six years after attending the graduate program.

Professional medical and chaplaincy programs are not eligible for GRADSO because these disciplines are covered by AMEDD and the Army Chaplaincy Corps mentioned earlier in this chapter. More specific information can be found here: http://www.career-satisfaction.army.mil/departments/goh_overview.html.

Also under the scope of the AEP are scholarships or fellowships within the Broad Opportunity Programs that target very narrow forms of education for specific types of education or training. These programs include:

- The Army Congressional Fellowship Program emphasizes the ties between the Army and Congress. The program is available to officers and senior NCOs who will receive a Master's of Legislative Affairs from George Washington University.
- The George and Carol Olmsted Scholars Program offers educational grants for officers to attend a two-year graduate program in a foreign country to study the language of that program.
- The Training Within Industry program offers officers and warrant officers the opportunity to advance their knowledge and skills in specific non-degree-granting education and training. The program is meant to keep officers trained in industry-specific practices and procedures in higher-level management positions. One hundred twenty-five officers are selected per year to learn state-of-the-art skills that allow them to bridge the gap of current advances in their industries as they relate to the overall Army mission. Often these fields include marketing, public affairs, physical security, and finance. A full list can be found at https://www.hrc.army.mil/Default.aspx?ID=12668. You will need a CAC or an AKO username and password to access this site.

The Army programs available for advanced education tend to be modified continually, so it is important that you stay in touch with your education center to stay updated. For example, the Performance Based Graduate School Incentive Program (PB-GSIP), a new program under the general ACS requirements, demonstrates the military's commitment to further the advanced education of its fighting force. The PB-GSIP allows fifty of the Army's top-performing active-duty captains and majors to attend a fifteen- to eighteen-month graduate program. Once selected, each officer must apply to three programs of their choice for the fall or spring semesters of the following year. The first MILPER message, 13-430, has been issued and outlines the requirements and objectives of the program. The officers will be chosen from the operations, support operations, and force sustainment functional categories for the program, and they will be able to obtain graduate degrees in business administration, history, psychology, public administration, computer science, international relations, philosophy, human resources, education, or sociology. PB-GSIP will pay up to $43,000 per year in tuition, but any officer who currently holds a master's degree is not eligible to apply.

Soldier for Life: Transition Assistance Program

The Veterans Opportunity to Work Act of 2011 (the VOW Act) greatly expanded the military's transition process for service members entering the civilian workforce. The intent of the law is not only to reduce veteran unemployment, but also to better prepare service members for a successful transition to civilian life. The Soldier for Life: Transition Assistance Program (SFL: TAP, formerly known as Army Career Alumni program, or ACAP) has been enhanced to address a number of the needs service members may have when attempting to establish their lives after leaving the military. Take advantage of these improved services; invest your time and effort into preparing more effectively for life post-Army.

When a soldier enrolled in the SFL: TAP program, the Army would formerly begin the transition process ninety days prior to a soldier's date of separation. This time frame has been expanded to eighteen months to give service members more time to organize a plan of action for a smooth transition. All tracks include a two-day workshop, personalized assistance from an SME, and specific benchmarks that must be met to successfully transition from the military.

The program also now includes four distinct tracks for service members to follow based on their interests: the required Employment Track and three voluntary tracks: Entrepreneurial, Technical, and Higher Education.

- The Employment Track—all transitioning service members must attend. Requires creating an updated résumé, attending job interview rehearsals, going to job fairs, and submitting job applications to potential employers. This track is mandatory for all soldiers.
- The Entrepreneurial Track (also known as Boots2Business), conducted by the Small Business Administration, includes topics such as recognizing business opportunities, understanding markets, the economics and legalities of starting a business, and seeking funding. This track is for those who wish to start a business immediately or at some point down the road after separation from the service. More information can be found at www.boots2business.org and www.sba.gov/vets.

- The Technical Track focuses on attending vocational, technical, and trade schools to learn a specific industry-based skill. Common examples include the automotive field, welding, HVAC (heating, ventilation, and air-conditioning), solar panel installation and maintenance, and cell phone tower repair. The track will address how to find the necessary education or training and how to determine if specific licensing or certification is required in your industry. Benefits, such as the GI Bills, are discussed to assist you in making your goals a reality.
- The Higher Education Track focuses on those service members who wish to attend a postsecondary educational institution such as a community college or university. Your military transition education counselor teaches the class and serves as your advisor during the process of finding and enrolling in a school. The class itself covers four main topics including evaluating and determining personal and career goals, finding and investigating postsecondary educational institutions that may fit these goals, how to fund this education, and how to navigate the admission process. After the class the military transition education counselor advises you on how to achieve your goal of becoming a student veteran once separating.

If interested, soldiers can participate in all three of the voluntary tracks.

During the Higher Education Track, career and personal goals are commonly addressed by examining the career you are interested in and the educational demands required to meet this goal. The needs of you and your family are also addressed and how this may play into school selection. For example, I (Paul) was helping a retiring soldier who had a very unusual sleep disorder that required constant monitoring. As a result, he had to live close to a particular medical facility to receive special treatment. This was the largest determining factor in choosing an institution, because the school had to be near this facility.

Finding and screening potential schools based on career and personal goals is the next objective of the class. You will utilize various college search strategies to find potential schools and then discuss methods and techniques to determine if the value of that school meets your academic and professional needs. The military transition education counselor can help you review your previous credits and your JST to see which degree plans may accommodate these credits.

As a veteran, you may have access to many potential sources of funding, many of which are mentioned in this book. The Higher Education Track class will address all of these sources of funding with the goal of maximizing the amount of money available for you to help pay for school and put money in your pocket. The class will review the different GI Bills, financial aid through FAFSA, state programs (veteran- and non-veteran-specific), scholarships, and any other sources of funding that might be uncovered throughout the process.

The last portion of the class covers the admission process and includes how to apply to a college, write an admissions essay, obtain letters of recommendation, study for and take an admissions test such as the SAT or ACT, and transcript requests. This is an essential section because the admissions process can vary widely across schools, and certain deadlines may require action up to ten months before the first day of class rolls around.

If you wish to attend college after leaving the military, you should take advantage of the new TAP program. This opportunity gives you the assistance and support that most civilian students desperately need, but do not have available. You can take advantage of the new program even after separating from the service. Those that retire have access to TAP services for life, and those separating but not retiring have access to these services up to 180 days from separation. Find your nearest SFL: TAP office at https://www.acap.army.mil/acap_centers.

Chapter Six

Cost and Payment Resources

Students need to consider cost when choosing an institution. If pursuing school while on active duty, soldiers should try to choose institutions that fall within the parameters of Tuition Assistance (TA). Those who have already transitioned off active duty should consider GI Bill coverage while researching potential schools. Why pay for school when you have a benefit that can cover the full amount? Service members who maintain vigilance regarding their benefits can come out of their educational experience completely debt free.

The following topics will be covered within this section:

- Financial Goals
- Army Tuition Assistance and GoArmyEd
- National Guard Tuition Assistance
- Montgomery GI Bill
- Post-9/11 GI Bill
- Montgomery GI Bill vs. Post-9/11 GI Bill
- Student Loan Repayment Program
- Reserve Component VA Education Benefits
- GI Bill Top-Up
- GI Bill Application and Conversion Process
- Post-9/11 Transferability to Dependents
- Yellow Ribbon Program
- VA GI Bill Feedback System
- Federal Student Aid
- States Offering In-State Tuition to Veterans
- State-Based Veteran Education Benefits
- Scholarships (Including Dependents)
- Textbook Buying Options
- Free Subject Matter Study Support

FINANCIAL GOALS

Transitioning from the service is a difficult process. Veterans who prepare for it in advance will find the experience to be less stressful, enabling them to focus on their studies more effectively. Forming a plan in advance will help to minimize potential distractions. Veteran students that minimize their risk of distraction during the school year will achieve a higher degree of academic success. Successfully educated or trained veterans will be more productive in their future endeavors and able to enrich their surrounding civilian communities.

Bypassing the work option, veterans have three main sources of income while attending school, not including any potential scholarships they might apply for and receive. These sources include:

- GI Bill housing stipend
- Federal Student Aid (Pell Grant)
- Unemployment

If a veteran is able to maximize benefits under each of these three options, he or she will have a good starting base and hopefully not have to worry about daily stressors, such as paying for rent, gas, and food.

The housing stipend on the Post-9/11 GI Bill typically is not enough to take care of one individual's personal needs, especially because "break pay" money is not paid while the student is not physically in school. The section in this chapter on the "Post-9/11 GI Bill" explains that the housing allowance is prorated, and veterans will most likely not be receiving as much money as they expect.

Federal Student Aid Pell Grant money can be a great benefit for veterans attending school. Think about having an extra $5,730 per academic year to help with education-related expenses above and beyond the GI Bill. How much better off would you be for spending thirty minutes to fill out the FAFSA? The time will be well spent, especially if you are awarded assistance.

Your previous year's tax information is required to fill out the FAFSA, so you need to pay attention upon your initial separation from active duty. If you have recently separated from the military, your tax information may not reflect your current financial situation. For example, if Specialist Croft separates in July 2015 and plans on beginning college in August 2015, he will submit his 2014 taxes on the FAFSA that reflect his military pay. The main problem is that he will no longer be working and receiving this level of pay. In most cases, a veteran's pay is drastically reduced upon separation. If Specialist Croft does not receive an award or does not receive the full amount, he needs to visit his financial aid counselor at his school and request to have his listed income level readjusted. Hopefully, upon readjustment of his income, he will be eligible for the maximum Pell Grant award. Be aware that Pell Grant money is based on your tax information, so it will fluctuate from person to person depending upon household finances.

The Unemployment Compensation for Ex-Servicemembers program may help eligible separating service members qualify for some level of unemployment. Unemployment will vary state by state because state laws determine how much money an individual can receive, the length of time the veteran will remain eligible, and any other eligibility conditions. Veterans must have been honorably separated in order to be eligible. Information on unemployment can be located on the Department of Labor's website (http://workforcesecurity.doleta.gov/unemploy/uifactsheet.asp).

Contact your local State Workforce Agency (http://www.servicelocator.org/OWSLinks.asp) upon separation to determine eligibility and apply. Make sure to have a copy of your DD 214.

Some military members may receive a service-connected disability percentage; others may not. When you separate from the military, you will be screened by the VA to determine whether you sustained any injuries or contracted any diseases while on active duty, or if any previous health-related issues were made worse by active military service. If you receive a minimum rating of 10 percent or higher, you may be eligible to receive a tax-free stipend from the VA every month. Zero percent ratings do not have a monetary stipend attached; however, in the "State-Based Veteran Education Benefits" section of this chapter, you will see that many states offer benefits that are tied to these disability ratings. For example, in California a 0 percent rating equals free schooling for your children at state-supported institutions. If you receive a percentage rating, this may help with your expenses. Be aware that ratings can take as long as twelve months to be determined, and there is such a thing as no rating.

Make sure to be screened prior to exiting the military. If you are not sure where to find your local VA office, it might even be on the base where you are stationed. The Disabled American Veterans and the Veterans of Foreign Wars maintain offices at several Army bases and may assist you as well. Many academic institutions have visiting representatives from these organizations. They will help you with your initial claim if you did not make it while still on active duty. They can also help you submit for a claims adjustment if your medical situation has changed.

Also remember to save for your child's future education as well. The education-based saving accounts known as 529s are a common tool that many parents use to save for their child's higher education pursuits. Operating similarly to a retirement account, if the money is withdrawn for purposes not associated with school you will pay taxes on this amount. The 529 accounts can be used for children or any designated beneficiary. Speak with your local education counselor or your financial advisor for more advice.

ARMY TUITION ASSISTANCE AND GOARMYED

At some point in your Army career you may decide that the suggestion by supervisors in your chain-of-command to go to school is making more and more sense. Thankfully, you can preserve your GI Bill benefits because the Army provides Tuition Assistance (TA) for about 2,500 different schools. The entire list of eligible schools can be found here at https://www.goarmyed.com/public/public_degree_plan_browse.aspx.

Currently, TA will pay for up to sixteen semester hours (SH) per fiscal year, and up to $250 per SH. This means you can receive a maximum of about $4,000 in TA a year. If the cost of an SH at your school is only $100, you will still only receive sixteen SH for a total of $1,600 that year. TA will also pay for one associate's, one bachelor's, and one master's degree. If you already have an associate's degree, the Army will not pay for another one, even if they didn't pay for the first. The same holds true for those who already hold a bachelor's or master's degree.

If you have a master's degree, you are not eligible for any TA, except for some very specific credentials. These exceptions include a chaplain's certificate, a teacher certification for one state, prerequisites for the Interservice Physician Assistance Program and the Army Medical Department Enlisted Commissioning Program, host nation languages for Outside of the Continental United States, and both immediate and emerging strategic languages. The Army will pay for one certificate or diploma at any point in your Army career, and in some very narrow circumstances, even if you already hold a master's degree.

Eligibility to use TA is based on many factors, but the biggest one holding up young soldiers is that they cannot take advantage of this program until they have been out of Initial Entry Training for one year. For most enlisted soldiers and warrant officers this is Advanced Individual Training, and for officers it is Basic Officer Leader's Course. Many people join the Army for educational benefits, but keep in mind that you may not have access to TA for half of your initial contract.

Other situations that may make you ineligible are a suspension of favorable personnel action such as an offense punishable under Article 15, failing your Army Physical Fitness Test, or being placed in the Army Weight Control Program. You may also become ineligible based on what level of degree you are pursuing. If your GPA drops below a 2.0 as an undergraduate, or 3.0 as a graduate, you will lose the ability to apply for TA. Soldiers may lose eligibility for many other reasons, and soldiers sometimes go on and off a "hold" status throughout their careers. The biggest thing to remember is that losing your TA and going on hold does not prevent schools from receiving TA for classes you have already applied for; it just prevents future enrollments from that point forward.

Every process to use TA is centralized in the GoArmyEd portal found at www.goarmyed.com. Every transaction is electronic and functionality in the portal is entirely in the hands of the soldier. Because the administrative process of using TA through the portal is highly efficient, soldiers may never step into an education center to seek assistance. After creating an account you will be prompted to log in, then you will be presented with various links. Look for the "Request TA..." link at the top left corner of your screen. Remember this action; selecting this link will always bring you to the next step of the process and toward the final goal of completing your degree.

If you are selecting "Request TA..." for the first time, you will be prompted to do six registration steps. The first is navigating through slideshows and a training video of how to use the portal. While it is tempting to click "Next" repeatedly and complete the process as fast as possible, much like other available online military training, following along to learn a basic understanding of the portal process will greatly benefit you later. This is your TA, your degree, and your future headache if you do not know how to solve problems in GoArmyEd.

Army TA has many deadlines and requirements, and an education center may not always be handy to problem solve every issue that may come up in the portal. I (Paul) know countless soldiers who were just three hours too late to enroll in a class that started at midnight, then had to foot the bill themselves with the school or delay the progression of their degree until the next term. Prior, proper planning will help you avoid this mistake.

After the training you will be prompted to input a home school and a degree plan. The Army will only pay for classes that advance you toward a specific degree from a specific school, so you must know where you wish to attend and have chosen a degree pathway before you begin. The next step requires you to input information into an electronic form titled the Common Application that resembles a college application. Some schools in GoArmyEd such as Central Texas College, University of Maryland University College, and Troy University will automatically accept you into their schools based on this application.

When you click "Submit" on the last registration step, you have created your first Customer Relationship Management (CRM) case. Your CRM case will be sent to your servicing education center, which maintains every active CRM case created by its soldiers. Once they receive your request to use TA, they will activate your account and then you will be ready to begin using TA. The process is quite simple. If you encounter problems, or some mysterious message pops up on your homepage, you still have the opportunity to create your second CRM case. Commonly called "Helpdesk Cases," or just "tickets," the CRM case system allows users to select from a potential list of problems to determine the route a case takes. Cases may go to the GoArmyEd Helpdesk if they involve a technical issue or to the education center if they involve a TA policy issue.

Even if the wrong pathway is selected, trained staff at each end can redirect your case to the appropriate office based on your description of the problem in the text window. If you call the GoArmyEd Helpdesk (800-817-9990) for assistance, they can create a case for you that will be routed to your local education center or perhaps a technical subject math expert. Save yourself a conversation and create the CRM case from the start.

Cases can have nontechnical and nonpolicy questions answered. Not sure which degree or school to choose? Create a case. Education counselors complete the legwork of reviewing each case as it comes in. Counselors can provide advice, tips, and Internet links to help you make the right decision.

I (Paul) have been assisting one sergeant first class continually with numerous issues for some time. I have never met him since he has never needed to step into my office. He simply creates a CRM case and signs off with "Hi Paul!" at the end of his case, knowing that I will be the counselor seeing his case very soon.

With your account now activated, you can begin requesting TA to pay for your classes. The process to request TA will be based on both the type of school you have selected and the type of degree. Of the 2,500 schools mentioned above about 150 of the institutions are Letter of Instruction (LOI) schools, meaning they have signed a Letter of Instruction with the Army. These particular schools upload their classes directly into GoArmyEd, and you can enroll in a specific class by searching for it within the system. A list of these schools can be found here: https://www.goarmyed.com/public/public_degree_plan_search.aspx.

If a class can be found on the school's website, it can also be found in GoArmyEd. A full list of available classes can be found here: https://www.goarmyed.com/public/public_earn_degree-course_schedules.aspx.
This is a unique search engine because nowhere else on the Internet can you search the class schedules of 150 schools simultaneously. Users can search by class as opposed to a particular institution. Looking for a school that offers a beginning Korean course online? It's cake with this search engine.

Schools that have not signed the LOI are referred to as non-LOI institutions. These schools do not upload their classes into GoArmyEd, and requests for these schools will automatically be sent to and reviewed by Certified Enrollment (CE) personnel. CEs work at education centers and review requests for certain regions. The process begins in the same fashion, by selecting "Request TA...," but you will be prompted to input the details of the class and attach a Verification of Cost document to your request. This document verifies your enrollment in the course and displays five crucial pieces of information.

1. Your name
2. Course title
3. Start and end dates of the class
4. Number of credit hours earned for the course
5. The cost per credit hour

If any one of the required elements is missing, your TA request will be denied.

The Verification of Cost document is typically an invoice or receipt, a memo from the school, or a screenshot of your online account displaying this information. While students at LOI schools can enroll in classes through GoArmyEd the day before class, students at non-LOI schools must create their requests at least ten days prior to the first day of class to ensure their request is reviewed by the CE. If you're unsure whether the institution you have chosen is an LOI or non-LOI school, just click "Request TA…" and the system will tell you what to do.

GoArmyEd schools have two types of degree pathways configured within the system. The biggest distinction between these degrees is whether the last step before requesting TA will require you to create a Course Planner. All students attending non-LOI schools must submit Course Planners. Course Planners are similar to an Amazon.com wish list. You tell the Army which future classes you wish to take. At least 50 percent of the remaining classes left to finish your degree must be detailed. After inputting these classes the list will automatically be submitted to your education center's Course Planner queue (different from the CRM case queue). Education center personnel will review the classes you are requesting based on the requirements of your chosen degree. Remember, TA will only pay for classes that advance a student toward a specific degree. If your classes are approved you can then go back in and request TA for the courses for which you received the approval.

Some degrees from LOI schools are called integrated degrees. In other words, the course requirements of the degree have already been input by the school into GoArmyEd, and these courses do not require education center personnel to verify the pathway. Not all degrees from LOI schools are integrated. If you're not sure if you have to complete a Course Planner, click "Request TA…" to find out.

While using GoArmyEd can appear daunting at first, keeping the following information in mind will greatly streamline the process.

- Do the initial training
- Create CRM cases
- Find out what type of school and degree you have selected to pursue through GoArmyEd

Knowing this information in advance will help you avoid a frustrating experience and potentially assist you in missing TA request deadlines. TA cannot be approved retroactively, and there are no exceptions to the GoArmyEd process. The Army holds you responsible for knowing how the portal works.

In September 2015 a new tool called VIA will be introduced to the GoArmyEd registration process that is intended to better inform your decision-making process when selecting a school and degree. It is supposed take into account your career goals, interests, and class format preferences and combine it with data from multiple sources to recommend a school and degree that may best fit your needs. Data is sourced from GoArmyEd, the Department of Education, the Bureau of Labor and Statistics, the Department of Labor, and the Department of Defense, as well as a personality test you must complete during registration. As of this writing, little is known about the specifics of this required feature and how it will affect your experience using GoArmyEd or potentially enhance your research of different schools and degrees. Speak with your local education center so counselors can help you interpret its recommendations.

NATIONAL GUARD TUITION ASSISTANCE

Soldiers in the National Guard have access to traditional tuition assistance through GoArmyEd. The process is identical to an active-duty soldier using TA; however, many states offer state-specific assistance with tuition for National Guard soldiers, which can increase the number of different combinations of available benefits. Guardsmen must calculate the costs of attending a particular school and how to maximize the coverage of the different benefits.

Currently, Arizona, Guam, Idaho, Oregon, Tennessee, and Washington do not have separate state TA programs outside of GoArmyEd (though Tennessee offers a stipend through the National Guard Association of Tennessee). All states allow you to take advantage of both TA from GoArmyEd (frequently termed FTA, or Federal Tuition Assistance) and State Tuition Assistance (STA) during the same fiscal year. Whether you can use both at the same time will usually depend on the cost of the school and the specific state program. Lastly, keep in mind that many states have limited budgets per year, so applying as early as possible should be the goal.

Alabama

The Alabama National Guard Educational Assistance Program provides a $500 stipend per term (not to exceed $1,000 a year) to Guardsmen while attending school. Speak with your unit to activate the benefit. Visit http://www.ache.alabama.gov/Content/Departments/StudentAsst/StudentAsst.aspx for more information.

Alaska

Alaska will pay up to twelve SH per term, not to exceed $250 a credit, for any school that is part of the public University of Alaska system. For other schools in Alaska, the state will pay up to $4,500 total for all courses during the Alaskan fiscal year (July 1 to June 30). Both programs will pay for one degree at each level. Visit http://guardedu.alaska.gov/index.htm for more information.

Arkansas

The Guard Tuition Assistance Program awards up to $2,500 per semester to Guardsmen, awarded only during the fall and spring semesters. The program requires that you have less than fifteen years in service and be a full-time student. Visit http://www.arguard.org/education/GTIP.htm for more information.

California

The California National Guard Education Assistance Award Program program will pay 100 percent of the tuition at any public university in California. Reservists are also eligible to apply. You must be enrolled in at least three units per term and maintain a 2.0 GPA to be eligible. Visit https://www.calvet.ca.gov/VetServices/Pages/CNGEAAP.aspx for more information.

Colorado

Colorado's program for Guardsmen pays 100 percent of tuition for a specific list of preapproved schools. Applications for the program must be submitted by July 1 for the fall semester, December 1 for the spring semester, and May 1 for the summer semester. Visit http://www.colorado.gov/cs/Satellite/DepartmentOfMilitaryAndVeteransAffaris/CBON/1251622368078 for a list of eligible schools and more information.

Connecticut

Connecticut provides free tuition for all public schools in the state for its Guardsmen. Contact your school for more information to apply. Beware that this program does not cover fees. Visit http://www.ct.edu/admission/veterans#benefits for a list of public schools and more information.

Delaware

Guardsmen in Delaware can receive tuition money for both public and private schools in the state. The program is a reimbursement process, so you must typically be able to afford your own tuition to begin the school term. The program will pay for one associate's and one bachelor's degree. Exceptions must be granted to pursue a certificate. Similar to FTA through GoArmyEd, if you already have an associate's or bachelor's degree, Connecticut will not pay for another one. This benefit can be combined with the Montgomery GI Bill. Visit http://www.delawarenationalguard.com/members/jfhq/education/statetuition.cfm for a list of eligible schools, amount of tuition reimbursed per school, and additional information.

District of Columbia

The District of Columbia will pay up to $1,500 toward any school or degree level if FTA through GoArmyEd does not suffice. Therefore, Guardsmen in the District of Columbia potentially have access to a total of $5,500 toward tuition per fiscal year. Contact your school, whether it is a public or private institution, to activate the benefit. Visit http://ova.dc.gov/page/dc-veteran-benefit-entitlements for more information.

Florida

The "Educational Dollars for Duty" program covers 100 percent of tuition at any public institution in Florida and will cover tuition at a private school up to the average cost of the tuition at a public school for that year. The program will pay for an associate's, bachelor's, or master's degree, but not a doctorate. Visit http://dma.myflorida.com/floridas-tuition-assistance-program/ for more information.

Georgia

Georgia does not have a traditional state tuition assistance program, but does have the Georgia HERO Scholarship available for eligible Guardsmen. The Georgia Military Scholarship awards up to $2,000 a year for four years if the participant has been deployed to a war zone. Children of Guardsmen that

have deployed can also apply. Visit http://myarmybenefits.us.army.mil/
Home/Benefit_Library/State__Territory_Benefits/Georgia.html for more information.

Illinois

Guardsmen can attend public schools in the state for up to four years with
100 percent of the tuition covered using the Illinois National Guard Grant.
You must have been in the Illinois Guard for at least one year before being
eligible to use this benefit. Visit http://www.isac.org/students/during-college/
types-of-financial-aid/grants/illinois-national-guard-(ing)-grant-pro-
gram.html for more information.

Indiana

The Indiana National Guard Supplemental Grant pays full tuition at any
public school in the state. The benefit can cover both full-time and part-time
students and pays up to thirty SH per year for the fall and spring semesters.
Visit http://www.in.gov/sfa/2339.htm for more information.

Iowa

The National Guard Education Assistance Program can pay between 50 and
100 percent of the tuition at a public or private school, depending on the
amount of funding available. Those eligible must not already have a bachelor's degree or have used the program for eight or more semesters. Other
sources of funding may decrease the amount awarded, and the program will
not pay more than the cost of tuition. Visit http://www.iowanationalguard.
com/Family%20and%20Services/Education/Pages/Tuition-Assistance.aspx
for more information.

Kansas

Guardsmen can receive either 100 percent, or some portion, of tuition not to
exceed the cost of in-state tuition at a public institution in Kansas. Amounts
awarded are based on the number of Guardsmen who apply and available
state funding. Visit http://www.kansastag.gov/NGUARD.asp?PageID=500
for more information.

Kentucky

Kentucky covers up to 100 percent of the cost of in-state tuition at a public
school in Kentucky. Both part-time and full-time students can receive cover-

age. Visit https://ky.ngb.army.mil/tuitionstudent/frmLogin.aspx to log into the system to apply for TA and view a list of participating schools.

Louisiana

The State Tuition Exemption Program provides 100 percent tuition for any public school in the state. The student must be pursuing an associate's, bachelor's, or master's degree and currently reside in Louisiana. Visit http://geauxguard.com/resources/education/state-tuition-exemption-program/ for more information.

Maine

Maine provides 100 percent of tuition for Guardsmen at any public school in the state. Visit http://www.legion.org/education/statebenefits/maine for more information.

Maryland

Two programs are offered for Guardsmen of Maryland. The first is state tuition assistance that can cover 25 to 50 percent of the cost of attending one of the "Partners in Education" schools. The second is the State Tuition Assistance Reimbursement (STAR) program that covers any additional tuition not covered by the first program or FTA through GoArmyEd. Documents for the STAR program must be submitted to the state Education Office within forty-five days after the start of the semester and the remaining tuition will be reimbursed to the Guardsman. Visit http://www.md.ngb.army.mil/absolutenm/templates/?a=808 for the list of "Partners in Education" schools and more information.

Massachusetts

Massachusetts will pay for 100 percent of tuition at any public school in the state. The program will pay for up to 30 SH a year for the fall, spring, and summer semesters for a total of 130 SH. Guardsmen must be pursuing an associate's, bachelor's, master's, or doctoral degree. Visit http://www.mass.gov/veterans/education/financial-assistance/tuition-and-fee-waivers-for-guard-members.html for more information.

Michigan

The State Tuition Assistance Program provides up to $4,500 a year for any Guardsman to attend a public, private, vocational, or trade school in the state. The Michigan National Guard has also entered into partnerships with various schools to provide additional funding to Guardsmen. Visit http://www.michigan.gov/dmva/0,4569,7-126-2360_68898---,00.html for more information on the tuition assistance program and http://www.michigan.gov/dmva/0,4569,7-126--16725--,00.html to view the schools and their specific scholarships for Guardsmen.

Minnesota

The Minnesota State Tuition Reimbursement program requires that you use the FTA through GoArmyEd first, and then allows Guardsmen to request reimbursement for any tuition not covered. This amount cannot exceed the cost of in-state tuition at the University of Minnesota–Twin Cities campus, which maxes at $17,000 per year for an undergraduate program and $36,000 for a graduate program. This program will pay for a maximum of 144 SH over the career of the Guardsman. Visit http://www.minnesotanationalguard.org/education/state/benefits/ for more information.

Mississippi

The State Educational Assistance Program (SEAP) is for Guardsmen who have used all of the eligible FTA funds through GoArmyEd. SEAP provides an additional $4,500 per year, up to $250 a SH, and only pays for regionally accredited schools. Visit http://ms.ng.mil/resources/edu/Pages/TuitionAssistance.aspx for a list of participating schools and more information.

Missouri

Missouri's program will pay for a total of thirty-nine SH per year consisting of fifteen SH in the fall, fifteen SH in the spring, and nine SH in the summer. For Guardsmen with less than ten years of service it will pay for any public school in the state up to the maximum rate based on the rate of tuition for the University of Missouri system, which is currently $274 per SH. After ten years of service it will pay for 50 percent of this rate. You must maintain a 2.5 GPA to remain eligible. Visit http://www.moguard.com/moguard-tuition-assistance.html for more information.

Montana

Montana does not have a separate state TA program and all FTA is granted through GoArmyEd. However, the Montana National Guard Scholarship Program can provide up to $1,500 per semester toward any Montana public university, two-year program, or VA-approved training program. Guardsmen must have less than seventeen years of service and not be in the rank of E8 or higher, O3 or higher, or WO4 or higher to be eligible. Visit http://www.montanaguard.com/hro/education.cfm for more information.

Nebraska

The Nebraska National Guard Tuition Assistance Program will pay up to 75 percent of the tuition at any school in Nebraska (public or private) or up to 75 percent of the maximum rate of tuition at the University of Nebraska at Lincoln, whichever is lower. It will also only pay for up to a bachelor's degree. Commissioned and warrant officers are not eligible for this program. A separate program for reservists, entitled the Reserve Tuition Credit Program, can pay up to 50 percent of tuition for any public school in Nebraska. Visit http://ne.ng.mil/Resource/Pages/TA-Register.aspx for more information.

Nevada

Guardsmen have access to a tuition waiver program that covers the cost of tuition at any public school in the state. This is only for the fall and spring semesters, but another program can reimburse you the cost of tuition if you attend during the summer, and the program will reimburse the cost of textbooks throughout the entire year. Currently, there is no SH cap on this program. Visit http://www.nv.ngb.army.mil/nvng/index.cfm/departments/education/ for more information.

New Hampshire

New Hampshire waives tuition for Guardsmen at any public institution in the state, but FTA through GoArmyEd must be used first. This program will typically waive the remaining tuition. The National Guard Scholarship Program can also provide up to $500 a year to pay tuition for any public or private school in New Hampshire. Visit https://www.nh.ngb.army.mil/members/education for more information.

New Jersey

The New Jersey National Guard Tuition Program (NJNGTP) provides fifteen SH free per semester at any public institution in the state. You are required to submit an application through FAFSA to be eligible; therefore, any grants received will be applied toward the cost of tuition before NJNGTP funds will cover the remaining balance. Visit http://www.state.nj.us/military/education/NJNGTP.htm for more information.

New Mexico

The New Mexico National Guard Tuition Scholarship Program pays up to $4,500 at a rate of $250 per SH per year for any program leading to the successful completion of a degree at the undergraduate level. This program can only be used toward public schools in New Mexico. Visit https://www.nm.ngb.army.mil/education.html for more information.

New York

The Recruitment Incentive and Retention Program is a scholarship that provides up to $4,350 a year toward tuition. It can be used at any school, but TA through GoArmyEd must be used first. The number of scholarships awarded is limited. Visit https://dmna.ny.gov/education/?page=rirp for more information.

North Carolina

The North Carolina Tuition Assistance Program will pay a specific amount of tuition depending on which North Carolina school the Guardsman attends. It can pay for both public and private schools in the state. Visit http://www.nc.ngb.army.mil/Services/Pages/Edu.aspx for more information, the list of approved schools, and the amount awarded per school.

North Dakota

North Dakota's program will only cover the difference of tuition not covered by FTA through GoArmyEd for any public or private school in the state. This difference will be reimbursed to the Guardsman after the successful completion of the term. Visit http://www.ndguard.ngb.army.mil/recruiting/benefits/educationalbenefits/tuitionassistance/Pages/default.aspx for more information.

Ohio

The Ohio National Guard Scholarship Program will pay full tuition at any public school in Ohio, or up to the average cost of tuition at an Ohio public school toward a private school. The program will only pay for the undergraduate level. Visit http://ong.ohio.gov/scholarship_index.html for more information.

Oklahoma

The Tuition Waiver Program will pay full tuition at any public school in the state. Unless the Guardsman already holds a bachelor's or a master's degree, undergraduate-level school will be covered. It will pay for up to eighteen SH per semester and for up to six years after the date of the very first TWP application. Visit https://secure.okcollegestart.org/Financial_Aid_Planning/ Scholarships/Military_Scholarships/National_Guard_Tuition_Waiver.aspx for more information.

Pennsylvania

The Pennsylvania National Guard Education Assistance Program will pay for 100 percent of tuition at a public school in the state, and up to the highest cost of tuition at a public university toward a private school. You must have signed a six-year contract with the Pennsylvania National Guard. Visit https://www.pheaa.org/funding-opportunities/aid-for-military-national-guard/national-guard-eap.shtml for more information.

Puerto Rico

The Puerto Rico National Guard Tuition Assistance Fund will pay up to $50 per SH at the undergraduate level and up to $75 a SH at the graduate level. It will pay for a total of eighteen SH per academic year, but there is a $5 monthly payment that must be paid to take advantage of this program. A version of this program can also pay the same amounts for the dependents of Guardsmen. Visit https://www.pr.ngb.army.mil/ and select the FIGNA link for more information.

Rhode Island

The State Tuition Assistance Program pays for the tuition of up to five classes per semester (not to exceed twelve SH) at any public school in the state. Guardsmen must serve one year from the last day of class for every twelve credits paid for by the program. Visit http://www.riarmynationalguard.com/free-college/ for more information.

South Carolina

The National Guard College Assistance Program awards up to $4,500 of funding per year ($2,250 per semester) at any public school in the state. The program does not pay for graduate-level programs, nor will it pay for an associate's or a bachelor's degree if the Guardsman already holds a bachelor's degree. Visit http://www.che.sc.gov/Students,FamiliesMilitary/MilitaryEducationTraining/NationalGuardCollegeAssistanceProgram.aspx for more information.

South Dakota

South Dakota pays for 50 percent of the tuition at any public school in the state. It will pay for up to 128 SH at the undergraduate level and thirty-two SH at the graduate level. Visit http://sdguard.com/guard-benefits/ for more information.

Tennessee

No traditional STA program exists in Tennessee, but the National Guard Association of Tennessee offers a $1,500 stipend per year for Guardsmen. There are a variety of scholarships for the dependents of Guardsmen, soldiers that were deployed and their dependents, and for NGAT members. Visit http://www.ngatn.org/association/scholarship-program for more information.

Texas

The State Tuition Reimbursement Program will pay up to $4,500 per semester at schools in Texas for up to ten semesters. Transcripts must be submitted after the completion of class for reimbursement of the Guardsman to occur. Visit http://www.txarng.com/strp for the list of eligible schools and more information.

Utah

The Utah State Tuition Waiver covers the cost of tuition at any public school in the state. The Guardsman must be attending school full-time and not currently hold a bachelor's degree. Visit http://www.ut.ngb.army.mil/education2/ for more information.

Vermont

The National Guard Educational Assistance Program is an interest-free loan given to the Guardsmen to attend any school in Vermont, whether public or private. Other sources of tuition-paying funding are applied first, which may lower the amount of the loan given. Visit https://www.goarmyed.com/public/facility_pages/NG_Vermont_Education_Services_Office/default.asp   for more information.

Virginia

The State Tuition Assistance Program will award funds toward the tuition of any school in Virginia, public or private. The amount varies by year depending on availability of funds. Guardsmen must also agree to serve in the Virginia National Guard for two years from the last day of the last class paid for by the program. Visit http://vko.va.ngb.army.mil/VirginiaGuard/education/index.html for more information.

West Virginia

The West Virginia Education Encouragement Program covers up to $6,500 annually of tuition and fees toward a public or private school in the state. Visit http://www.wv.ngb.army.mil/education/benefits/default.aspx for more information.

Wisconsin

The Wisconsin National Guard Tuition Grant can reimburse Guardsmen up to 100 percent of tuition at public and private schools in the state, or up to the cost of tuition at the University of Wisconsin at Madison, whichever is less. It will only pay for a degree at the undergraduate level and for a total of eight semesters. The Wisconsin school system has a reciprocity agreement with many schools in Minnesota, as well as limited agreements with schools in Iowa, Illinois, and Michigan, which may also be eligible for the program. Visit http://dma.wi.gov/dma/shr/tuition_grant_information.asp for a list of eligible schools and more information.

Wyoming

Wyoming will pay for the cost of tuition at any public school in the state and some pre-approved technical programs. It will also only pay for one degree, but it can be at any level, including PhDs and certificates. Guardsmen must also agree to serve in the Wyoming National Guard for two years after the last semester that was paid by the program. Visit http://www.wyoguard.com/education/assistance/ for more information.

Contacting your National Guard Education Center can also be a great way to get specific information. A full list of NG Education Centers can be found at this link: https://www.goarmyed.com/public/public_goarmyed-education_centers.aspx (they are designated with the letters "NG" before the name). Each center has its own GoArmyEd page with contact information to reach a counselor.

MONTGOMERY GI BILL

Not all service members have a Montgomery GI Bill (MGIB). When you entered the service, if you elected to opt in to MGIB and paid $100 per month for your first year of service to total $1,200, you might qualify for

MGIB. You must be separated with an honorable discharge as well; that goes for most benefits. Double-check your eligibility on the GI Bill website (http://www.benefits.va.gov/gibill/).

As of October 1, 2014, MGIB will pay $1,717 per month for up to thirty-six months for school. MGIB does not have a separate housing and book stipend like the Post-9/11 GI Bill. It is a flat payment amount. MGIB can be used for academic degrees, certificate programs, on-the-job training (OJT), correspondence classes, apprenticeship programs, and flight training. Benefits are good for ten years after separation from the military. Some service members participated in the $600 Buy-Up Program under MGIB. For those who did, an extra $150 per month will be added to their MGIB payments. That amount per month pays you back your $600 investment in four months. Every month after that point is money you are profiting from the program. If you cannot remember if you paid the optional Buy-Up Program, check with DFAS (Defense Finance and Accounting Service). You must pay the $600 at DFAS, and it is important you keep your receipts and provide them to the VA because you must prove to them that you took part in the program. For those who did not pay the money, check with the veterans' representatives at the school you are interested in attending before running off to pay it now. If you select Post-9/11, you forfeit the $600 that it takes to fully fund the Buy-Up. Smaller Buy-Up packages can be bought for prorated amounts. If you rate it and decide to stay under MGIB, you will most likely want to pay the Buy-Up for increased monthly payments.

Currently, if you paid into MGIB, remain under MGIB, and exhaust all thirty-six months of the benefit, you may be able to extend out an extra twelve months on Post-9/11. Contact the VA for final eligibility determination on this pathway. Typically, this requires that you have one period of qualifying service between August 1, 2009 and July 31, 2011, or completed two periods of qualifying service active duty after August 1, 2011. Multiple periods of active duty before August 1, 2009 will also make you eligible. This may enable you to save some benefit for a master's degree or a certificate program after completing a bachelor's degree. The problem is that in most cases, MGIB will not cover all of your bills.

You must decide whether you want less money consistently over forty-eight months or more money over thirty-six months using the Post-9/11. Graduate programs tend to be considerably more expensive than undergraduate programs, and if you use all thirty-six months of the Post-9/11 getting your bachelor's, you may need to use loans to get a graduate degree. Think wisely and be as creative as possible with the combination of benefits that are at your disposal.

You must also verify your enrollment at your school using the Web Automated Verification of Enrollment system to receive your $1,717 per month. This system can be found here: https://www.gibill.va.gov/wave.

Many veterans are concerned that they must pay the full cost of tuition up front when using the MGIB, and this might be the case for you.

If you have determined that the MGIB will net you more money than the Post-9/11 at your particular school, you must be adamant about using this benefit and not let the school interfere. Many schools prefer the Post-9/11 because tuition is paid up front; however, schools have been using the MGIB since its inception in 1985 and are always looking to attract students. In this thirty-year period many schools have offered to delay payments until the veteran receives enough money from the MGIB to pay tuition or may place veterans on an interest-free payment plan. Be your own best advocate and research all possible options, including discussing your situation with the school, before committing to any one pathway.

In the early 1990s the Army began offering an enlistment incentive program called the Army College Fund (ACF) for Military Occupational Specialities with critical shortages. This program was originally designed to increase the overall worth of the MGIB by distributing the total worth of the ACF over the thirty-six months. Unfortunately, the program was discontinued in October 2011, but soldiers can still take advantage of it if they were given this program. Check DA Form 3286 Annex A of your contract, because many soldiers are not even aware that they have it.

There is a lot of confusion about how much more you may actually receive. If you enlisted between April 1, 1993 and September 30, 2004, your total MGIB was lumped together with your ACF. In 2000, the MGIB was worth $23,400, but in 2014 it is worth $61,812. This just shows you how much the average cost of education has ballooned in the last fifteen years! The large increases you may believe you were given may not reflect the exact amount of extra benefit you may receive. This amount is also dictated by how long you served, even beyond your original contract. Search iPERMS for your original contract, find DA Form 3286, and send a copy to the VA to inquire how much your ACF is worth today. In many cases the ACF will still increase your overall MHA if you switch to the Post-9/11. If you need more guidance on the process, visit your local education center for advice.

POST-9/11 GI BILL

The Post-9/11 GI Bill is truly an amazing educational benefit available to eligible veterans. To determine your eligibility, visit http://www.benefits.va.gov/gibill/. Basically, to rate 100 percent of the Post-9/11, you need to meet these criteria:

- Served thirty-six consecutive months after September 11, 2001
- Received an honorable discharge

There are other categories for approval, but, like I have stressed at other points in this book, always check to determine your specific eligibility. In this case, contact the VA at (888) GIBILL-1.

The Post-9/11 GI Bill has three financial components built into the program: books and supplies, housing, and tuition.

Books and Supplies

The books and supplies stipend is prorated at $41.67 per credit hour for a maximum of $1,000 per academic year. A regular full time student who enrolls in a minimum of twelve credits per semester would receive the full $1,000. The stipend is broken into two payments per academic year and lumped in with the first month of the housing stipend for each semester.

You should take note that $1,000 is not actually a great amount for books. Books can run over $200 per class. Many universities list the approximate costs of textbooks for the school year on their websites. For example, California State University, Long Beach estimates their books at $1,828 for the 2014–2015 academic year. According to their calculations, $1,000 won't cut it for books. You definitely need to check into other options. The "Textbook Buying Options" section in this chapter is dedicated to helping you find used or rental books.

Housing

The housing stipend gets slightly more complicated. Referred to as the Monthly Housing Allowance (MHA), it is equivalent to the salary for an E-5 with dependents and applies for everyone. That is great if you separated anywhere near E-5, but if you separated as a general, you will need to do some adjusting with your budget (sorry—that is my bad sense of humor!). DO NOT use an online calculator other than the one offered on http://www.benefits.va.gov/gibill/, which is actually the US Department of Defense calculator (direct link: https://www.defensetravel.dod.mil/site/bah-Calc.cfm). This is the only valid website when it comes to determining your MHA based on the zip code of your school. That is right; the MHA is based on the zip code of your school, not your abode.

If attending school strictly online, the Post-9/11 housing rate was set at $754.50 as of August 1, 2014. This amount can vary each year. Check the website, http://www.benefits.va.gov/GIBILL/resources/benefits_resources/rates/ch33/ch33rates080114.asp, for current rates.

Tuition

Tuition under the Post-9/11 GI Bill can get complicated to explain. I am going to keep it simple. If you follow the most basic of parameters, you will not pay a dime for your school. Go outside of these parameters and you run into technical billing questions; in these cases, you should contact the school you are interested in attending for further information. If you are pursuing an undergraduate or graduate degree, plan on attending a state school in the state where you have residency, and finish your degree within the thirty-six months of benefit you have allotted, your schooling should be covered. The thirty-six months is enough for most bachelor's degrees if you stay on track because it equates to nine months of school per year over the course of four years (assuming that you do not attend in the summer, though you may do so if interested). If one of these factors changes, so might your bill. Veterans who chose to attend private school received a maximum of $20,235.02 for the academic year 2014–2015 (http://www.benefits.va.gov/GIBILL/re-sources/benefits_resources/rates/ch33/ch33rates080114.asp).   Anything above that amount and you run the risk of having to pay out of pocket. Many schools participate in the Yellow Ribbon Program (http://www.gibill.va.gov/benefits/post_911_gibill/yellow_ribbon_program.html), and it may help cover private school costs that come in above the maximum VA-allotted threshold for out-of-state tuition charges.

What about out-of-state tuition, you ask? Out-of-state tuition is what non-residents must pay a public school when enrolled. Tuition can be much higher for non-residents because they have not contributed to the tax pool of that state and do not deserve the resident rate of tuition. However, the Veterans Access, Choice, and Accountability Act of 2014 (https://veterans.house.gov/the-veterans-access-choice-and-accountability-act-of-2014-highlights) was passed in July 2014, and as of the academic year 2015–2016, schools that take Post-9/11 dollars will need to list veterans as in-state residents for tuition purposes. If you attend a public college within three years of your separation date and use a GI Bill for payment, out-of-state tuition charges should not be a problem as of the start of the Fall 2015 semester. If you decide to remain off your GI Bill in the beginning, schools do not have to extend the honorary in-state residency benefit to you. Spouses and children who are using transferred GI Bill benefits are also covered under this benefit.

As stated above, the VA will pay you the full-time housing allowance if you pursue school at the full-time rate. The VA considers twelve credit hours to be full-time. However, if you have no previous college credit and intend on pursuing a bachelor's degree, twelve credits per semester will not suffice. Most bachelor's degrees require students to complete 120 semester credit hours of specific subject matter in order to have the degree conferred on them. That equates to fifteen credit hours each semester, or five classes.

The college year runs similar to the high school year, two semesters each year over the course of four years. So, 120 SH breaks down to fifteen SH each semester to total thirty credits each year (freshman year: 30; sophomore year: 30; junior year: 30; senior year: 30; total: 120). If you follow the VA's minimum guidelines of twelve credits each semester, or four classes, you will run out of benefits at the end of your senior year but only have earned ninety-six semester credit hours, which are twenty-four credits shy of the 120 required. You will be out of benefit but will not have obtained your degree. The academic counselors at the school you attend will help you with your degree plans. If you need to make changes or have questions, contact them for further advice.

MONTGOMERY GI BILL VS. POST-9/11 GI BILL

There are a few situations in which it makes more sense for the veteran to remain under MGIB instead of opting for Post-9/11. There are three big ones. The first is if your MHA is low. This may occur in areas where the cost of living is not that high, such as large rural areas where the MHA rarely breaks the $800 or $900 mark. Be aware that you still need to calculate the cost of your tuition and fees into the total overall money being spent. You might make more initially, but after paying your school and book bills find yourself coming up short. Typically, the cost of the school needs to be very low in order for this tactic to be beneficial.

Another situation occurs if a veteran determines that an online program is the best fit. Students pursuing online-only school under the Post-9/11 GI Bill currently receive $754.50 per month (2014–2015 school year) for a housing stipend. The amount is half of the national average of the housing stipend paid for the face-to-face rate. You must attend a minimum of one face-to-face class every semester in order to rate the full MHA assigned to the zip code of the school. In a few cases, veterans who decide that they can only attend online school may do better by remaining under MGIB and paying the $600 Buy-Up prior to separation. In the case of strictly online school, it is difficult to run numbers in this book because there are too many unknown factors. Examples of this include tuition charges, MHA attached to the school's zip code, and fluctuations in GI Bill payouts.

However, here is a hypothetical example: Sergeant Smith decides to attend a fully online academic program. The cost of the school per credit hour is $250. He is taking two classes over an eight-week semester. The total cost for his two classes will be $1,500. The MHA for strictly online school at this point in time is $754.50 per month. Sergeant Smith paid the $600 Buy-Up

Program at DFAS before separating. His combined monthly payout under MGIB and the Buy-Up Program for academic year 2014–2015 is $1,867. In the span of his eight-week classes, he will take in $3,734. After paying his $1,500 bill for his two classes (two classes on an eight-week-semester schedule is considered full-time), he is left with $2,234. That is roughly $725 more than what he would take home if he had elected Post-9/11 and only received the $754.50 that is allotted for strictly online school ($2,234 − $1,509 = $725). MGIB, in this case, looks like the better choice.

If considering online-only school, make sure to verify all tuition and fee charges prior to making a decision. The above-listed example only worked out to the student's benefit because the tuition charges were capped at $250 per credit hour. If your tuition and fee charges amount to a larger sum, MGIB might not be the best choice for payment.

A third example is if the cost of tuition at the school is low. Some veterans attending school in rural areas might find staying under MGIB more beneficial than converting to Post-9/11. For example, Corporal Jones will attend Coahoma Community College in Clarksdale, Mississippi. The MHA for the school under Post-9/11 is $1,038 per month. After nine months of school for her first year she would have received $9,342. Under MGIB with the $150 Buy-Up paid, she would take in $16,803, but she may need to pay her school up front both semesters. The current cost of Coahoma Community College per semester is $1,050 (http://www.coahomacc.edu/admissions/financialaid/admissions/tuitionfees/index), but make note that this does not include some of the extra fees the institution will charge per semester or per year, or book expenses. So for one academic year, Corporal Jones will pay $2,100 for her tuition charges, but she will still take in more money under MGIB than had she elected Post-9/11. Here are the calculations:

Post-9/11 MHA for nine months= $9,342
MGIB with the Buy-Up for nine months= $16,803
Minus tuition charges for the academic year $16,803–$2,100=$14,703
Difference between Post-9/11 and MGIB $14,703–$9,342= $5,361

As a veteran, it is important that you follow through with your own research on state and federal benefits. States are often updating and adding benefits for veterans. The monetary amounts attached to the federal GI Bills change as well. The only way to stay current with the information is to become fluent with the websites and check back regularly.

The fourth situation occurs when soldiers attend school in a state with a full state-based benefit. The "State-Based Veteran Education Benefits" and the "National Guard Tuition Assistance" sections of this chapter will review both of these circumstances and demonstrate why a veteran might elect to remain under MGIB. States can also offer non-military-specific programs that may pay tuition. California, for example, has the Board of Governors

Waiver (BOG), which pays tuition at any community college in the state if you are eligible. The Post-9/11 will not pay tuition twice, so the benefit is effectively worth less in this situation, thereby potentially increasing the overall worth of the MGIB in comparison. Be careful in this situation though. Even though the BOG might pay the school, in many areas of California the housing stipend under Post-9/11 is significantly higher than the $1,717 that MGIB currently pays out per month.

Prior to electing either GI Bill, it is best to discuss all available options. Contact your state VA to determine your available state benefits and learn how to use them. Contact the veterans' department at the institution you would like to attend and request guidance. Typically, the veterans' representatives can offer great advice pertaining to the best benefit pathway. They have already blazed the trail and learned the ropes for themselves. Never forget that you can use the MGIB if it is going to be worth more at your initial school, and then switch to the Post-9/11 if you decide to go to a more expensive school or a school with a higher MHA at a later date. You will simply have the remaining months left out of the total thirty-six months. The VA also offers guidance and can be reached at (888) GIBILL-1.

You can get a head start on financial planning by using the Comparison Tool on the main GI Bill website found here: http://www.benefits.va.gov/gibill/comparison. This new and highly dynamic tool that the VA is constantly updating is a reliable resource to assist you in your research. You can configure the rate of going to school, the number of terms you may be attending, and the length of each school's term. This allows you to pinpoint a fairly accurate idea of what the benefit will be worth to you as you attend school for that year. This also allows for easy comparison to the MGIB, which is worth $1,717 a month.

After inputting the required information you can view the "Total GI Bill Benefits" number given by the tool, which is worth nine months of schooling (one academic year). On the dropdown menu select any GI Bill to see what it is worth at that institution, and compare this "Total GI Bill Benefits" for each school. Here's a tip: since the MGIB is worth $1,717 a month, every nine-month period will be worth $15,453, so just compare this number to what the "Total GI Bill Benefits" Post-9/11 amount is for that school. Voilà, the VA made it easy!

STUDENT LOAN REPAYMENT PROGRAM

The Student Loan Repayment Program (SLRP) is offered to soldiers instead of the MGIB at enlistment and can pay off federal student loans. Two versions of this program exist, one for active-duty soldiers and one for reservists.

The active-duty SLRP is an option that will typically pay slightly over $65,000, depending on your contract. It will only pay the principal amount on federal loans; you are responsible for paying the interest. Loans that are currently in default cannot be covered. For active-duty personnel, these must be loans obtained before joining the Army and only a third of this amount will be paid every year over your three-year contract.

During this time you will not build time toward Post-9/11 GI Bill eligibility. Once your three years is over, any amount of active-duty time between ninety days and thirty-six months will earn you some portion of the Post-9/11 GI Bill. You do not need to contribute the $1,200 during your first year of service toward the Montgomery GI Bill to be eligible for Post-9/11. The SLRP is typically obtained at initial enlistment as an incentive.

The Reserve SLRP works differently in that it can pay for future loans. This allows reservists to strategize their benefits by taking on loans for school while in drilling status, knowing they have a benefit that will pay off this amount. Reservists can also use any GI Bill they qualify for simultaneously. This incentive typically comes in $10,000 and $20,000 versions depending on the contract. Reservists use the same paperwork and forms as the active-duty component, but they submit it electronically while active-duty soldiers use a paper mailing system.

Both active-duty personnel and reservists must fill out the DA Form 2475 *each* year for *each* loan they have. Be aware that federal loans are broken down by the subsidized and unsubsidized categories and are considered different loans. Some soldiers have multiple loans within each category. You must also obtain the promissory note from your lender for *each* loan.

The 2475 has three primary sections. Section one is typically filled out by your S1 or unit personnel officer. You must complete sections two and three. Your lender must fill out section four. Many soldiers submit the 2475 to the lender once sections one to three are completed and request that the lender submit the form for them. I (Paul) would not rely on the lender to comply. Ask your lender to give you the 2475 once they complete section four so you can ensure it is completed, then submit the paperwork yourself. Once the completed forms are obtained from the lenders, active-duty soldiers must submit each 2475 with their promissory notes by mailing them to

Commander, AHRC
ATTN: AHRC-PDP-E
1600 Spearhead Division Avenue
Fort Knox, KY 40122

Details of both the active-duty and reserve process can be found here: https://www.hrc.army.mil/TAGD/Loan%20Repayment%20Program.

Keep an eye on your military email; you should receive an email ten months from the date of entry into the military, the Basic Active Service Date or Pay Entry Base Date for the reserve component, reminding them to complete the SLRP process. If you require assistance contact your nearest active-duty or reserve education center by finding them here: https://www.goarmyed.com/public/public_goarmyed-education_centers.aspx (Army Reserve Education Centers begin with an AR).

RESERVE COMPONENT VA EDUCATION BENEFITS

Guardsmen and Reserve soldiers may potentially have access to two additional VA educational benefits that can make their combination of benefits complicated, but also more worthwhile: Chapter 1606, or the Montgomery GI Bill–Selected Reserve (MGIB-SR), and Chapter 1607, or the Reserve Education Assistance Program (REAP). These benefits allow soldiers to use up to twelve months of the benefits described and still preserve all thirty-six months of their other benefits, such as the Post-9/11, thereby extending the total number of months of benefits available. This pathway is not possible with the MGIB-AD.

Chapter 1606, or the MGIB-SR, may be offered to reserve component soldiers who have signed at least a six-year enlistment contract. Once you complete your Advanced Individual Training and continue to remain in good standing, your unit will provide you the DD 2384-1, or NOBE (Notice of Basic Eligibility), which you will return to your unit for them to notate your eligibility in your personnel file. While the MGIB-SR is not a particularly generous benefit, it may allow service members to extend the number of months they may have available in order to attend school for up to forty-eight months, the typical maximum amount of months available for federal education benefits for the life of a soldier.

The MGIB-SR currently awards $367 a month to full-time students, but if tuition is already covered by another program, students can pocket this money while extending the number of months available to them for their education. Additionally, some soldiers are awarded a "kicker" as an enlistment incentive in their reserve component contract. I (Paul) have seen amounts as high as an additional $400 on top of the original $367 per month.

The REAP, or Chapter 1607, is another benefit that is often described as the predecessor to the concept of the Post-9/11 GI Bill. This is because when it launched in 2005 reserve component soldiers who were activated in response to war or national emergency for certain lengths of time potentially became eligible for amounts of 40 to 80 percent of the worth of the current MGIB-AD monthly amount, currently set at $1,717. If you were activated for between ninety days and a year, you are eligible for 40 percent, or $686.80

per month as a full-time student. If you were activated for more than a year, you are eligible for 60 percent, or $1,030.20. If you were activated for more than two years, you are eligible for 80 percent, or $1,373.60.

The catch in this situation is that all periods of active duty must be *consecutive*; they cannot be combined such as with eligibility for the Post-9/11. There is a provision that *successive* periods of active duty may be combined to determine maximum eligibility. Two successive years of active duty for those in the reserve component is rare, even when military activities during Operation Iraqi Freedom and Operation Enduring Freedom were at their peak. In such situations it may also be possible to be eligible for the entirety of the MGIB-AD. Consult with the VA (888-GIBILL-1) to determine MGIB-AD eligibility if you find yourself in this position, as the same active-duty time cannot be used concurrently toward both programs.

A significant change to REAP in 2008 broke from the pattern of requiring successive active-duty periods to allow those individuals activated for a combined total of three years or more, even if not consecutive, to be eligible at the 80 percent rate. Soldiers can participate in the Buy-Up Program described in the MGIB-AD section by contributing up to $600 to receive up to an additional $150 per month while using the program. If you are eligible for the MGIB-SR and were awarded the "kicker," that can also increase the REAP monthly amount.

Under both the MGIB-SR and the REAP, soldiers can only receive a maximum of forty-eight months of VA benefits. Deciding which benefit is more advantageous usually depends on whether you are using the benefit on active duty or as a veteran and the cost of tuition and fees at your school. You will receive the maximum amount of the MGIB-SR on active duty, but REAP will be calculated similarly to the MGIB-AD and Post-9/11, which in many cases is not the full worth of the benefit. When not on active duty REAP may be more advantageous because the monetary value of the benefit may exceed the MGIB-SR. To get the most from your benefits, you should calculate what your MGIB-SR and REAP are worth, adding any "kickers" and the Buy-Up Program, and how this may compare to your rate of eligibility under Post-9/11. I (Paul) have worked with quite a few soldiers in the reserve component who had served for one deployment and whose amount of REAP exceeded the 40 to 60 percent worth of the Post-9/11 benefit at the school they had elected to attend.

Sometimes, reserve component soldiers who opt to receive less money while they attend a cheap school, such as a community college, in the first twelve months of schooling can preserve all thirty-six months of the potentially more generous Post-9/11 to use for some portion of an expensive advanced degree, even if their eligibility is rated at only 60 percent. Creatively combining these VA benefits with the other benefits described in this chapter, such as reserve component STA or veteran state programs, can potentially assist soldiers in maximizing the amount of money available to them in the long run.

GI BILL TOP-UP

If a soldier is attending school while on active duty and chooses a school that costs more than the amount allotted under TA, GI Bill Top-Up can be used to top off the TA. The soldier would activate his or her GI Bill, and tap into it as a funding resource for the portion of the class that was not covered by TA. This would affect the soldier's overall remaining benefit amount upon separation from the military.

TA only covers up to $250 per credit hour. If a soldier chooses a school that costs $350 per SH and is taking a three-SH class, he or she will be responsible for $300 out of pocket for the entire class after using TA. In this case, Top-Up could be used to cover the amount.

Using Top-Up may be necessary in some cases, but soldiers generally avoid using any GI Bill on active duty because of the manner in which the benefit is calculated. Tapping into Top-Up early will pull on the soldier's available GI Bill months, thereby reducing the amount of benefits remaining after separation from the military. Top-Up was originally created in 2001 to keep soldiers from having to lose more months than what the VA pays out on active duty. The VA wants you to save your benefit for after you separate, so the benefit is calculated differently on active duty, and not to your advantage. Top-Up avoids this problem because you will only lose the amount above what is covered by TA, but Top-Up does not function correctly under the Post-9/11 GI Bill, nor does it operate under the MGIB-SR or REAP. Under Post-9/11, Top-Up users lose benefits based on months; under MGIB users lose benefits based on cost amount. Under MGIB, if the cost of the class is $250 above the allotted TA amount, then you only lose $250 of your benefit. If MGIB is worth $1,717 for thirty days, then $250 is about five days of benefits used. Under the Post-9/11, it is your status as a student multiplied by the number of days in class that is used. If you are a 50 percent time student enrolled in a class that is two months long, then that is one whole month of the Post-9/11 spent. Talk to an education counselor, a GI Bill counselor (888-GIBILL-1), and the VA certifying official at your school before making a decision about which benefit to use in this case. Remember that once you elect to use the Post-9/11 GI Bill, you cannot go back to MGIB. You can still switch later to the Post-9/11 if that is the better benefit at that time.

Many institutions across the country cost less than or equal to the amount covered under TA. If the institution you are planning on attending is over the $250 threshold and recommending GI Bill Top-Up, please speak to an academic counselor for advice prior to making any final decisions.

Three situations come to mind when I discuss using Top-Up for service members.

1. If the individual is about to run out of TA money, is at the end of his or her degree, and is separating from active duty soon. In this case, it is important to note that the individual will obtain the degree prior to separating, and will be able to list the accomplishment on his or her résumé. This enables the veteran to get into the workforce faster.
2. In most master's degree programs, the cost is above and beyond the $250 per credit hour that TA can cover. Completing an advanced degree while still on active duty will be an enormous benefit to separating service members.
3. If the service member is looking to attend a prestigious university and cannot cover the costs out of pocket. In this case, I would typically recommend attending a local community college (many have fully online, fast-paced programs available) for as long as possible prior to transferring into the university. At least this way, the individual would not be drawing from his or her GI Bill for such an extended period of time.

For undergraduate study, try all possibilities prior to looking into Top-Up. The Pell Grant is often a viable option (check the "Federal Student Aid" section). Ultimately, the decision to use Top-Up must be the service member's, but the guidelines above are solid and should be considered prior to making a move.

GI BILL APPLICATION AND CONVERSION PROCESS

The application process for the GI Bill is not complicated; however, it does currently take approximately four to six weeks to receive the Certificate of Eligibility (COE) statement. Make sure to allot time for the wait prior to starting school. If you find yourself in a time crunch, check with your school to see if the institution might take a copy of the submitted application and let you get started.

If you have MGIB and you are positive you want to convert to Post-9/11, the process can be done at the same time you activate the benefit for a specific school. This process can occur before or after you separate from the military, so it would be wise to be absolutely certain of what school you will be attending before deciding which GI Bill to use. If you choose to switch to the Post-9/11, but you decide to attend a different school at a later date, you will not be able to switch back if the MGIB is more advantageous at your new school.

To activate the GI Bill, you will need to access the Veterans Online Application (VONAPP; see http://vabenefits.vba.va.gov/vonapp/). You can also access it by going to the main GI Bill website (http://www.benefits.va.gov/gibill/): select the "Post 9/11" link on the right-hand side, select "Get Started" on the left-hand side, select "Apply for Benefits," and lastly select "Apply Online." You will need three pieces of information before you proceed:

- Your school's name and address
- A bank account and routing number (VA is direct deposit)
- An address you will be at in the next four to eight weeks

The easiest way to prepare for the application process is to be accepted to your intended institution prior to applying to activate your benefit, but you can change the required information at a later date by contacting the VA at (888) GIBILL-1.

The VA does not send hard checks anymore. Inputting your bank account and routing numbers enables them to directly deposit your MHA and book stipend money. You may change this information at a later date using the VA's Direct Deposit form if you change your bank.

The address you list will be where your COE is delivered. Soldiers living in the barracks might want to send their COEs to their parents or another reliable family member's address. Just make sure that the individuals located at the listed address keep an eye out for the document and inform you when it arrives. You will need to take that document to the veterans' representative at your school as soon as you receive it, because it is the school's ticket to receive payment from the VA. This is part of the process for you to receive the housing allowance if you are using the Post-9/11

Process of Applying

Upon entering the VONAPP website (http://vabenefits.vba.va.gov/vonapp/), you will be asked if you are a first-time VONAPP user; answer accordingly. Next, you will be asked if you possess an eBenefits Account. I find this to be a difficult way to enter the site. If you select that you do not have an eBenefits account, you will need to create a VONAPP account (this seems to be a much easier pathway!). Be aware that you will need an eBenefits account for all other VA-related concerns, but applying directly through VONAPP will not disrupt that process. Once settled, select the "22-1990 Education Benefits" form to proceed. The first question on the form will ask you which GI Bill you wish to use, and if you elect to receive a benefit you do not currently have, it will also ask you which GI Bill you will be giving up. The VONAPP website will also ask you to provide information about your active-duty tours, prior education and training, upcoming start date for your school and training, pursuit of study (associate degree, bachelor's degree, graduate degree, or apprenticeship/on-the-job training), and so on. The form is not overly complicated, so do not overthink the answers to your questions. There are actually only a few pieces of information that the VA is really interested in, such as your personal information and the GI Bill you are electing to use, so it is very hard to make a mistake with your answers.

If you are concerned about the questions on the 22-1990 or whether you are making the correct choices, contact the VA at (888) GIBILL-1. The veterans' representatives at your intended school are usually good sources of information as well. Check with your base's education center to see if they keep paper copies of the 22-1990s if you would like to see the required information in advance.

Once you receive the COE, you need to take it (a copy!) to the veterans' representatives at your school. You will also need to send a copy of your DD 214 to your local VA processing center. When you finish filling out and submitting the 22-1990, the main page on the VONAPP will maintain two links (side by side) with required, printable information: one is your submitted application, and the other is your local processing center, which is often not in the same state. Some institutions will also want a copy of your DD 214 for verification purposes.

If you have used the VA benefit before and are transferring to a new school, you will need to fill out the 22-1995 form, but only if you are not changing GI Bill chapters. The 22-1995 form can be found on the VONAPP website.

POST-9/11 TRANSFERABILITY TO DEPENDENTS

Active-duty service members may be eligible to transfer their Post-9/11 GI Bill benefits to dependents. The transfer process requires a four-year commitment to stay in the military. If benefits are successfully transferred, certain rules apply while the service member remains on active duty.

To be eligible to transfer benefits, service members must be eligible for Post-9/11 and:

- have completed six years of active-duty service to transfer
- have four years remaining on contract (enlisted) or commit four more years (officer)

Exceptions to serving the four additional years commonly include Mandatory Retirement Dates, Retention Control Points, or Medical Evaluation Boards. Transfer must be approved while the service member is still in the armed forces. The best time to complete the process is at the same time as a re-enlistment or extension package that gives the individual the required amount of payback time. To transfer benefits, follow these steps:

- Verify your time in service.
- Visit the website (at http://www.benefits.va.gov/gibill/post911_gibill.asp).
- Click on the "Transfer of Entitlement" option.
- Follow the directions ("Apply Now").
- You will find yourself on the MilConnect webpage and will need to enter your Common Access Card card or DFAS account information.
- Click on the "Go to Transfer of Eligible Benefits" link on the right-hand side.
- Apply the needed information and submit—but you are not finished.
- Obtain a Statement of Understanding from the website or the local education center aboard your base.
- Fill out all required information and talk to your military career counselor to verify time in service.
- The battalion commanding officer signs off on a soldier's application, and then the document must be routed through S1.
- Once transfer is approved, eligibility documents will be found in the Transfer Education Benefits website (https://www.dmdc.osd.mil/milconnect/help/topics/transfer_of_education_benefits_teb.htm) for each individual.

Service members may revoke transferred benefits at any given time. Designated months may also be changed or eliminated through the website while on active duty or through a written request to the VA once separated.

Dependents who have received transferred benefits will need to apply to use the benefits through the VONAPP website (http://www.benefits.va.gov/gibill/post911_gibill.asp) in the "Post 9/11, Apply for Benefits" section. Dependents may also print the form (22-1990e) and send it in to their nearest VA regional office. The form may be found online (at http://www.vba.va.gov/pubs/forms/VBA-22-1990e-ARE.pdf) and regional offices may also be found online (at http://www.benefits.va.gov/benefits/offices.asp). Eligible dependents may include the service member's children or spouse. Dependents must be in the Defense Enrollment Eligibility Reporting System (DEERS).

Spouses

- May use the benefit immediately
- Are not entitled to the MHA while the service member remains on active duty, but are entitled once the service member separates

- Are entitled to the book stipend
- May use the benefit for up to fifteen years from the service member's End of Active Service date, just like the service member

Children

- May use the benefit only after the service member has attained ten years on active duty
- May use the benefit while the parent is on active duty or after separation
- Must have obtained a high school diploma or equivalency certificate, or have turned eighteen
- May receive the MHA while a parent remains on active-duty status
- Are entitled to the book stipend
- Do not fall under the fifteen-year delimiting date; however, benefits must be used prior to turning twenty-six years old.
- Must have been given the benefit before the age of twenty-one. An extension can be granted by DEERS to transfer benefit before the age of twenty-three if you are still on active duty.

Soldiers can commit the required payback time of four years after separating from active duty and dropping into the Reserves. See http://www.gibill.va.gov/benefits/post_911_gibill/transfer_of_benefits.html as well as the DoD Fact Sheet on Post-9/11 GI Bill Transferability at http://www.benefits.va.gov/gibill/docs/factsheets/Transferability_Factsheet.pdf for more information.

THE YELLOW RIBBON PROGRAM (HTTP://WWW.BENEFITS.VA.GOV/GIBILL/YELLOW_RIBBON.ASP)

The Yellow Ribbon Program (YRP) is designed to cover tuition above and beyond the maximum allowable rate for a private school or foreign school.

YRP is not automatic, and there are many stipulations to watch out for prior to determining if the benefit will work for your particular purpose. YRP does not pay the student any money.

Eligibility

- Must qualify for 100 percent of the Post-9/11 GI Bill
- Active-duty members of the military are not eligible, nor are their spouses; however, children of active-duty service members may qualify (if the active-duty parent is eligible for 100 percent of 9/11).

YRP potentially enables veterans to cover costs above and beyond the Post-9/11 GI Bill parameters. Not all schools participate, and a school's participation for one year does not guarantee participation in subsequent years. You do not need to maintain full-time status in order to be eligible for YRP. Summer terms may be eligible as well, but check with your particular institution.

Schools must reestablish their YRP program with the VA every year. This means, and I have seen it happen, that a school may participate one year but not the next. You could get left hanging. For example, a corporal attended a well-known private school in Georgia. The school participated during her first year, but not the following years. She was out of pocket roughly $22,000 per year for her school at that point—ouch!

Schools may participate on different levels by limiting the amount of YRP spots available and the amount of money they offer. This can restrict veterans from considering certain institutions based on financial constraints. The following is a hypothetical breakdown:

- School A participates in YRP with unlimited spots and unlimited money. Therefore, you shouldn't pay out of pocket. But you still run the risk of the school choosing not to participate in upcoming years.
- School B participates with twenty spots and $4,000 per student. Therefore, you may or may not get one of those twenty spots (remember that it is first come, first served!), and the VA will match the $4,000, effectively giving you an extra $8,000 toward tuition (this is a rough explanation of how it actually works).

You must also check to see how the program at your school is participating. Consider the following hypothetical situation:

- School C: The graduate-level school of business participates with seventeen spots and $11,000 per student.
- School C: The graduate-level school of education participates with four spots and $6,000 per student.

Notice that different programs within the same school may participate with different amounts of money and available spots.

Lastly, a school may participate differently at the graduate level than it does at the undergraduate level. See the following example:

- School E participates at the undergraduate level with five spots and $8,000 per student.
- School E participates at the graduate level with three spots and $1,000 per student.

While it can become complicated to determine the benefit you may be eligible for, the vet reps at the school can usually offer sound advice. You can search YRP participating schools by state (at http://www.benefits.va.gov/GIBILL/yellow_ribbon/yrp_list_2014.asp). However, I always recommend contacting the VA directly for solid confirmation that the school you are applying for does participate and to what degree.

Do not make the mistake of thinking that a small, off-the-beaten-path school might not fill their YRP seats. I spoke with a small college in Washington State that participates in the YRP, wondering if they often fill their openings. Prior to speaking to the veterans' representative, I thought to myself that it was nice they had allotted so many spots even though they probably do not need them. I mean, how many veterans are relocating to this rural area? I was so wrong! The school had a waiting list for its YRP spots that was in the double digits. Apparently, while the school was located in a rural area, it was also the closest school to one of the state's main snowboarding mountains and maintained a fairly large veteran population. On the flipside, I was happy to hear that our veterans were getting some much-needed R&R after their military service along with a good education.

If you intend on transferring, you must speak with your new school regarding YRP eligibility at their institution. Eligibility at one does not guarantee eligibility at another. If you take a hiatus from your school and were enrolled in YRP, you may get dropped for subsequent semesters. Before you make any decisions, talk with your academic advisor and/or veteran department. The more informed you are, the better you can plan.

VA GI BILL FEEDBACK SYSTEM (HTTP://WWW.BENEFITS.VA.GOV/GIBILL/FEEDBACK.ASP)

The VA has recently implemented voluntary guidelines entitled the Principles of Excellence along with a system to handle complaints when schools violate these guidelines. Educational institutions that have agreed to abide by the specific guidelines of the program are agreeing to do the following:

- Inform students in writing of the costs associated with education at that institution.
- Produce educational plans for military and veteran beneficiaries.
- Cease all misleading recruiting techniques.
- Accommodate those who are absent due to military requirements.
- Appoint a point-of-contact who offers education-related and financial advice.
- Confirm that all new programs are accredited before enrolling students.
- Align refund policies with Title IV policies (Federal Student Aid).

Schools that participate in the Principles of Excellence program can be found on the VA website (http://www.benefits.va.gov/gibill/principles_of_excellence.asp).

Complaints should be submitted when institutions participating in the program fall below the above-listed set of standards. Complaints are filed on subjects such as recruiting practices, education quality, accreditation issues, grade policies, failure to release transcripts, credit transfer, financial topics, student loan concerns, refund problems, job opportunities after degree completion, and degree plan changes and subsequent requirements. To file a complaint, visit the website and follow the directions.

FEDERAL STUDENT AID

Soldiers have other sources of funding to pursue above and beyond TA and the GI Bills. Student Aid money is offered by the US federal government, states, schools, and nonprofit organizations. Federal Student Aid (FSA) money is the most actively sought after money and is available through the US Department of Education. Active-duty and veteran service members can apply for FSA and should be encouraged to do so to cover any extra costs they are unable to get funded. For example, TA cannot cover books or supplies. Under the Post-9/11 GI Bill, if a student attends school full-time he/she will receive $1,000 per academic year toward books and supplies. In most cases, this is not enough to cover book expenses. FSA might be a viable option to help in these circumstances if a soldier qualifies.

Prior to choosing a school, it is important to consider the costs associated with attending each institution. Although you have different types of educational benefits available to use because of your military status, these benefits do not cover all expenses in most cases. School expenses can vary significantly from institution to institution. Prospective students should consider expenses above and beyond the tuition and fees. Books, travel, and equipment costs can add up and create a substantial financial burden for service members.

The US Department of Education recommends that if attending a particular school is going to require you to pay money above and beyond the amounts covered under your available benefits,

> You'll want to make sure that the cost of your school is reasonable compared to your earning potential in your future career. In other words, you want to make sure that you can earn enough money to cover any student loan payments you may need to make, along with living expenses, after you graduate. [1]

Schools that participate in FSA programs are required to provide potential students information about costs and to provide a net price calculator on their websites. Students can also access the College ScoreCard (http://college-cost.ed.gov/scorecard/index.aspx), provided by the US Department of Education's College Affordability and Transparency Center, to help in making more informed decisions regarding an institution's value and affordability.

Prior to applying for FSA, it is important to understand what it is, how it works, and what you would want to accept. FSA, or Title IV Programs as they are categorized, comes in three forms: work-study, loans, and grants. For active-duty and veteran students using their GI Bills, loans are usually not necessary. In fact, it is best to avoid them at all costs. In most cases, active-duty service members have access to TA money and veterans typically have access to their GI Bills. Loans have to be repaid with interest, and you should think carefully before accepting them. VA Work-Study is discussed in depth in chapter 10.

Pell Grant money should be the goal for most service members. Pell Grant money does not need to be repaid and is awarded for first-time bachelor's or associate's degree-seeking students only. In certain instances, students might receive a Pell Grant award if they are attending a post-baccalaureate teacher certification program. The maximum Pell Grant award was set at $5,730 for the 2014–2015 academic year. That amount was based upon maximum financial need and a full-time rate of pursuit.

In order to be eligible to apply for FSA, students must meet the following parameters:

- Most programs require demonstrating financial need
- Must be a US citizen or eligible noncitizen
- Have a valid Social Security number (exceptions apply)
- Be registered with the Selective Service
- Be enrolled or accepted at minimum of half-time as a regular student into an eligible degree or certificate program
- Maintain satisfactory progress

FSA applicants will also need to sign statements stating:

- Student is not defaulting on any federal student loans
- Student does not owe money on any federal grants
- Student will only use aid money for education-related expenses
- Student must demonstrate evidence of eligibility by having a high school diploma, GED, or completed homeschool program approved by state law

Financial need eligibility is based upon, "your Expected Family Contribution, your year in school, your enrollment status, and the cost of attendance at the school you will be attending."[2] The Expected Family Contribution (EFC) is a number that the financial aid department employees use to help determine the amount of financial aid you would potentially need to attend that particular school. The information that you file when completing the Free Application for Federal Student Aid (FAFSA) is used within a special formula that was established by law to determine your EFC. Financial information pertaining to your taxed and untaxed income, benefits, and assets can all be taken into account, as well as your family size. More detailed information on how the EFC is calculated can be found on the following Department of Education (DOE) website: http://ifap.ed.gov/efcformulaguide/attachments/091913EFCFormulaGuide1415.pdf.

Your enrollment status is simply your rate of pursuit. Award amounts are based upon the degree to which you pursue school and are reported by your school to the DOE. Full-time school is usually difficult for active-duty soldiers to maintain considering mission demands. Veterans must attend school at the full-time rate in order to rate full-time Post-9/11 GI Bill benefits.

The cost of attendance (COA) is the actual amount of money it will cost in order for you to attend an institution. Typically, for traditional educational programs the COA is calculated on a yearly basis. The estimate includes:

- tuition and fees;
- the cost of room and board (or living expenses for students who do not contract with the school for room and board);
- the cost of books, supplies, transportation, loan fees, and miscellaneous expenses (including a reasonable amount for the documented cost of a personal computer);
- an allowance for child care or other dependent care;
- costs related to a disability; and/or
- reasonable costs for eligible study-abroad programs.[3]

After determining the COA, your EFC is subtracted from your COA to determine your financial need.

Service members need to reapply for FSA every year even if they were not awarded Pell Grant money the previous year. Economic circumstances for military members can change drastically from year to year, thereby changing financial need determination. For example, certain billets have different pay attached to them or you might have been in a combat zone. Also, you might get married, divorced, separate from the military, or have a child, all of which can affect your financial situation. I often work with higher-ranking service members who tell me they make too much money and will not be eligible for a Pell Grant award. I have worked with E-9s that have received the full award and E-2s that have been denied, so let the DOE tell you what might be available to assist with your educational expenses.

If you are separating from the Army, filled out your FAFSA, and did not receive an award, or received very little, visit with the financial aid department at your school. They have the ability to fix your FAFSA based upon your new income levels. In many instances, this can drive the previous number up, helping you cover your expenses.

If a student is awarded Pell Grant money, the amount is sent to the school, and the school pays the student. If any money is owed toward tuition and fees, schools remove that amount from the award prior to turning the remainder of the money over to the student. Award money is typically turned over to students in check, cash, or bank deposit. Federal Pell Grant money is paid out in at least two disbursements. Most schools pay students at least once per semester. Since most veteran students' tuition is covered by the GI Bill, most veterans should get to keep the full amount of the award. Remember this prior to choosing an institution that may not be fully covered under Post-9/11 or MGIB.

If you have depleted your military-based educational benefits and are considering taking out student loans, be sure to research and understand where a student loan is coming from prior to accepting any money. Student loans can be federal or private depending on the source. Federally backed loans and private loans have many differences. Here are just a few of the reasons that federally backed loans can offer greater flexibility than loans from private sources.

- Federal loans can offer borrowers fixed interest rates that are typically lower than private sources of loans.
- Borrowers are given a six-month grace period upon completion of the degree to begin repayments. Often, private school loans will require payments to be made while the student is still attending school.
- Only federally backed loans are subsidized, meaning the government pays the interest for a period of time.
- Interest may be deductible, not an option for private loans.
- Federal loans can be consolidated into a Direct Consolidation Loan, while private loans cannot.
- Private loans may require the borrower to have an established credit record. Most federal student loans do not require a credit check.
- Federal loans tend to have greater offer forbearance or deferment options.
- Private loans may demand that repayments begin immediately.

(Information taken from the following site: http://studentaid.ed.gov/types/loans/federal-vs-private.)

Federal student loans come in three shapes and sizes. Federal student loans can be Direct Subsidized Loans or Direct Unsubsidized Loans, Direct PLUS Loans (for advanced education), or Federal Perkins Loans.

According to the DOE, Direct Subsidized Loans have slightly better parameters for students with financial need. Direct Subsidized Loans are only available for undergraduate students, and the amount awarded cannot exceed the financial need. Interest on this type of loan is covered by the US Department of Education while students remain in school at a minimum of half-time and for the first six months after graduation (grace period).

Direct Unsubsidized Loans demand a demonstration of financial need and are available for undergraduate and graduate school. The amount borrowed is regulated by the school and is based upon the school's costs. Interest is the responsibility of the borrower at all times. If the borrower chooses not to pay interest while in school, the amount accrues and is added into the overall loan and will be reflected in payments when they come due.

Federal PLUS loans are available for graduate or professional degree-seeking students and parents of dependent undergraduate students. Schools must participate in the program for students to be eligible. Loans are fixed at a specific rate, and borrowers must not have an adverse credit history. For information regarding the current rates for loans, visit the DOE website (https://studentaid.ed.gov/types/loans/interest-rates#what-are-the-interest-rates-of-federal-student-loans).

The National Student Loan Data System (NSLDS), the DOE's central database for student aid, maintains information regarding Title IV loans and grants. If you have already received loans or grants and need information regarding your awards, you can access the information on the website (https://www.nslds.ed.gov/).

FSA has many resources available to assist service members. A review of Table 6.1, which can also be found on the DOE website (https://studentaid.ed.gov/sites/default/files/military-student-loan-benefits.pdf), will give you a brief overview of the available benefits.

The DOE also offers military students readmissions assistance if their schooling was interrupted due to military duty. More information regarding the assistance and the point-of-contact can be found at http://www2.ed.gov/policy/highered/guid/readmission.html.

If you plan on applying for FSA, you will need access to your taxes from the previous year. For example, if you are applying for student aid for the 2015–2016 school year, you will need your 2014 taxes. The FAFSA application opens in January of each year and must be re-applied for each year.

If you are not eligible for any money one year, do not let it deter you from applying in subsequent years. You may be eligible at another time. If you are under the age of twenty-three, but have already served on active duty, you will not need to enter your parents' tax information on the FAFSA. You will enter your personal tax information.

If you are interested in applying for FSA, but are unsure how to proceed, contact your local education center or the financial aid office of your school for further guidance.

Here is a quick checklist for applying for federal financial aid:

Table 6.1. Loan Assistance*

Benefit	Description
Servicemembers Civil Relief Act (SCRA) Interest Rate Cap	(SCRA) Interest Rate Cap Interest on federal student loans obtained prior to your military service is limited to 6% during periods of active duty. The interest rate limitation also applies to any private education loans you may have.
Military Service Deferment	You can postpone federal student loan repayment during certain periods of active duty, such as during war, other military operation, or national emergency, and immediately following active duty.
Public Service Loan Forgiveness	You may qualify for forgiveness of the remaining balance of your Direct Loans when you've made 120 qualifying payments after October 1, 2007, while employed in public service, including military service.
Deferments After Active Duty	You can postpone repayment while you prepare to return to school following your active duty.
0% Interest	While you are serving in a hostile area that qualifies you for special pay, you do not have to pay interest on Direct Loans made on or after October 1, 2008, for up to 60 months.
Repayment Based on Income	Repayment plans that base your monthly payment on your income are available. Under these plans, you may qualify for a low or zero payment amount with the possibility of forgiveness of the remaining balance in the future.
HEROES Act Waiver	While you are on active duty, the DOE waives many of the documentation requirements attached to program benefits. For example, if you are on a payment plan based on your income and military service prevents you from providing updated information on your family size and income, you can request to have your monthly payment amount maintained.
Department of Defense (DoD) Repayment of Your Loans	In certain circumstances, as determined by the DoD, all or a portion of your loans may be repaid by the DoD.

Veterans Total and Permanent Disability Discharge	If you have a service-connected disability, you may qualify for discharge of your federal student loans.

*For Members of the U.S. Armed Forces," Federal Student Aid, February 1, 2013, accessed December 2, 2014, https://studentaid.ed.gov/sites/default/files/military-student-loan-benefits.pdf.

1. Have your tax information from the previous year on hand.
2. Apply on http://www.pin.ed.gov for your PIN.
3. Apply for FSA through FAFSA (http://www.fafsa.ed.gov; you will need to list your school).
4. Verify your submission with your school's financial aid office.
5. Keep an eye out for your financial aid award letter, and monitor your student account on your school's website.
6. Hopefully receive a payment!
7. The http://www.fafsa.ed.gov website offers many helpful hints if you get stuck while filling out the FAFSA. The application will take twenty to thirty minutes to complete online.

More information on FSA can be found through the following resources:

- The Federal Student Aid Information Center: (800) 4-FED-AID (800-433-3243)
- Federal Student Aid: https://studentaid.ed.gov/
- Free Application for Federal Student Aid: https://fafsa.ed.gov/
- Veterans Total and Permanent Disability Discharge: http://disabilitydischarge.com/home/
- Servicemembers Civil Relief Act (SCRA): Dmdc.osd.mil/appj/scra/
- YouTube: http://www.youtube.com/user/FederalStudentAid

STATES OFFERING IN-STATE TUITION TO VETERANS

As noted above, veterans beginning school on or after fall of 2015 will receive honorary in-state residency at any state school across the country as long as they are entering the institution under their Post-9/11 GI Bill and are within three years of their date of separation from the service. Some soldiers prefer to stay off their Post-9/11 GI Bill for the first year or two of college. Potential reasons to take this pathway might include a student pursuing a degree that requires more than the typical load of 120 SH, or students trying to save benefits for graduate degrees at a later date.

As of right now, only some states offer in-state tuition to out-of-state residents. Some university systems will also grant in-state tuition for veterans. There are always qualifying criteria you must abide by, so, as I keep stating throughout this book, always check with the state VA or with the vet reps at the school to verify your eligibility.

Here is some information for states that currently offer in-state residency to veterans. Some of these states offer other veteran benefits as well. There are specific steps (like registering to vote or getting a driver's license) tied into eligibility for the in-state tuition, and sometimes it is up to the school to participate. Check with the veterans' representatives at the institution you wish to attend to determine how to get going with the process for that particular state.

- Alabama: In-state tuition for veterans who reside in Alabama and were honorably discharged within the five years immediately preceding their enrollment into a state institution of higher learning. Reservists and service-connected disabled veterans are eligible as well.
- Arizona (602-255-3373): In-state tuition for veterans who registered to vote in the state and meet at least one of the following parameters: an Arizona driver license, an Arizona motor vehicle registration, demonstrate employment history in Arizona, transfer their banking services to Arizona, change their permanent address on all pertinent records, or demonstrate other materials of whatever kind or source relevant to domicile or residency status.
- California (916-653-2573): The state of California offers honorary residency to veterans who were stationed in California for one year prior to separation from the military, separate, and stay in the state to attend an institution of higher education.
- Colorado (303-866-2723): In-state tuition for qualifying veterans and dependents. Veterans must be honorably discharged and maintain a permanent home in Colorado. Enlisted service members who are stationed in Colorado and receiving the resident student rate (themselves or their dependents) will be able to maintain that rate upon separation from the military if they continue to reside in the state.
- Florida: In-state tuition for honorably discharged veterans at state community colleges, state colleges, and universities.
- Idaho (208-577-2310): In-state tuition for qualified veterans and qualifying dependents. Veterans must have served at least two years on active duty, have received an honorable discharge, and enter a public school within one year of separating from the service. Dependents must receive at least 50 percent of their support from the qualifying veteran.
- Illinois: Any individual using the Post-9/11 GI Bill will receive the in-state tuition rate.

- Indiana: Veterans enrolled in undergraduate classes no more than twelve months after honorably separating from the armed forces or Indiana National Guard are eligible for in-state tuition.
- Kentucky (502-573-1555): In-state tuition for qualifying veterans.
- Louisiana: In-state tuition for veterans who served a minimum of two years on active duty and received an honorable discharge. Veterans who have been assigned service-connected disability ratings and are either already enrolled or applying for enrollment in a state institution are eligible as well.
- Maine: Honorably discharged veterans enrolled in a program of education within the University of Maine system, the Maine community college system, or the Maritime Academy are eligible for in-state tuition.
- Maryland: In-state tuition for honorably discharged veterans of the armed forces. Veteran must reside in Maryland and attend a state institution of higher learning.
- Minnesota: In-state tuition at the undergraduate rate for veterans. If the veteran was a resident of the state upon entering the service and begins a state college/university graduate school program within two years of separating from the service, he or she will receive the in-state tuition rate.
- Missouri: In-state tuition for veterans who received honorable or general discharges from the service. Benefit can be utilized at the state two-year or four-year institutions. Two-year institutions also offer the in-district rate.
- Nevada: In-state tuition for veterans who were honorably discharged and matriculated no more than two years after their date of separation from the armed forces.
- New Mexico (505-827-6374): In-state tuition for qualified veterans.
- North Dakota : In-state tuition for veterans who served 180 days or more on active duty and separated under other than dishonorable conditions. Dependents who received transferred Post-9/11 benefits may also be eligible.
- Ohio: In-state tuition for qualified veterans.
- Oregon: Honorably discharged veterans who establish a physical presence in Oregon within twelve months of enrolling in school may be eligible for in-state tuition and fees.
- South Dakota: Bill 13-53-19.1 exempts veterans from having to meet the twelve-month residency requirement for in-state tuition.
- Tennessee: In-state tuition for veterans discharged within two years who did not receive a dishonorable separation.
- Texas: In-state tuition for veterans who qualify for federal education benefits. Dependents may qualify as well.
- Utah (801-326-2372): In-state tuition for qualifying veterans at certain schools. Veterans must demonstrate that they are taking the required steps to gain residency.

- Virginia: Veterans released or discharged under conditions other than dishonorable are eligible for in-state tuition.
- Washington: Veterans (and their dependents) who served a minimum of two years in the military and received an honorable discharge will be granted in-state tuition as long as they enroll in school within one year of their date of separation from the service.

A few state-based university systems across the country may also offer veterans in-state tuition without a state-based benefit in place:

- University of Alaska school system: http://www.alaska.edu/alaska/about-ua/
- Mississippi Institutions of Higher Learning: http://www.ihl.state.ms.us/board/downloads/policiesandbylaws.pdf
- University of Wisconsin school system: https://docs.legis.wisconsin.gov/statutes/statutes/36/27/2/b/4
- Kentucky Public Universities: http://www.lrc.ky.gov/record/11rs/HB425.htm
- University of Iowa school system: http://www.registrar.uiowa.edu/LinkClick.aspx?fileticket=EnXD7AdsnJ0%3d&tabid=94
- University System of Georgia: http://www.usg.edu/policymanual/section7/C453/
- University of Rhode Island: http://www.uri.edu/gsadmis//documents/residency/BOG-va.pdf
- University of Delaware: http://www.udel.edu/registrar/students/residency.html#section6

STATE-BASED VETERAN EDUCATION BENEFITS

Many states offer veterans state-based education benefits that are above and beyond available federal benefits. Some of these benefits can be used quite liberally and others have very tight restrictions. In a few instances, it is possible to double-dip from MGIB and a state-based benefit to maximize benefits. This can potentially mean more money in the student's pocket or longer-lasting education benefits.

Prior to electing to use the Post-9/11 GI Bill, you need to determine if you have a state-based benefit available to use and how it works. Sometimes veterans can bring in more money by staying under MGIB as opposed to Post-9/11. Electing chapter 33 (Post-9/11) is an irrevocable choice and all available options should be considered prior to electing the benefit.

While your school's veterans' department might have information regarding your state-based benefits, it is best to make contact with your state's

Department of Veterans' Affairs Office (http://www.va.gov/statedva.htm). The state VA can explain all of your available benefits, not just the education-related options, as well as verify your eligibility. Usually, a quick visit to the website can give you a general understanding of the state-offered benefits, but connecting with a benefit specialist is the best way to gain in-depth knowledge. Sometimes there are programs available that are not listed on the website because they are location specific. A benefit specialist will be able to assist you with any information that might be available in your location or might be more specific to your needs.

I (Jillian) list and describe many of the state-based benefits later in this chapter. Remember that states may cancel, change, or add benefits throughout time. While I strive to be as accurate as possible, this book was compiled and written in 2014, and things change. Since you are the veteran, you need to double-check what you have available at any specific time.

Here is an example of a veteran who did better by staying under MGIB instead of electing Post-9/11 and used state-based benefits:

Sergeant Smith enlisted in Illinois. In 2014, after serving four years of honorable service in the Army, he is about to separate and return home. Sergeant Smith is interested in attending University of Illinois in Urbana-Champaign and needs to determine his available education options.

Sergeant Smith learns about the two federal GI Bills and the Illinois Veteran Grant (IVG) after reading this book. Sergeant Smith needs to determine if he paid into MGIB, which would have been $100 per month for the first year of his enlistment to total $1,200. He believes he did but cannot remember for sure. He will double-check his contract through iPERMS by looking for the DD 2366, but continues planning as if he did pay the $1,200 into MGIB.

Sergeant Smith might also be eligible for IVG. Only the Illinois state VA can ultimately determine his eligibility, and he will need to verify with them if he will be able to use the benefit prior to following through with the details.

IVG will cover the cost of tuition and certain fees for eligible veterans at state-supported universities and community colleges within the state of Illinois. If Sergeant Smith does qualify for IVG, he might do better financially by using it in tandem with MGIB, as opposed to opting for Post-9/11.

Here is the IVG eligibility list from the Illinois State VA (also at https://www2.illinois.gov/veterans/benefits/Pages/education.aspx) that I reviewed with Sergeant Smith (remember, things change!):

- Veteran must have received an honorable discharge.
- Veteran must have resided in Illinois six months prior to entering the service.

- Veteran must have completed a minimum of one full year of active duty in the US Armed Forces (this includes veterans who were assigned to active duty in a foreign country in a time of hostilities in that country, regardless of length of service).
- Veteran must return to Illinois within six months of separation from the service.

Sergeant Smith falls within the above-mentioned parameters, feels confident that he will qualify for the IVG, and proceeds accordingly.

Looking up the MHA stipend for the Post-9/11 GI Bill (at https://www.defensetravel.dod.mil/site/bahCalc.cfm), Sergeant Smith finds the MHA stipend for the academic year 2014 is $1,179. This tool can also be found by visiting the main Post-9/11 GI Bill webpage (http://www.benefits.va.gov/gibill/).

The towns of Champaign and Urbana are in a rural region of central Illinois; hence, the housing allowance under Post-9/11 is on the low side. Sergeant Smith feels he could do better if he elects to stay under MGIB, instead of choosing Post-9/11. Here are his calculations:

- Post 9/11 MHA: $1,179
- MGIB payments (as of October 1, 2014): $1,717
- Sergeant Smith will qualify for IVG, which will pay most of his public university's tuition and fees.
- If Specialist Smith pays the $600 Buy-Up to MGIB prior to separation, it will increase his monthly MGIB payments by an extra $150 per month, so his monthly take-home amount would be $1,867, or $688 more than the $1,179 he would receive under Post-9/11. If none of the amounts change over the thirty-six months that Sergeant Smith has allotted, he would take home $24,768 more under MGIB than he would under Post-9/11.
- One drawback is that IVG can be used for a master's degree as well. If Sergeant Smith double dips on his federal and state-based benefit at the same time, he may not retain any benefits that could have been used for graduate school. That is a personal decision.

Sergeant Smith reviews his calculations and realizes that he still needs to verify his IVG with the Illinois state VA and his GI Bill eligibility with the federal VA. He also needs to contact the veterans' representatives (vet reps) at University of Illinois to discuss which GI Bill the veterans already attending the school have chosen and any recommendations that the vet reps may have for him. Sergeant Smith must decide whether he minds depleting both of his benefits simultaneously.

In the case of Illinois veterans who meet IVG requirements, they must decide if the extra payoff they obtain by depleting both benefits at the same time is worth it. Many veterans may want to pursue a graduate degree with that benefit at a later date, and others may be more interested in maximizing their benefits immediately. Also remember that Sergeant Smith is going to attend a school in a rural area. If you are from Illinois and elect an institution closer to Chicago, your MHA amount will be much higher than the listed amount for University of Illinois in Urbana-Champaign. In this case, double dipping is not necessary.

Many institutions of higher learning have also adopted scholarships for disabled or wounded veterans. For example, the University of Idaho has the Operation Education scholarship that may provide financial assistance for eligible service-connected disabled veterans and their spouses (http://www.uidaho.edu/operationeducation). Check with the institutions you are interested in attending to obtain information regarding policies or programs that may benefit you.

The following states offer education benefits at this time. Most of the information is taken directly from the state VA websites.

Alabama (http://www.va.state.al.us/otherbenefits.aspx and http://www.va.state.al.us/gi_dep_scholarship.aspx)

Purple Heart (PH) recipients may be eligible to have tuition and fees waived for undergraduate studies. Spouses of state residents with service-connected disability ratings of 20 percent or higher may qualify for three standard academic years without payment of tuition, mandatory textbooks, or instructional fees at a state institution of higher learning, or for a prescribed technical course not to exceed twenty-seven months of training at a state institution. Dependent children are eligible for five standard academic years or part-time equivalent at any Alabama state-supported institution of higher learning or a state-supported technical school without payment of any tuition, mandatory textbooks, or instructional fees. Dependent children must start school prior to age twenty-six. Veterans must have honorably served at least ninety days of continuous active federal military service during wartime, or be honorably discharged by reason of service-connected disability after serving less than ninety days of continuous active federal military service during wartime. They must be permanent civilian residents of the state of Alabama for at least one year immediately prior to (1) the initial entry into active military service or (2) any subsequent period of military service in which a break (one year or more) in service occurred and the Alabama civilian residency was established. Permanently service-connected veterans rated at 100 percent who did not enter service from Alabama may qualify but must first establish at least five years of permanent residency in Alabama prior to application. *Note*: If you are a veteran with a PH and MGIB, you may want to stay on MGIB instead of electing Post-9/11.

The following subsection is a breakdown of current payout under MGIB versus Post-9/11 with a veteran using his or her Alabama state benefit under MGIB at a community college.

Northeast Alabama Community College

MGIB currently pays out $1,717/month + $600 (buy-up) = $1,867/month
    Total for 4 months = $7,468
    MHA under Post-9/11: $990 × 4 months = $3,960
    Veterans who qualify for the state-based PH waiver earn $3,508 more in four months under MGIB than if they opted for Post-9/11 ($7,468–$3,960=$3,508). Remember that the state pays the school tuition in this case.

California (http://www.va.state.al.us/gi_dep_scholarship.aspx and https://www.calvet.ca.gov/VetServices/Pages/Non-Resident-College-Fee-Waiver.aspx)

Veterans receive in-state tuition if they have been stationed in California for one year prior to separation, separate in the state, and remain in California for school. Dependent children of service-connected disabled veterans receive a tuition waiver at state-supported schools. The California benefit has four different pathways for eligibility: Medal of Honor recipients and their children, National Guard, children of veterans with service-connected disabilities (the most common category), and spouses (veteran is totally disabled, or whose death was service connected). Let's discuss the most common category: children. California veterans who rate a 0 percent disability rating or higher may qualify for their children to receive waivers of tuition at state community colleges and universities. Please note that a 0 percent disability rating is an actual rating. Fees for books, housing, parking, and so on are not included in the waiver. The state of California does not care where you enlisted. If you separate, have a service-connected disability, and become a California resident, you may be eligible.

This is a great way to have your children's college covered. Many veterans use the benefit to send their children to state schools to pursue higher education and not worry about the bills. The universities in the state are used to children using this benefit, and the veterans' representatives at the institutions know how to facilitate it for dependent children.

To read a more thorough breakdown of eligibility, check at https://www.calvet.ca.gov/VetServices/Pages/College-Fee-Waiver.aspx. For the most common pathway, children are eligible if they make less than $12,119 per year (changes yearly to reflect cost of living), meet in-state residency requirements determined by the school, and provide proof of relationship to the veteran.

Connecticut (http://www.ct.gov/ctva/cwp/view.asp?A=2014& Q=290874)

Eligible veterans receive tuition waivers at Connecticut state community colleges and state colleges/universities. Only the cost of tuition is waived. Other charges such as books, student fees, and parking are not waived. Students must be matriculated into a degree program.

To be eligible veterans must be honorably discharged, have served at least ninety days of active military duty during war, residents of Connecticut at least one year prior to enrolling in college, and residents of Connecticut at the time they apply for the state benefit.

Florida (http://floridavets.org/?page_id=60)

Recipients of the PH and other combat-related decorations superior in precedence to the PH receive a waiver of undergraduate-level tuition at state universities and community colleges. The waiver covers 110 percent of the required credit hours for the degree or certificate. The veteran must be admitted as a part- or full-time student in a course of study leading to a degree or certificate, must have been a Florida state resident at the time the military action that resulted in the awarding of the PH (or other award) took place, must currently be a Florida state resident, and must submit DD 214 documenting PH or other decoration to school.

Illinois (http://www2.illinois.gov/veterans/benefits/Pages/ education.aspx)

The Illinois Veterans' Grant (IVG) is a tuition (and certain fees) waiver for undergraduate and graduate studies at state-supported institutions for veterans who served during a time of hostilities. Eligibility and residency requirements for veterans: received an honorable discharge; resided in Illinois six months prior to entering the military; have served a minimum of one year on active duty with the armed forces, or was assigned to active duty in a foreign country in a time of hostilities in that country, regardless of length of service; and returned to Illinois within six months of separation from the military.

Many Illinois veterans choose to stay under the MGIB as opposed to Post 9/11 to fully maximize dollar amounts under their available benefits. If you plan to attend school in a rural area—for example, University of Illinois in Urbana-Champaign—double-dipping on MGIB and IVG can produce more money on a monthly basis. If you do this, be aware that you will be depleting both state and federal benefits at the same time. That means you may not have any benefit left for a master's degree later.

The Children of Veterans Scholarship authorizes each county in the state to provide one scholarship yearly at the University of Illinois for children of veterans of World War I, World War II, the Korean War, the Vietnam Conflict, Operation Enduring Freedom, or Operation Iraqi Freedom. Children of deceased and disabled veterans are given priority. These children can receive four consecutive years tuition-free (undergraduate, graduate, or professional studies) at the University of Illinois (Urbana-Champaign, Chicago Health Sciences Center, or Springfield Campus). See http://www.osfa.uiuc.edu/aid/scholarships/waivers_COV.html.

Indiana (http://www.in.gov/dva/2378.htm)

Indiana PH recipients receive free tuition at the resident tuition rate for 124 semester credit hours at state-supported postsecondary schools for undergraduate study only.

Eligibility and residency requirements for veterans who entered the service on or before June 30, 2011: entered service from a permanent home address in Indiana; received the PH; honorably discharged.

Be aware that the law is different for those who entered the service on or after July 1, 2011. For those entering through June 30, 2011:

- Free resident tuition for the children of disabled veterans or PH recipients.
- Benefit includes 124 semester hours of tuition and mandatory fees at the undergraduate rate.
- Benefit can be used for graduate school, but the difference between the undergraduate and graduate rate is the responsibility of the student.
- Available to biological and legally adopted children of eligible disabled Indiana veterans.
- Child must produce a copy of birth certificate or adoption papers.
- Veteran must have served during a period of wartime.
- Veteran must have been a resident of Indiana for a minimum of three consecutive years at some point in his or her lifetime.
- Veteran must rate a service-connected disability (or have died a service-connected death), or received the PH (demonstration of proof is necessary for either).

Under the new law, for a veteran who entered service *on or after* July 1, 2011:

- Free resident tuition for the children of disabled veterans or PH recipients.
- Benefit includes 124 semester hours of tuition and mandatory fees for undergraduate study only.
- Benefit is based on the level of disability the veteran rates (see below).
- Student must maintain a mandatory minimum GPA (see below).
- The program limits the student to eight years.

- Available to biological and legally adopted children of eligible disabled Indiana veterans.
- Child must produce a copy of birth certificate or adoption papers.
- Veteran must have served during a period of wartime.
- Veteran must rate a service-connected disability (or have died a service-connected death) or have received the PH (demonstration of proof is necessary for either).
- Student must apply prior to turning thirty-two years old.

Disability rating prorated schedule for tuition for new law—taken directly from the website.

- Children of veterans rated 80 percent service-connected disabled or higher by the VA or whose veteran parent is/was a recipient of the Purple Heart Medal will receive 100 percent fee remission.
- Children of veterans rated less than 80 percent service-connected disabled will receive 20 percent fee remission plus the disability rating of the veteran.
- If the disability rating of the veteran changes after the beginning of the academic semester, quarter, or other period, the change in the disability rating shall be applied beginning with the immediately following academic semester, quarter, or other period.

GPA requirements under new law:

- First-year student must maintain satisfactory academic progress.
- Second-, third-, and fourth-year students must maintain a minimum cumulative GPA of 2.5.

Maryland (http://veterans.maryland.gov/education-supports-and-scholarships/\)

The Edward T. Conroy Memorial Scholarship provides aid for qualifying veterans or children of veterans to attend a Maryland state school (community college, university, or private career school) as part-time or full-time students, undergraduate, or graduate. The award is not based on economic need and is for tuition and fees for five years at the full-time attendance rate or eight years at part-time. More detailed information can be found on the website (http://www.mhec.state.md.us/financialAid/COARenewal/2013-2014/2013-2014%20conroy%20conditions%20of%20award%20renewal. pdf). To be eligible, you must be a Maryland resident and either a child of a veteran who has died or is 100 percent disabled as a result of military service, or a veteran who has a 25 percent or greater disability rating with the VA and has exhausted federal veterans' education benefits.

The Veterans of the Afghanistan and Iraq Conflicts Scholarship Program Award is 50 percent of tuition and fees and room and board at the in-state undergraduate rate at a school within the University of Maryland system (UMUC and University of Maryland, Baltimore, are exempt from this award). The maximum award for students residing on-campus was $10,655 for the 2014–2015 school year. All undergraduate majors are eligible. The award works for five years at the full-time attendance rate or eight years at part-time. Students must maintain a minimum 2.5 GPA. To be eligible, students must have served in Afghanistan (minimum sixty days) on or after October 24, 2001, or in Iraq on or after March 19, 2003 (minimum sixty days); be on active duty, or a veteran (honorable discharge), or the son, daughter, or spouse of the aforementioned group; and attend school part- or full-time and be degree seeking. Spouses and children must provide supporting documentation of relationship to veteran (birth certificate or marriage certificate). Veterans must provide supporting documentation of active-duty status (orders) or DD 214; and be a resident of Maryland (active-duty military stationed in the state at the time of application) to qualify.

Massachusetts (http://www.mass.gov/veterans/education/financial-assistance/tuition-waivers.html)

Massachusetts provides a waiver of full or partial tuition at state institutions of higher education on a space available basis for undergraduate study (fees are not included and can be very high). Graduate school waivers are dependent upon each university. Waivers are for degree or certificate programs. To be eligible, you must be a resident of the state for at least one year prior to the start of the school year; not be in default of any federal or state loans or financial aid; have served a minimum of ninety days and received an honorable discharge; and maintain a minimum of three undergraduate credits per semester and make satisfactory academic progress.

Minnesota (http://mn.gov/mdva/resources/education/minnesotagibill.jsp)

Eligible veterans receive a maximum payment of $1,000 per semester for full-time students and $500 per semester for part-time students, but no more than $10,000 per lifetime. Those veterans pursuing OJT or apprenticeship programs with eligible employers (see http://www.doli.state.mn.us/Appr.asp) can receive up to $2,000 per fiscal year. To be eligible, the veteran must be a Minnesota resident, under the age of sixty-two, and enrolled in a Minnesota institution, and have received an honorable discharge. The spouse of a disabled veteran (total and permanent) or surviving spouse or child of a veteran who died as a result of his or her service may also receive this benefit (must be eligible to receive benefits under Chapter 33/35). For those pursuing OJT or apprenticeships, the training must be documented, reported, and last for at least six months. Veterans must reapply every year to receive funding.

Missouri (http://www.dhe.mo.gov/files/moretheroesact.pdf)

The Missouri Returning Heroes' Education Act prevents Missouri institutions of higher education from charging eligible veterans more than $50 per credit hour. To qualify for the tuition limit, veterans must have received an honorable discharge, served in an armed combat zone for more than thirty days after September 11, 2001, and been a Missouri resident when they entered the service. To qualify vets must enroll in an undergraduate degree-seeking program and maintain a minimum 2.5 GPA every semester.

Note: Missouri residents who qualify for this benefit and MGIB should run the numbers before electing Post-9/11. Many of the veterans I (Jillian) counsel choose to stay under MGIB as opposed to Post-9/11 to fully maximize their dollars under their available benefits. Speak to a counselor at your closest education center on the base, or contact the veterans' representatives at your chosen school for advice. Remember, once you select Post-9/11 you can never return to MGIB, so make an educated decision.

Example: Private First Class Carlson meets the eligibility requirements as listed above. He will attend Three Rivers Community College in Poplar Bluff, Missouri. The housing allowance under Post-9/11 is $999 per month. The tuition per semester will be $750 (for fifteen credit hours) under his state-based benefit. If he elects to stay under MGIB, he needs to pay the Buy-Up at DFAS prior to his separation, and then he will receive $1,867 per month. After paying his tuition the first month, he will have $1,117 remaining, but every month past that point he will receive $1,867 for the rest of the semester. That means $868 more per month than if he elected Post-9/11. The process would repeat itself every semester. Veterans who elect this option must remember that they will only receive the book stipend under Post-9/11.

Montana (http://wsd.dli.mt.gov/veterans/vetedu.asp)

Eligible wartime veterans who have exhausted all federal education benefits may receive tuition waivers for up to twelve semesters of undergraduate study. Veterans must be honorably discharged state residents who have served in a combat theater in Iraq or Afghanistan after September 11, 2001, and have received the Global War on Terrorism Expeditionary Medal, Afghanistan Campaign Medal, or Iraq Campaign Medal.

New York (http://www.hesc.ny.gov/pay-for-college/financial-aid/types-of-financial-aid/nys-grants-scholarships-awards/veterans-tuition-awards.html and http://www.hesc.ny.gov/pay-for-college/financial-aid/types-of-financial-aid/nys-grants-scholarships-awards/msrs-scholarship.html)

Veterans' tuition awards are available for students attending undergraduate or graduate degree-granting schools, or vocational training programs at the part- or full-time rate. The award covers the full cost of the undergraduate tuition for New York residents at the State University of New York (SUNY) or the actual amount of the tuition (whatever is the lesser charge). "Full-time" is defined as twelve or more credits per semester (a maximum of eight semesters for undergraduate study and six for graduate study). "Part-time" is at least three but fewer than twelve credits per semester (within the same time frames).

The benefit was set at a maximum of $6,195 for the 2014–2015 school year. Veterans who qualify for the state benefit and MGIB may be able to double-dip (there is no double-dipping under Post-9/11, unless the veteran is not eligible for 100 percent).

To qualify for a tuition award, you must be a New York State resident matriculating in an undergraduate or graduate degree-granting institution, or in a state-approved vocational training program of at least 320 clock hours. In most cases you must have served in hostilities after February 28, 1961, as evidenced by receipt of an Armed Forces Expeditionary Medal, Navy Expeditionary Medal, or Marine Corps Expeditionary Medal.

The Military Enhanced Recognition Incentive and Tribute Scholarship provides financial aid for qualifying veterans and dependents of veterans. The award is a maximum of four years (five for approved five-year programs) of full-time study at the undergraduate level. The award works at SUNY or City University of New York schools for the actual tuition and mandatory fees, plus room and board (on campus) and books and supplies. Those who attend school off-campus will receive an allowance. Private school attendees will receive a sum equal to the public school costs. Only dependents of those New York residents who died or became severely and permanently disabled after August 2, 1990, while participating in hostilities or training for duty in a combat theater are eligible.

North Carolina (http://www.doa.state.nc.us/vets/scholarshipclasses.aspx)

Scholarships are available for dependent children of veterans who rate a minimum of 20 percent disability and served during wartime or received the PH. A maximum of one hundred awards per year are given. The award is for eight semesters completed within eight years. It covers tuition, an allowance for room and board, and exemption from certain mandatory fees at public, community, and technical colleges and institutions, or $4,500 per academic year at private schools. Recipients must be natural or adopted (prior to age fifteen) children of qualifying veterans, under the age of twenty-five, and residents of North Carolina at the time of application. The veteran must have entered service in North Carolina, or the applicant/dependent must have been born in North Carolina and maintained continuous residency in the state.

Oregon (http://www.oregon.gov/odva/BENEFITS/Pages/ OregonEducationBenefit.aspx)

The Oregon Veteran Educational Aid Program provides financial aid for veterans who have exhausted all federal education benefits. The maximum award is thirty-six months (award months equal months of service) of $150 per month for full-time students or $100 per month for part-time students. Face-to-face classes, home study, vocational training, licenses, and certificates from accredited Oregon academic institutions are eligible. Benefits are paid while pursuing classroom instruction, home study courses, vocational training, licensing, and certificates from accredited Oregon educational institutions.

To be eligible veterans must be Oregon residents, have served on active duty for a minimum of ninety days sometime after June 30, 1958, and received an honorable discharge.

Puerto Rico (Puerto Rico Public Advocate for Veterans Affairs, P.O. Box 11737, San Juan PR 00910-1737; (787) 758-5760)

Veterans attending the University of Puerto Rico and its regional colleges receive free tuition if they have exhausted federal benefits before completing a degree. Verify qualifying criteria with the institutions.

South Carolina (http://va.sc.gov/benefits.html)

Free tuition is available for children of veterans who have been awarded the PH for wounds received in combat. The award can be used at state-supported schools or technical education institutions. For a child to be eligible, the veteran mother or father must have been a South Carolina resident at the time of entry to the military and throughout the service period, or have been a South Carolina resident for a minimum of one year and still resides in the state. The veteran must also have been honorably discharged and served during a war period. The child must be twenty-six or younger.

South Dakota (http://vetaffairs.sd.gov/benefits/State/State%20Education%20Programs.aspx)

Eligible veterans who have exhausted all federal education benefits may receive full tuition. The award is prorated on the veteran's qualifying military service (one month for each qualified month of service, for a maximum of four years). The veteran has twenty years from the end date of a qualifying service period to use the entitlement. To be eligible the veteran must be a South Dakota resident and qualify for resident tuition. They must have a 10 percent (or more) disability rating with the VA, and must also have received an honorable discharge and a US campaign or service medal for participating in combat operations outside the United States (such as an Armed Forces Expeditionary Medal).

Tennessee (http://www.tn.gov/sos/rules/1640/1640-01-22.20090529.pdf)

The Helping Heroes Grant for Veterans is available yearly to a maximum of 375 qualifying veterans. The $1,000 per semester award is given on a first-come, first-served basis to students completing a minimum of twelve credit hours per semester. The award can be applied for until the eighth anniversary of the veteran's separation date, or when the student has received the award for a total of eight semesters. Recipients must be Tennessee residents for one year prior to application and be admitted to an eligible institution for an associate's or bachelor's degree. They must also have received an honorable discharge and either the Iraq Campaign Medal, Afghanistan Campaign Medal, or Global War on Terrorism medal on or after September 1, 2001. They may not be in default on any federal or Tennessee student aid programs and may not already have a bachelor's degree. They also may not be in jail (that's right, you heard me—this is specifically mentioned on the website).

Texas (http://veterans.portal.texas.gov/en/Pages/education.aspx)

The Hazlewood Act provides funds to cover tuition, dues, fees, and other required charges up to 150 semester hours at state institutions (see http://www.collegeforalltexans.com for a list of eligible schools) for those who have exhausted Post-9/11 GI Bill benefits. The award will not cover room and board, books, student services fees, or deposit fees. The waiver can be used for undergraduate and graduate classes. Teacher certification fees, aircraft flight training courses, and distance learning classes may also be covered (verify with the school). To be eligible veterans must have been Texas residents at the time of entry into the military, have designated Texas as home of record, or entered the service in Texas; they must also reside in Texas for the semester the funds are being claimed. Recipients must have

181 or more days of active duty and an honorable discharge, and may not be in default on state-guaranteed student loans.

Note: Veterans are not able to double-dip with Post-9/11 and Hazlewood at the same time. Texas schools maintain a great amount of control over Hazlewood Act usage. Always contact the vet reps at your institution of choice prior to making any final decisions.

Children may be eligible to have unused Hazlewood benefits transferred to them through the Legacy Program. The award can only be used at state-supported institutions. A list of eligible schools can be found at http://www.collegeforalltexans.com/index.cfm?ObjectID=D57D0AC5-AB2D-EFB0-FC201080B528442A under the Public School list. The award covers tuition, dues, fees, and other required charges up to 150 semester hours. The award will not cover room and board, books, nonmandatory fees, or deposit fees. To be eligible the veteran must have been a Texas state resident when he/she entered the military, designated Texas as home of record, or entered the service in Texas. The child must be the biological child, stepchild, adopted child, or claimed by the veteran as a dependent in the current or previous tax year; be under the age of twenty-five at the beginning of any term for which the benefit is being claimed (some exemptions may apply); make satisfactory academic progress; and provide proof of the veteran's honorable discharge.

The Combat Tuition Exemption provides tuition waivers (fees not exempted) for dependent children of service members deployed in combat zones. The child must be a resident of Texas, or a dependent of military personnel stationed in Texas (and thus entitled to receive the in-state tuition rate). (If an out-of-state resident, the child may need to provide a copy of the veteran's orders.) The veteran must be deployed in a combat zone during the time of enrollment.

Be aware that state reimbursement for this program is not available. It is up to each institution if they will grant this award.

Utah (http://veterans.utah.gov/state-benefits/)

Utah state residents who are PH recipients are eligible for tuition waivers at state schools. The award works for undergraduate and graduate programs. Veterans who are eligible for this benefit should be able to complete a bachelor's and master's degree with little or no debt.

Virgin Islands (http://www.militaryvi.org/benefits/)

Free tuition is offered for attendance at local public educational institutions and at the University of the Virgin Islands. This program is for veterans who entered the armed forces while residing in the Virgin Islands. Contact the schools for more information.

Washington (http://apps.leg.wa.gov/RCW/default.aspx?cite=28B.15.621)

Washington offers full or partial tuition waivers at state schools for undergraduate education for up to two hundred quarter credits (or equivalent semester credits). Some schools offer the waiver for graduate programs (check with your institution). Full- or part-time enrollment is eligible. The award may work at some private institutions. Be aware that the tuition may not be fully covered. To be eligible students must be Washington State residents; make satisfactory academic progress; have served in a war/conflict fought on foreign soil or in international waters, or in another location in support of those serving on foreign soil or in international waters; and have received an honorable discharge.

West Virginia (http://www.veterans.wv.gov/Pages/Veteran%27sRe-Education.aspx)

Through the West Virginia Veterans Re-Education Scholarship Program, eligible veterans can receive $500 per term (part-time students: $250). The amount cannot exceed a total of $1,500 per academic year. Program funding may be used to cover professional exam costs as well. Eligible veterans may use the scholarship in tandem with the Workforce Investment Act and/or Trade Adjustment Act if program cost exceeds the amount allocated under the latter two programs. To be eligible, the veteran must be a West Virginia resident; have received an honorable discharge; served 181 consecutive days on active duty; be eligible for a Pell Grant or unemployed; and have exhausted all federal GI Bill funds (including Vocational Rehabilitation, if eligible).

Wisconsin (http://www.wisvets.com/wisgibill)

The Wisconsin GI Bill tuition remission benefit program provides remission of tuition and fees at state institutions (University of Wisconsin and Wisconsin Technical Colleges) for eligible veterans and dependents. The award is good for a maximum of eight semesters (or 128 semester credits), undergraduate and graduate education, and professional programs. There are no income restrictions or delimiting periods. Many fees are not covered, such as books, meals, room and board, and online fees. The award cannot be combined with federal benefits. The veteran must have served since September 10, 2001, entered the service from Wisconsin, and must apply for Post-9/11 GI Bill benefits first, if eligible (remember to talk to an education counselor or the veterans' representatives before choosing which GI Bill to use). Children and spouses of the veteran with a combined rating of 30 percent or greater from the VA may also be eligible. To be eligible a child must be a biological child, adopted child, stepchild, or member of the veteran's household, and must be between the ages of seventeen and twenty-six and a Wisconsin resident. Spouses must also be Wisconsin residents for tuition purposes and must use the benefit within ten years of the veteran's VA rating.

The most clearly written information on eligibility for the state education benefits can be found on the website (see http://dva.state.wi.us/WebForms/WDVA_B0105_Wisconsin_Tuition_Programs_WI_GI_Bill_Color.pdf).

The State of Wisconsin does not allow veterans to double-dip on federal and state-based benefits. However, if veterans paid into MGIB and if the MHA under Post-9/11 at the school they want to attend is less than what they would have received under MGIB, the school will reimburse the veteran for the difference. Talk to the veterans' representatives at the institutions for more information.

The Veterans Education Reimbursement (http://www.WisVets.com/VetEd) grant program reimburses veterans after successful completion of coursework (at University of Wisconsin locations, Wisconsin Technical Colleges, or a private institution of higher education in Wisconsin or Minnesota) at the undergraduate level only. Reimbursement is prorated based on aggregate length of qualifying active-duty service. Veterans with a minimum of 30 percent of qualifying disability from the VA are reimbursed at 100 percent. Veterans must have entered active duty as Wisconsin residents, or lived in Wisconsin for twelve months prior to entering the service; must exhaust all other benefits first (including Wisconsin State GI Bill); must meet income requirements and provide proof of adjusted gross income from tax returns (annual income of veteran and spouse cannot exceed $50,000, plus $1,000 per dependent beyond two). If the veteran was discharged more than ten years prior to application, they will only be eligible for reimbursement at the part-time rate. They cannot hold a bachelor's degree, must not be delinquent on child support payments, and must maintain a 2.0 GPA.

Wyoming http://www.communitycolleges.wy.edu/Data/Sites/1/ commissionFiles/Programs/Veteran/_doc/statue-19-14-106.pdf and https://sites.google.com/a/wyo.gov/wyomingmilitarydepartment/ veterans-commission/res#TOC-Tuition-Assistance-for-Veterans- and-Surviving-Dependents)

Free tuition and fees is available for overseas combat veterans at the University of Wyoming and the state community colleges. Eligible veterans can receive ten semesters of schooling through this benefit. The veteran must have had residency in the state for a minimum of one year prior to entering the service; the home of residence on the DD 214 must be Wyoming; he/she must have received a medal signifying service in an overseas combat zone (such as the Armed Forces Expeditionary Medal); and must have been honorably discharged. He/she must also maintain a 2.0 GPA and complete the program in eight years or less.

State-Based Education Benefits Based on Severe Levels of Disability or Death

There are other state programs besides those listed above that offer education benefits for spouses and/or children. In the case of these programs, the veteran must be severely and permanently disabled, or have died while on active-duty service (in many cases, in combat or combat-related situations). I am not going to cover the specific details of these benefits, but below you will find a list of the states that offer this benefit and the links to their websites.

- Alabama: http://www.va.state.al.us/gi_dep_scholarship.aspx
- Alaska: http://veterans.alaska.gov/education-benefits.html
- Arkansas: http://www.veterans.arkansas.gov/benefits.html#edu
- California: https://www.calvet.ca.gov/VetServices/Pages/College-Fee-Waiver.aspx
- Delaware: http://veteransaffairs.delaware.gov/veterans_benefits.shtml
- Florida: http://floridavets.org/?page_id=60
- Iowa: http://www.in.gov/dva/2378.htm
- Kentucky: http://veterans.ky.gov/Benefits/Documents/KDVAInfoBookletIssueAugust2010.pdf
- Louisiana: http://vetaffairs.la.gov/Programs/Education.aspx
- Maine: http://www.maine.gov/dvem/bvs/VDEB_2.pdf
- Maryland: http://veterans.maryland.gov/wp-content/uploads/sites/2/2013/10/MDBenefitsGuide.pdf
- Massachusetts: www.mass.gov/veterans/education/for-family/mslf.html
- Michigan: http://www.michigan.gov/documents/mistudentaid/CVTGFactSheet_271497_7.pdf
- Minnesota: http://www.mdva.state.mn.us/education/SurvivingSpouseDependentInformationSheet.pdf
- Missouri: http://mvc.dps.mo.gov/docs/veterans-benefits-guide.pdf
- Montana: http://montanadma.org/state-montana-veterans-benefits
- Nebraska: http://www.vets.state.ne.us/waiver.html
- New Hampshire: http://www.nh.gov/nhveterans/benefits/education.htm
- New Jersey: http://www.state.nj.us/military/veterans/programs.html
- New Mexico: http://www.dvs.state.nm.us/benefits.html
- New York: http://www.veterans.ny.gov/

- North Carolina: http://www.doa.nc.gov/vets/benefitslist.aspx?pid=scholarships
- North Dakota: http://www.nd.gov/veterans/benefits/nd-dependent-tuition-waiver
- Ohio: https://www.ohiohighered.org/ohio-war-orphans
- Oregon: http://www.ous.edu/stucoun/prospstu/vb
- Pennsylvania: http://www.portal.state.pa.us/portal/server.pt/community/veterans_benefits/11386/disabled_benefits/567417
- South Carolina: http://va.sc.gov/benefits.html
- South Dakota: http://vetaffairs.sd.gov/benefits/State/State%20Education%20Programs.aspx
- Tennessee: http://www.state.tn.us/veteran/state_benifits/dep_tuition.html
- Texas: http://www.tvc.texas.gov/Hazlewood-Act.aspx
- Utah: http://veterans.utah.gov/state-benefits/
- Virginia: http://www.dvs.virginia.gov/veterans-benefits.shtml
- Washington: http://www.va.gov/opa/persona/dependent survivor.asp
- Wisconsin: http://dva.state.wi.us/Ben-education.asp#Tuition
- West Virginia: http://www.dvs.virginia.gov/education-employment/virginia-military-survivors-and-dependents-education-program/
- Wyoming: https://sites.google.com/a/wyo.gov/wyomingmilitarydepartment/veterans-commission/res

SCHOLARSHIPS (INCLUDING DEPENDENTS)

Although quite a bit of scholarship money is available for veterans, you must be proactive in your pursuit. No one is going to hand you the money without you making an effort. Applying for scholarships is not as difficult as it seems. Often you can use the same information for multiple applications, so keep everything you write. Most education centers have financial aid packets available for you to pick up or posted on their websites. These packets offer a good place to start your search.

Try to remember that the active-duty TA money only goes so far. TA does not cover books, tools, computers, and so on. You should run the numbers before you start. For example, California State University, Long Beach (CSULB) estimated the 2014–2015 school year book costs at $1,828. During that year for a veteran attending school full-time, the maximum book stipend awarded under the Post-9/11 GI Bill was $1,000 per academic year. That left a gap of $828 for the veteran attending CSULB to cover out of pocket. To help fill financial gaps like these, applying for scholarships is a wise move, although not your only option.

Scholarships come in all shapes and sizes. You will need to determine which scholarships may apply to you. Do not narrow yourself to veteran-based possibilities. You can apply for civilian scholarships as well. Most break down into specific categories, such as pursuit of study, age, gender, race, disability, state-based, or school-based.

You will also need to find out whether the scholarship only pays tuition or perhaps goes into your pocket similar to FSA. If you have decided to use the Post-9/11 and all of your tuition is already covered, applying for scholarships that pay tuition might not be beneficial, but if you are using the MGIB that means you can keep more of the $1,717 monthly stipend in your pocket each month. Often, scholarships that put money directly into your pocket are designated as "grants" or "prizes," but you must inquire with the organization giving the scholarship to determine how it can be used.

When you begin your search, remember it will take some time to find and determine eligibility. Start by making a quick search on your school's website. Many schools list scholarships specific to their institution right on their own pages. Check with your school's veterans' representatives, the financial aid department, and the local education center for possible scholarship opportunities. Libraries are also an underused resource for scholarship opportunities. Check opportunities based on options outside your military experience; then, check opportunities based on options within the military community.

Check for scholarships offered through local organizations such as Army and Air Force Exchange Service, Defense Commission Agency, and Army Emergency Relief first, because few are aware that they exist and competition is scarce. I (Paul) served on an installation with a Military & Civilian Spouses' Club offering $25,000 in scholarships for that year. Only five individuals applied and guess how much each applicant received. Yup, $5,000 each! Most scholarships will require an essay, so prepare the best essay possible, and then see if someone in the education center is willing to proofread it for you. Always start far, far in advance. Most scholarships are due during the spring semester in order to pay out for the following fall.

Be very careful of organizations that ask you to pay money in order to be eligible for a scholarship. Scholarship information is widely available, and you should not have to pay to find, receive, or complete an application. Most certainly, *never* give any credit card information. If you need help, contact your school's financial aid department.

Applying for scholarships can require a lot of legwork, and many students are not willing to put in the effort. This limits the pool of competitors and increases the chances of you being awarded a scholarship. Additionally, many veterans will not bother to explore other options outside of the GI Bill to increase their sources of funding, so military-related scholarships can have even fewer potential competitors. Use this to your advantage.

Lastly, remember that once you apply for a scholarship each subsequent scholarship becomes easier. Many essay requirements are similar and share a common theme of "How will you use your education to make the world better?" Essays can be modified slightly and used multiple times, as noted above. Plus, once you have been through the process of filling out an application, listing information and extracurricular activities, you can just copy and paste the same answers for each subsequent application. If transcripts are required, perhaps to demonstrate a GPA or degree progression, the same copy can usually be used repeatedly. Keeping these tips in mind will give you the psychological edge required to endure the legwork far beyond your potential competitors and increase your chances of a financial reward.

The following are just a few of the scholarships available to service members. Take a look and see what might be relevant to you. At the end of the section there are several scholarship search sites listed.

Military-Based Scholarships

American Legion Auxiliary
www.alaforveterans.org/Scholarships/Non-Traditional-Student-Scholarship/
Approximately five scholarships at $2,000 each are awarded to applicants who are members of the American Legion, American Legion Auxiliary, or Sons of the American Legion. Members must have paid dues for a minimum of two years prior to applying. Applicants must be nontraditional students (going back to school after an absence or starting later in life). Applications are due by March 1.

American Veterans (AMVETS)
http://www.amvets.org/pdfs/programs_pdfs/scholarship_application_
veteran.pdf
(877) 726-8387
Award amount is $4,000 over four years. Applicant must be pursuing full-time study at the undergraduate, graduate, or certification level from an accredited institution. Three scholarships awarded annually. Application is due by April 15. Applicant must be a veteran, be a US citizen, and have financial need. Required materials include the veteran's DD 21, official school transcripts, a completed (and signed) 1040 form, a completed FAFSA application, an essay of fifty to one hundred words addressing a specific prompt (see website), a résumé (see website), and proof of school-based expenses.

American Veterans (AMVETS) National Ladies Auxiliary
http://www.amvetsaux.org/scholarships.htmlpdf
(301) 459-6255

Two scholarships at $1,000 each and up to five scholarships at $750 each may be available. In order to be eligible, applicant must be a current member of the AMVETS Ladies Auxiliary; or a son or daughter, stepchild, or grandchild or step-grandchild of a member. Application can be filled out starting in the eligible individual's second year of undergraduate study at an eligible institution. Required documents include a personal essay of two hundred to five hundred words (see website for more information), three letters of recommendation, official transcripts, a copy of the member's membership card, and all required paperwork from the Ladies Auxiliary. Applications are due by July 1.

Armed Forces Communications and Electronics Association (AFCEA)
http://www.afcea.org/education/scholarships/undergraduate/military.asp
(703) 631-6100

Three scholarships are available to eligible veterans through the AFCEA: the Military Personnel/Dependents Scholarship, the Afghanistan and Iraq War Veterans Scholarship, and the Disabled War Veterans Scholarship (Afghanistan or Iraq).

The Military Personnel/Dependents Scholarship awards $2,000. Active duty, veterans, dependents, and spouses may apply, but they must be attending a four-year institution (no community college) full-time. Active duty and veterans can apply in their first year of school; however, spouses and dependents must be in their second year at minimum.

AFCEA scholarships require certain fields of study, such as electrical, chemical, systems, or aerospace engineering; mathematics, physics, science, or mathematics education; technology management; management information systems; or computer science. Majors of study that support US intelligence initiatives or national security may be eligible as well, if the subjects are applicable to the purpose of AFCEA. Transcripts and two letters of recommendation from faculty members are mandatory.

Army Aviation Association of America
www.quad-a.org

Association members, spouses, unmarried siblings, unmarried children, or unmarried grandchildren may be eligible. Scholarship may be used for undergraduate or graduate school. Includes an essay. Different forms of the scholarship exist and may be reserved for enlisted, warrant officer, or officer. Scholarship is based upon academic performance and award amounts vary.

Army Engineer Memorial Awards
http://www.armyengineerspouses.com/

Scholarship is open to children of officers (including warrant officers) in the Army Corps of Engineers or current Department of the Army, Army

Corps of Engineers employees. Service member must be on active duty, retire, or have deceased during active-duty service or after retirement. Children must be high school seniors. An essay is required and award amounts are $1,000 or $2,000.

Army Nurse Corps Association
   https://e-anca.org/ANCAEduc.htm
   The ANCA scholarship is open to US citizens who are attending an accredited institution and seeking a bachelor's degree or a graduate degree in nursing or anesthesia. Award is $3,000 and granted for one year. Students must:

* Currently be serving or have previously served in any branch, and at any rank, of a component of the US Army (active-duty Army, Army National Guard, and Army Reserve).
* Not be receiving funding by a component of the US Army, for example ROTC students and students using their GI Bill benefits (at the full rate) are not eligible.
* If relevant, have received an honorable discharge.
* Be nursing or anesthesia students whose parent(s), spouse, or child(ren) is serving or has served in a component of the Army.

Army Scholarship Foundation Scholarships
   www.armyscholarshipfoundation.org
   Applicants must be high school seniors, high school graduates, or undergraduate students who are dependent children of active-duty, active-duty reserve, or active duty National Guard, or spouses. Open to children of soldiers who received an honorable discharge, medical discharge, or were killed while serving. Awards are $500 to $2000 for undergraduate studies and students must maintain a minimum of a 2.0 GPA to be eligible. Students may reapply annually to renew the scholarship based upon their academic performance.

Association of the United States Army Scholarships
   http://www.ausa.org/about/scholarships/Pages/default.aspx
   The Larry Strickland Memorial Fund and Scholarship awards one noncommissioned officer a bronze eagle and $4,000 for education cost assistance that Tuition Assistance will not cover, for example book costs. The noncommissioned officer should exemplify the Army's vision and have a positive influence on others.

The Joseph P. and Helen T. Cribbins Scholarship is a $2,000 award based upon academic merit and personal achievement. Eligible soldiers are currently serving on active duty in the Army, Army Reserve, or Army National Guard of any rank, must be honorably discharged, must be attending an accredited school, and pursuing a degree in engineering or a related field (for example, computer science).

Disabled American Veterans (DAV) Auxiliary
    http://auxiliary.dav.org/membership/Programs.aspx
    (877) 426-2838, ext. 4020
Life members with the DAV Auxiliary who are attending a college or vocational school full-time can participate in the scholarship program. The scholarship maxes out at $1,500. Part-time pursuit of study may be eligible for $750. Applicants must maintain a minimum of twelve credit hours per semester to remain eligible. Renewals are not guaranteed.

Leave No Veteran Behind
    http://www.leavenoveteranbehind.org/
    (312) 379-8652
A retroactive scholarship that is designed to assist with student debt incurred prior to entering military service. Winners get their loan amounts paid off in full. In return for the award, selectees must commit to one hundred to four hundred hours of community service. The community service work must take advantage of the awardee's military skills and civilian education. Applicants must suffer from economic hardship, have student loans, have completed some degree of higher education, and have been honorably discharged.

Military Order of the Purple Heart
    www.purpleheart.org/scholarships/Default.aspx
    www.purpleheart.org/Downloads/Forms/ScholarshipApplication.pdf
    (703) 642-5360
    scholarship@purpleheart.org
Be aware that this scholarship demands a $15 payment at time of submittal. Applicant must be a Purple Heart recipient and a member of the Military Order of the PH, or the spouse, widow, child (including step or adopted), or grandchild. Student must currently be a high school senior or attending college as an undergraduate student full-time (or attending trade school), and have a minimum 2.75 GPA on a 4.0 scale. Applicant must submit an essay of two hundred to three hundred words (see site for prompt), two letters of recommendation, all other required materials, and the $15 fee (check or money order).

Pat Tillman Scholarship

> http://www.pattillmanfoundation.org/tillman-military-scholars/apply/
> (480) 621-4074
> info@pattillmanfoundation.org

Award amount varies every year. This year's awards per scholar averaged $11,000 (money above and beyond your GI Bill). Active-duty personnel, veterans, and spouses of both categories are eligible to apply. Applicant must be attending school full-time at a four-year university or college (public or private) at the undergraduate or graduate level. This scholarship is a great opportunity for graduate school students, because options at that level are more difficult to find. Applicant must apply for Federal Financial Aid (FAF-SA). Digital files of the applicant's DD 21 or personal service record and résumé will be required in order to submit, as well as responding to the two essay prompts. Those who proceed further will need to turn in their financial aid award letter (from attending institution), SAR report from FAFSA, and a photo highlighting the applicable individual's military service. The application opens in January and closes the following month. Check the website for more information.

Veterans of Foreign Wars

> http://www.vfw.org/Scholarship/
> (816) 756-3390, ext. 220

Twenty-five annual scholarships are awarded to members of Veterans of Foreign Wars who served or are currently serving in one of the branches, or members of their immediate family. Five scholarships per branch will be awarded at $3,000 apiece. If already separated, the EAS date must have been within thirty-six months before the December 31 annual deadline.

Veterans United Foundation Scholarship

> http://www.veteransunited.com/about/scholarships/

This scholarship awards a maximum of twenty scholarships per year with an award amount of $2,000 to assist with tuition and books each semester. Essays are required for submission. Eligible applicants must be pursuing an associate, bachelor's, master's, or doctoral degree, or be planning on attending school the following academic year. A connection to the US Military must be demonstrated through one of five specific pathways. Applicant must be:

- A current active-duty service member
- A veteran of the US Armed Forces
- A spouse of a service member or veteran
- Surviving spouse or child of a fallen service member
- A child of a service member or veteran

Applicants must also maintain a cumulative 2.5 grade point average on a 4.0 scale at all times.

School-Based Scholarships

Many schools offer internal scholarships. Speak to the financial aid department of your chosen institution to find out about opportunities. This section demonstrates just a few of the scholarships available around the country.

Florida

Santa Fe College

Jeffrey Mattison Wershow Memorial Scholarship

http://m.sfcollege.edu/development/index.php?section=info/JeffreyMattisonWershowMemorial

Applicant must have received an honorable discharge (but can still be on active duty) and must maintain a 2.5 GPA for award renewal. Award amount is $1,600 per year, or $800 per semester. Application demands a thousand-word essay pertaining to student's education (see website) and three letters of recommendation (see website).

Idaho

Idaho State University

Iwo Jima Scholarship

http://www.isu.edu/scholar/forms/IwoJimaAnn.pdf

The Iwo Jima Scholarship may be available to a descendant of World War II veterans (preference for those who served at Iwo Jima). Applicant must have a 3.0 GPA to be eligible, and preference is given to engineering majors. Personal statement and discharge papers are required (see website).

Kansas

Johnston County Community College

Veterans Scholarship

http://www.jccc.edu/admissions/financial-aid/aid-types/scholarships/jccc-scholarships/veterans/avetrn.html#.VTCI2nlFBhE

This scholarship is designed to assist veterans who are reentering the workforce or higher education after being discharged from active duty or deployment. Funding is available to veterans who have been discharged within six months of the first day of classes of the semester they plan to enroll at Johnston County Community College (JCCC). The scholarship will be applied to tuition and book costs, with no cash going directly to the student. Books must be purchased at the JCCC bookstore.

Maryland

Wor-Wic Community College

Salisbury Optimist Scholarship
http://www.worwic.edu/StudentServices/FinancialAidScholarships/LocalNeedBasedScholarships.aspx
Applicant must be a resident of Wicomico County, Maryland; must enroll at the college within two years of returning from the military; and must demonstrate financial need. A GPA of 3.0 is necessary to apply.

Michigan
Michigan State University
MSU Disabled Veteran's Assistance Program
http://finaid.msu.edu/veterans.asp
New and returning undergraduate veterans with a military-related disability who are Michigan residents and working on their first baccalaureate degree may qualify for an aid package that covers all costs.

Minnesota
University of Minnesota Duluth
LaVerne Noyes Scholarship
http://www.d.umn.edu/onestop/student-finances/financial-aid/types/scholarships/umd-current.html
This scholarship is available to students attending the University of Minnesota Duluth. Applicant must be a direct blood descendant of a military member who served in the US Army or Navy in World War I and died in service or received an honorable discharge. Applicant must demonstrate financial need. Award is $1,000.

New York
Cornell University Law School
Dickson Randolph Knott Memorial
http://www.lawschool.cornell.edu/alumni/giving/endowed_funds/scholarships_g-l.cfm
Applicant must be a military veteran enrolled in the law school (see website for more information).

Monroe Community College
Donald W. Holleder Endowed Scholarship
http://www.monroecc.edu/depts/finaid/documents/scholarshipbrochure-listing2012_2013.pdf
Applicant must demonstrate financial need, and preference is given to Vietnam veterans and their dependents. Award is for $600 per year.

Hilbert College
Sgt. Martin F. Bogdanowicz Memorial Scholarship

http://www.hilbert.edu/admissions/student-aid/scholarships-grants
Scholarship is for entering freshman veterans (or their children).

Ohio

Cedarville University
James Cain Special Education Award
http://www.cedarville.edu/courses/catalog/2011-2012/financial-information.pdf
Full-time sophomore, junior, or senior students at the university majoring in special education (intent on teaching kids with special needs) may apply. Applicant must demonstrate financial need, and preference is given to certain populations, including those who have served in the military.

Texas

Angelina College
Disabled American Veterans Scholarship
http://www.angelina.edu/generalbulletin/scholarship-info/
Applicant must be a descendant of a member of the DAV. Award is $500 per semester for full-time study.

Texas Christian University
Adrienne Miller Perner Scholarship
http://www.dance.tcu.edu/financialaid.asp
(817) 257-7615
Amount varies. Applicant must be a child or grandchild of a career military service member. Applicant must also be female and majoring in ballet. Scholarship is based on talent or community work.

Utah

Westminster College
Doris Edwards Miller Endowed Scholarship
http://www.westminstercollege.edu/pdf/financial_aid_current/0910schlplist.pdf
This scholarship is available to veterans or their children, but both must demonstrate need. Full-time enrollment is mandatory in order to be eligible for this scholarship (eight at $3,500 each).

Scholarship Possibilities for Dependents

Below is a list of scholarships available for spouses and dependent children. Always check with the Military & Civilian Spouses Clubs at the base where you are stationed if you are still on active duty with the Army. The clubs usually have scholarship possibilities every year. Organizations such as The

National Military Family Association also keep lists of scholarships or funding opportunities for spouses which can be found here: http://www.militaryfamily.org/spouses-scholarships/

Ladies Auxiliary VFW

Continuing Education Scholarship

https://www.ladiesauxvfw.org/programs-page/scholarships/

Spouses, sons, and daughters of members may be eligible if they are pursuing a college degree or career pathway at a technical school.

Fisher House

http://www.militaryscholar.org/

Run by the commissaries. A minimum of one $2,000 scholarship is awarded through every commissary location, although more might be possible depending on funding. Award may be used for payment of tuition, books, lab fees, or other education-related expenses. Scholarship is open to children of active-duty, retired, or reserve service members. Applicant must have a minimum of a 3.0 GPA on a 4.0 scale.

The Joanne Holbrook Patton Military Spouse Scholarships

https://militaryfamily.scholarships.ngwebsolutions.com/CMXAdmin/Cmx_Content.aspx?cpId=561

For spouses of active-duty, retired, and reserve service members. Award may be used for tuition, fees, or school room and board. The scholarship offers assistance for GED or ESL, vocational training or certification, undergraduate or graduate degrees, licensure fees, and clinical hours for mental health licensure. Applicants can attend face-to-face schooling or online.

American Legion

http://www.legion.org/scholarships

Samsung American Legion Scholarship

For high school juniors who complete a Boys State or Girls State program. Scholarship is for undergraduate study only and is based on financial need. It can be used for tuition, books, fees, or room and board. Applicants must have completed a Boys State or Girls State program, be direct descendants or legally adopted children of wartime veterans (must be eligible for American Legion membership), and be in their junior year of high school. Award is up to $20,000 for an undergraduate course of study. Winners are selected based upon academic record, financial need, and participation in community activities. Application requires several mini-essays.

Legacy Scholarship

http://www.legion.org/scholarships/legacy

Eligible applicants are children or adopted children of military members who died while on active duty on or after September 11, 2001; are high school seniors or already graduated; and are pursuing an undergraduate degree.

The Baseball Scholarship
http://www.legion.org/scholarships/baseball
baseball@legion.org
Applicant must have graduated high school, be on a team affiliated with an American Legion post, and be on a 2013 roster filed with the National Headquarters. High school transcripts, three letters of testimony, and a completed application must be filed.

National High School Oratorical Contest Scholarship
http://www.legion.org/scholarships/oratorical
oratorical@legion.org
Scholarship money (up to $18,000 for first place) can be used at any college or university within the United States. Scholarship has hundreds of small rewards involved at local levels.

Department of Michigan-American Legion Auxiliary
http://michalaux.org/scholarships/
Medical Career Scholarship
Applicants should be daughters, granddaughters, great-granddaughters, sons, grandsons, or great-grandsons of honorably discharged or deceased veterans of specific conflicts (World War I, World War II, Korea, Vietnam, Persian Gulf, etc.) and be living in Michigan. Award is $500 for tuition, room and board fees, books, and so on. Scholarship must be used at a school in Michigan, and applicants must be in their senior year of high school (top quarter of their class) and preparing to enter college. This is a need-based scholarship.

Scholarship for Nontraditional Students
One two-year scholarship of $500 per year will be awarded. Applicant must be the descendant of a veteran, over the age of twenty-two, and attending college or trade school for the first time or attending college after a significantly long break. The award may be used toward tuition and books at a school in the state of Michigan. Entries are due by March 15. Application includes short essays.

National American Legion Auxiliary
Children of Warriors Scholarship National Presidents' Scholarship

https://www.alaforveterans.org/Scholarships/Children-of-Warriors-National-Presidents--Scholarship/

Fifteen scholarships were awarded in 2012–2013. Applicants must be daughters or sons, stepdaughters or stepsons, grandsons or granddaughters, step-grandsons or step-granddaughters, or step great-grandsons or step great-granddaughters of eligible American Legion members. Applicants should be in their senior year of high school and complete fifty hours of volunteer service. Completed applications and all documentation (includes an essay) are due to the local American Legion Auxiliary Unit by March 1, and winners are announced on March 15.

Spirit of Youth Scholarship

https://www.alaforveterans.org/Scholarships/Spirit-of-Youth-Scholarship-Fund/

Five awards at $5,000 each for this scholarship. Applicants must be seniors in high school and junior members of the American Legion Auxiliary for the past three years, hold current membership, and continue membership throughout awarding years. A 3.0 GPA is mandatory for individuals applying for this scholarship. Applications are due by March 1; winners are announced March 15. ACT or SAT scores, high school transcripts, four letters of recommendation, a completed FAFSA application, and essays are required.

Another extremely noteworthy option:

The American Military Retirees Scholarships:
http://amra1973.org/Scholarship/

Federal sites for scholarship searches:
http://www.careerinfonet.org/scholarshipsearch/ScholarshipCategory.asp?searchtype=category&nodeid=22
http://studentaid.ed.gov/

Other useful search sites:
https://www.horatioalger.org/scholarships/index.cfm
http://www.collegescholarships.org/scholarships/army.htm
http://www.finaid.org/military/veterans.phtml
www.scholarships.com
www.collegeboard.org
http://www.scholarships4students.com/council_of_college_and_military_educators_scholarship.htm
http://scholarshipamerica.org/
www.careeronestop.org
www.collegedata.com

http://www.finaid.org/scholarships/
http://fedmoney.org/
www.militaryonesource.com

TEXTBOOK-BUYING OPTIONS

Who knew books could be so expensive? Welcome to college! The cost of books can often get out of control. The Post-9/11 GI Bill maxes out at $1,000 per academic year for books and supplies, and often that does not begin to cover the bill. If you are still on active duty, then you already know that TA does not cover books.

College books are notoriously expensive. Unlike high school, a year of college requires an incredible amount of books. Professors have to find supplemental materials to feed your brain and back up the information with proof. Books are still the most common, easiest way of accomplishing this task.

Now you know why you need them, but not why college books are so expensive. A few reasons come to mind: for example, copyrighted material, specialized material, and online supplements. College books can hold an incredible amount of copyrighted material. Publishers have to cover the copyright fees, as well as all other fees, within the cost of the book. Information within college books is usually quite specialized and often not found elsewhere. This means the books do not have another avenue for sales and contributes to a highly competitive market, driving the cost up. Many books also have online supplements attached to them, and those fees must also be included in the cost.

Last—although I hate addressing this reason, but feel I (Jillian) must—many professors have written books. Can you guess which books could be included in your reading list? Terrible, I agree . . . since professors get royalties just like other authors. Let's think more positively about the situation. Sometimes these books can be some of your most informative and easily organized reference material. Professors often write books based on the knowledge they have derived from their years in the classroom and field experience to help themselves or others teach. Many schools take pride in having such accomplished professors on staff. Speaking from personal experience, getting published is no easy feat. This practice may sometimes help a professor cut down on the book expenses for his or her students because the book follows along closely with the class's learning expectations, thereby allowing the student to purchase one or at least fewer books than previously necessary.

Although many other reasons contribute to book costs, I'll get down to the reason you are reading this section: how to pay for them. The first trip to the bookstore can be excruciating as reality sets in. Do not stress yet; other options may exist. Since many books top the $100 range (sometimes closer to $200!), students should spend as much time as feasible trying to find books from alternate sources. I still recommend checking out the campus bookstore first. Some schools maintain significant used textbook sections. You will need to get to the store as early as possible to take advantage of this possibility; the discounted books will be the first ones to leave the shelves. Check to see if you can sell your books back at the end of the semester as well. Most likely, the amount the store will offer you will be greatly reduced. Remember that a little cash is better than none, and you can roll that money into your textbooks for the following semester.

Next, you can try either renting or buying the books used online. Which path you choose depends on whether you want to keep the books. Personally, because books change every few years and the information within them becomes outdated at such a fast pace, I only kept my French books. The language was not going anywhere, so I figured I would hold on to them for future reference.

There are an astounding number of sites on the Internet that sell or rent used textbooks. Even some bigwigs have gotten into the game. Amazon has a used textbook section that may suit all of your needs. The section (at http://www.amazon.com/New-Used-Textbooks-Books/b?) enables users to refer friends and earn $5 credits. While it may not seem like much, if you are the first in your group to start referring friends, you could end up with a stash of extra money to help cover your own textbook expenses. Amazon also allows users to sell books back to the store for Amazon gift cards. If you would prefer to rent (yes, for a full semester!), the site has that option available to users. If you are an Amazon Prime member (payment required: join as a student and receive a discount), you can receive your shipment in two days; otherwise, orders over $35 receive free shipping but will run on regular shipment time frames. Lastly, you can rent or buy Kindle Textbooks for Kindle Fire tablets, or put the Kindle application on your iPad, Android tablet, PC, or Mac, and read it on your own device. You can rent the eTextbooks for an amount of time you specify. When you pick a book, Amazon lets you set the return date, although the price does go up the longer you keep the book.

Barnes & Noble (B & N) offers the same services as Amazon (see http://www.barnesandnoble.com/u/textbooks-college-textbooks/379002366/). You can receive a check from the store and even get a quick quote by entering some easy information on the website. The eTextbooks offered through B&N can be viewed with a seven-day free trial before purchasing on your PC or Mac (not available for the actual NOOK device or mobile phones). This may come in handy if you are looking for an older version to save money. Make sure you compare the older version against a new version (find a friend!)

before purchasing. The eTextbooks are viewed through NOOK Study (free app). You can highlight, tag, link, and conduct searches on textbooks downloaded with this app.

If I were currently attending school, I would ask for gift certificates to these two stores for every single holiday that came around. The generosity of family could keep me going with school textbooks for quite some time.

You may also want to check out the publisher's website. Very often the book's publisher will sell the ebook or text version for a greatly reduced rate. Sometimes there is no telling what pricing or distribution disputes are ongoing that will affect the prices of textbooks from various vendors.

Now, these are not the only possible sources to rent or purchase textbooks. Below are just a few other possible sources. Always compare prices at different sites to make sure you are getting the best deal possible before you proceed.

- Amazon Student Website: www.amazon.com/New-Used-Textbooks-Books/b?ie=UTF8&node=465600
- Barnes & Noble: http://www.barnesandnoble.com/u/textbooks-college-textbooks/379002366/

Compare book prices:

- http://www.bookfinder4u.com
- http://www.textbookrentals.com

Rent, sell, or buy back books:

- http://www.chegg.com
- http://www.campusbookrentals.com
- http://www.bookrenter.com
- http://www.valorebooks.com
- http://www.skyo.com

Here are my last few ideas on this subject. You may be incredibly shocked to learn that sometimes the library is a good place to start. Check out both your college's library and your community library. The book, or even a very similar recent past edition, may be available to rent for free. Or you can make friends with someone who already took the class and has not returned his or her book, and offer that individual a decent price. Check with the college's bookstore for class reading lists, or send an email to the professor to find out the reading list in advance, then double down on your mission.

FREE SUBJECT MATTER STUDY SUPPORT

This section will be short and sweet. I packed it full of free websites and preparatory programs that can help in your educational pursuits. Often, all it takes is a little extra help, or a different explanation of the same material to clear the cobwebs and make progress in a subject. I find the websites listed below to have the best information/explanations to help promote learning.

Military-Based Study Support

Peterson's, a Nelnet Company

www.petersons.com/dod

Peterson's is a solid site for subject-matter proficiency exams and AS-VAB test preparation. You can continue to use this site upon separation from the Army. You and your dependents (free for them as well) can access CLEP prep, DSST prep, and ASVAB prep.

This site also has options to help users narrow their searches—for example, by undergraduate and graduate school, vocational-technical school, or Servicemembers Opportunity Colleges. Under the undergraduate and graduate school search tabs are listed helpful articles that may give you more guidance in your pursuit of an appropriate school, an appropriate program, or preparing for the admissions process, which can take a very long time and be time-consuming.

Lastly, on the home page of Petersons is a link labeled OASC, Online Academic Skills Course. The program is intended to boost the user's reading comprehension, vocabulary, and math abilities. The preassessment will determine the user's strengths and weaknesses and help design an appropriate learning plan. As a user progresses through OASC, learning is supported by interactive exercises and quizzes.

eKnowledge Corporation & NFL Players

SAT & ACT test preparation
www.eknowledge.com/military
(770) 992-0900
LoriCaputo@eknowledge.com

This program is a combined effort of the Department of Defense and some patriotic NFL players. eKnowledge Corporation donates SAT and ACT test preparation software to military families and veterans. The software usually runs approximately $200, but it is free for service members and their families. The programs include classroom instruction, interactive learning participation, and 120 classroom video lessons.

Veterans Attending School with the GI Bill—Tutoring Available

Veterans attending school on a GI Bill at one-half time or more in a postsecondary program at an educational institution may be eligible for an extra tutoring stipend from the VA. The VA will pay up to $100 per month for tutoring on top of your regular GI Bill payments. The subject must be mandatory for program completion. Total amount cannot exceed $1,200. Student must need help in the subject, and even if currently receiving a passing grade, can receive the assistance if the current grade will not count toward program completion. Use the VONAPP system to fill out the DD 22-1990T and inquire with your school to see if they participate in this VA program. Often, tutors can be found for free at your school. Commonly, the tutors are students of the subject they give tutoring for and often are receiving "tuition remission" or a deduction of their tuition costs. Regardless, even if fees are charged, rarely does it exceed $100 a month, unless you need extremely extensive tutoring.

Under Post-9/11, there is no entitlement charge (deduction of remaining months of benefit). Under MGIB, there is no entitlement charge for the first $600. See http://www.gibill.va.gov/resources/education_resources/programs/tutorial_assistance_program.html

Non-Military-Supported Free Subject Matter Help

Here is a list of free non-military-related study websites I like to use when I need extra help. I have used all of them at some point and found each beneficial for one thing or another. Hopefully, you will find them constructive too.

Math

Khan Academy (www.khanacademy.org)

The very first website that should be on anyone's list for math is Khan Academy. This is far and away the most amazing math help available without paying for one-on-one tutoring. You can register for the site through Facebook or Google, and it is incredibly easy to use (and of course *free*!). Videos guide the user through different problems, and discussion question threads allow the user to ask questions. The site offers other subjects besides math. Science and economics, humanities, computer science, and some test prep help are available as well.

PurpleMath (www.purplemath.com)

Purple Math offers a wide array of math topics. You can find anything you might need on the site. The main page is a bit jumbled, and many of the links take you to external sites. Stick to the main Purple Math page. The examples arc written step-by-step to show you how to proceed for each particular problem.

English

Grammar Bytes (www.chompchomp.com)

I (Jillian) dig this website. The layout is easy to understand without any mumbo jumbo to sort through. Each section has a print tab that organizes the material in an easily printed (no pictures or extra garbage to waste ink!), easily read manner. The subject matter is comprehensive, and the site even contains YouTube videos.

Purdue Owl (http://owl.english.purdue.edu/owl/)

As an English teacher, I love Purdue Owl. Everything I need is on this site. Plus the site offers instructive writing help, such as thesis statement development, dealing with writer's block, and creating an outline to start a paper. If you are in need of American Psychological Association (APA) or Modern Language Association (MLA) formatting help, go to this site. APA and MLA are formatting structures that most higher education classes demand be used in writing papers.

Guide to Grammar Writing (http://grammar.ccc.commnet.edu/grammar/)

This is a no-nonsense website that has all of the basics organized in a user-friendly manner. The Editing and Rewriting Skills section has a checklist that is similar to the one I use when writing and grading papers. The checklist also offers the user links to some of the most common grammatical problems facing writers.

The Grammar Book (www.grammarbook.com)

Another good no-nonsense English grammar website. The explanations are brief and easy to understand. The examples are to-the-point and easy to follow. The Quizzes tab also has two sections of comprehensive free activities to test your aptitude.

Massive Open Online Courses

Massive Open Online Courses (MOOCs) are the newest venture in college-level virtual education. Alarmed at the rising cost of tuition and declaring that education unto itself should be free, professors across a variety of prestigious universities began offering college-level courses online that were open to anyone with Internet access. Organizations such as www.coursera.org, www.edx.org, and www.udacity.com offer free courses in many common classes found on college campuses. They function like many standard online courses, and if you get bored or no longer have the time to attend, just walk away. The beauty of MOOCs is that they allow you to enroll in a course and expose yourself to material that you will encounter later in a class that costs real money with a real grade on the line. Nervous about taking business law or statistics because it is required for your degree? Check out a class in that subject through a MOOC so you can gain confidence and a better understanding of the material before stepping into the classroom. While these classes are not currently worth college credit, you can often voluntarily choose to pay a small fee for a certificate if you successfully complete the class. If nothing else, this could be a bullet point on your resume.

Citation Formatting for APA and MLA References

- http://citationmachine.net/index2.php
- https://www.calvin.edu/library/knightcite/

APA format guidance:

- American Psychological Association: www.apastyle.org
- Purdue Owl: https://owl.english.purdue.edu/owl/resource/560/01/

MLA format guidance:

- Cornell University Library: http://www.library.cornell.edu/research/citationmanage/mla
- California State University Los Angeles: http://web.calstatela.edu/library/guides/3mla.pdf
- Purdue Owl: https://owl.english.purdue.edu/owl/resource/747/01/

Chapter Seven

Prior Learning Credit

Prior learning credit is college credit that is granted for learning that occurred after a student completed high school. Many schools award prior learning credit even though it is not widely advertised. Institutions of higher learning often award prior learning credit for service members. Schools always demand evidence of the learning that took place. For soldiers, that evidence is demonstrated through an evaluation of their Joint Services Transcript. If granted, these credits can result in service members expediting their college degrees. This chapter includes information on the following topics:

- Prior Learning Credit
- American Council on Education
- Joint Services Transcript
- Servicemembers Opportunity Colleges
- Subject Matter Proficiency Exams

PRIOR LEARNING CREDIT

Prior learning credit is credit for coursework that is earned in a nontraditional manner. Institutions that offer traditional and nontraditional education for training, learning, and/or knowledge already gained might offer students credit through this pathway. Schools that offer credit through a formal assessment pathway are providing a beneficial service to their student population. Nontraditional credit awards can assist students in fast-tracking their educations while helping them save money, provide incentives for students to finish their degrees, and put more control back into the students' hands.

Assessment methods for prior learning credit typically fall into three different categories: credit earned through examinations such as Common Level Examination Program (CLEP), portfolio-based assessment, and any other credit earned without examinations used to demonstrate proficiency. For military personnel, prior learning credit is most often granted after reviewing the service member's Joint Services Transcript (JST). Each school will have its own policies on this type of credit and they can vary greatly. Although prior learning credit is becoming more popular, double-check with the institution you are interested in to determine whether they will consider granting you credit based on your experiences.

Schools do not typically advertise their ability to offer prior learning credit, so it might not be widely detailed on their website. Veterans are often granted credit in this fashion, so it is wise to follow through. Contacting the school to determine whether the institution will review your military transcript might get you free credit based upon learning you have already completed. Not every school awards JST-based prior learning credit; however, more institutions are opting to participate every year. Schools that award prior learning credit through military training and learning place value on the knowledge a service member has gained through his service and demonstrate the institutions' capacity for understanding the rigorous demands that active service has placed upon the student.

Why do you care if the school you have chosen awards prior learning credit? Because it will help fast-track your degree. You only have thirty-six months of GI Bill benefit available to use. Think about the flexibility you will gain if you attend an institution that awards prior learning credit. You might be able to save some benefit for a master's degree, a certification program, or simply to build a small buffer into each semester's class load. Consider the process as a beneficial pathway to helping you achieve your degree, but don't pick a school based solely on this criterion. Remember, the point of going to school is to feed your brain.

AMERICAN COUNCIL ON EDUCATION

The American Council on Education (ACE; http://www.acenet.edu/Pages/default.aspx) works with the Department of Defense to translate military training and experiences into potential credit. ACE has evaluated the ratings or MOSs, formal courses, and mandatory training requirements from the different branches to determine what might be eligible for academic credit. ACE makes its recommendations, which are reflected in a soldier's JST. Schools that elect to award credit must first determine how to convert the recommendations into credit that their institution offers. Just because your JST reflects ACE recommendation does not mean your school will adhere to the recommendations and award you credit. Remember, prior learning credit is granted at the will of the institution.

ACE credit recommendations are based on nontraditional learning, meaning it was not completed in an academic environment. ACE credit evaluators are professors who are teaching within the field they are assigned to evaluate. These professors understand that learning can be completed through traditional and nontraditional methods, and they take that into account while conducting evaluations of military credit. Evaluations are ongoing in order to maintain a status that accurately reflects current military training requirements. During the evaluations, faculty members review the military coursework length, learning outcomes, and instruction, and then offer credit recommendations that describe the training in a manner that institutions of higher learning can understand and relate to coursework already offered at their school. Not all military training is awarded credit recommendations.

If you are interested in finding out what type of credit is recommended for a particular course or rating, you can search on the ACE website, http://www.acenet.edu/news-room/Pages/Military-Guide-Online.aspx. You can search by military course numbers, course titles and locations, subject level, or by the ACE identification numbers that can be found on your JST.

Familiarize yourself with the website so you can become a better-prepared student. Your school might not award credit through JST evaluation; however, it may be willing to award prior learning credit in another manner. What if you read the class description of a course listed on your education plan and you realize that it is similar to training you completed while in the Army? You might be able to petition your school for prior learning credit based upon demonstration of the knowledge. That might earn you college credit without you actually attending the class.

The following is a detailed example of how to use the ACE website to find information regarding your training—it will help you become a better researcher.

Sergeant Stevens visits the ACE website to learn more about the aircraft electrician course that he attended in September 2010. He clicks on the "Higher Education Topics" link at the top of the page, then scrolls down to the "Military Students and Veterans" link located under "Attainment and Innovation." Once on the new page, he clicks on the "Military Guide" on the right-hand side and now finds himself on the search page. Sergeant Stevens will search on the "Courses" tab for his information.

He selects his branch, lists his course, inputs the month and year, and initiates the search. The search produces several results. Sergeant Stevens scrolls down until he finds the correct course. He notices that the dates listed for his course encompass the dates he attended the course. He clicks on the description and is brought to a page that details the course parameters, learning outcomes, and credit recommendations.

If Sergeant Stevens would like to search his military occupational specialty, he would return to the main search page and click on "Search Occupations," choose "Army Enlisted" under "Occupation," list 15F under "Occupation Title," and input the time frame (2010) that he completed his occupational training. Only one result comes up during the search. The search results also yields the ACE ID, in this case MOS-15F-004.

Some schools do not automatically award credit through the JST. If that is the case with your institution, you might still be able to complete a written request for prior learning credit based upon the information housed in your JST. Before you write a submission request for prior learning credit, always double-check with your academic counselor to determine if the school will consider the request and how to make the request. Some institutions have very specific pathways that must be completed to be considered for the free credits and fees that must be paid.

Civilian institutions are familiar with ACE and find their recommendations to be highly credible. If you decide to petition your institution for prior learning credit based upon your military service, make sure to reference ACE and detail the information pertaining to your MOS or course offered on its website on your petition. This way your knowledge is validated through a reputable organization and lends your petition more weight.

JOINT SERVICES TRANSCRIPT

The Joint Services Transcript (JST; https://jst.doded.mil/) replaced the Army/American Council on Education Registry System, or AARTS. The JST document compiles the ACE credit-recommended coursework information into a transcript that academic institutions can read. The document endorses a soldier's military experiences as valuable in an academic setting.

If your school recognizes the JST, you will want to send an official copy to the institution for credit evaluation. The official JST can be requested by you, or someone at your education center. The official request goes to Fort Knox, and then it is sent to the institution. The requests are free, and you do not need to be on active duty; veterans can use the site as well. If you want to pull your unofficial JST, visit the website, create an account, then click the "Transcripts" link at the top of the page.

ACE recommended credit means you might be able to collect free college credit as discussed in the section regarding the organization. Remember that free credit helps you fast-track your degree. That means getting into the workforce faster, saving GI Bill benefit, or simply giving you a small buffer in the number of classes you need to take each semester in order to graduate.

Let's discuss the credit load concerns. Your GI Bill has thirty-six months of benefit available for you to use. That equates to nine months per year over the course of four academic years. That is enough benefit to attain most bachelor's degrees, which require 120 semester credit hours to graduate. But those semester hours are not in random classes. Your academic counselor will build a degree plan for you based upon your academic goals, meaning the degree you want to attain. Upon completion, most classes earn you three credits; some math classes and most sciences will earn you four credits because they often have a mandatory one credit hour lab attached to them. In order to attain your declared degree (if it requires 120 semester hours), your semesters will look like this:

Fall semester freshman year: 5 classes x 3 credits = 15 credit hours
Spring semester freshman year: 5 classes x 3 credits = 15 credit hours

This totals thirty semester credit hours earned for your first year of school. Complete the same process for your sophomore, junior, and senior years. You end up with 120 semester credit hours, and you will have earned your degree.

Here is where it gets tricky. The VA considers twelve credit hours every semester (on a normal sixteen-week semester schedule) to be full-time. Full-time semesters equal full-time housing allowance under Post-9/11. If you only complete the bare minimum according to the VA to maintain your full-time benefits, you will not collect the number of credits you need in order to graduate. Twelve credits per semester will only total ninety-six credits at the end of your senior year of college. You will be out of benefit, but you will not have attained your degree yet.

Because the VA considers four to six classes to be full-time, you could take four classes one semester and six the next to make up the difference. If you are awarded JST credit this might not affect your credit progression. For example, if Specialist Ramirez attends ABC University and is awarded fifteen JST credits, he has two choices in building his semester schedules. He could consider those fifteen credits as a full semester and continue along a normal pathway to graduate early, or he could use the free JST credit as a built-in buffer to enable him to build a slightly less intensive semester schedule. He would have the ability to schedule four classes per semester for his first two and one-half years, still maintain full-time GI Bill benefit, and still be on track to graduate because he would have been fifteen credits shy of where he should be, but he made up the missed credit with the free JST credit he was awarded.

While there are many available options, only you can determine the best pathway for your academic career. Discuss your needs with an academic counselor at the school and consider all applicable pathways before you decide. Most of the service members I (Jillian) work with opt to fast-track their educations. They use the JST credit they are awarded to fill semesters in order to graduate early. This is most beneficial as it can save your benefit toward another pathway such as a master's degree or a certification.

Typically, when attending college, students have three different types of credit they must earn: general education, core, and elective. General education credits typically include math, English, history, arts, health, natural science, and social and behavioral sciences. Core credits include all classes specific to your particular major—for example, business classes if you are a business major. Elective credits are your free choices. They give you a well-rounded education. Your educational pathway will demand a certain number of elective credits depending upon your major course of study. Choosing a major that is heavy on core classes, such as engineering, will reduce the number of elective credits.

JST credit is typically applied to the free-choice elective credits section. Although each school determines what it accepts and how the free credit will be applied, some schools offer MOS-related degrees that enable JST credit to be applied to core credits. The overall value of a soldier's JST will depend upon his desired educational pathway at an institution that is open to accepting military credit, his MOS, and his completed training. Typically, the longer you are in the military, the more JST credit you are able to pick up. Remember, because acceptance of the JST is at the discretion of each institution, some schools will not accept any JST credit. Ahhh . . . the horror!

Searching out schools based upon the amount of JST credit the institution is willing to award you is not the best pathway for choosing a school. Make a decision after doing a holistic review of all of your personal needs, school offerings, and personal career goals. I would be skeptical of an institution that made big promises and offered you excessive amounts of JST credit. The point in attending school is to get an education and to feed your brain. Choose a school that fits all of your needs, not just the need to finish fast.

Learning to read the JST is not an exciting task, but it will make you a better-informed student. If you have already pulled your transcript, find it and follow along. If not, go to https://jst.doded.mil/smart/signIn.do, create an account, and print your "Combo Report." The JST is divided into the following six sections:

1. Military Course Completions
2. Military Experience

The "Military Course Completion" and the "Military Experience" sections host all of the training and courses the service member completed during his active-duty service. The military course ID, the ACE identifier, course title, location, description, credit areas, dates taken, and ACE credit recommendation are listed in this section. You can search by the military course ID and the ACE identifier on the ACE website to access more detailed information.

The "Description" section gives a quick rundown of the specific areas of academic course work that ACE is recommending. The "ACE Credit Recommendation" section lists the number of credit hours ACE recommends for the breakdown of each course. The section marked "Level" will have an L, U, or V listed. The L stands for lower-level credit or anything at the freshman or sophomore level of college. The U stands for upper-division credit or anything at the junior or senior level of college. The V is for vocational education.

3. College-Level Test Scores

The "College-Level Test Scores" section lists any CLEP, DSST, or DLPT exams the service member completed while on active duty and the scores received.

4. Other Learning Experiences

This section houses all of the training the service member completed that does not receive credit for one or more of these reasons: ACE has not evaluated the specific course, attendance dates are missing, the course might have been evaluated but not for the dates the service member attended, or ACE did not evaluate the course at the location the service member attended. This section also lists any training that might receive credit but currently does not due to a mistake in the transcript updating process. This will be demonstrated by a 4 code listed to the right of the course. If you are still on active duty and see 4 codes listed, bring your JST in to the local education center and request help to fix the error.

5. The Summary

The "Summary" section is the part of the transcript the schools are going to review. This section breaks down all of your potential credits and houses all of your juicy stuff! Everything you completed while on active duty that ACE recommends for credit is listed in this section. The credits and levels are listed as well as the Servicemember Opportunity College (SOC) category code, which details the subject areas where SOC recommends credit. For example, below is a list of the four common credit recommendations for attending basic training listed by course:

- First Aid = 1 SH, L
- Marksmanship = 1 SH, L
- Military Science = 2 SH, L
- Physical Conditioning = 2 SH, L

6. Academic Institution Courses

You may believe there are errors on your JST. Click the "How to make updates and corrects to your JST transcript" link on the main page after logging in. The first recommendation the JST website makes is checking to make sure your Army Training Requirements and Resources System (ATRRS) transcript is updated correctly (this can be accessed through AKO). Speak to your unit S1 to ensure everything is in order in your Army personnel file. It is also possible that your particular service school made an error and did not report your training in ATRRS, so it will be up to you to contact that specific service school to ensure they make the correct updates. Lastly, you can always email the Army JST team at usarmy.knox.hrc.mbx.tagd-jst@mail.mil. The JST team might recommend that you try the first two suggestions before they problem solve the issue on their end. You can always contact your local education center for assistance in this process. Remember, if it isn't on your JST, your school will not be able to see it; hence, you might miss some credit.

The Joint Services Transcript is not strictly for academic credit or degree completion. The JST can be used in many different areas such as employment and skills documentation, state credential verification, and résumé development. If you are putting together a résumé, you can reference your JST for work history. Education centers, Transition Assistance Program offices, and the Army Family Readiness Group may offer résumé-writing seminars and review your résumé, but each installation's services will vary widely. Make sure to bring your JST and VMET (https://www.dmdc.osd.mil/tgps/) with you if you schedule an appointment.

SERVICEMEMBERS OPPORTUNITY COLLEGES

SOC was created to assist active-duty service members and their spouses in their pursuit of education. SOC operates in collaboration with higher education associations, the Department of Defense (DoD), and active and reserve components of the military. The Defense Activity for Non-Traditional Education Support (DANTES) manages the contract that is funded through the DoD. The group aims to improve higher education opportunities for active-duty military members.

Service members often face roadblocks when pursuing higher education during their active-duty time. The SOC Consortium tries to eliminate many of these roadblocks by working with educational institutions and creating higher degrees of flexibility. The point is to facilitate military degree completion as opposed to simply compiling course credits. The program is available to family members as well.

Attending SOC schools can benefit active-duty soldiers and veterans. The schools are familiar with the difficulties of pursuing college credit while on active duty, and many have created degrees that relate to specific MOSs to assist in the degree completion process.

Institutions build MOS-related degrees to enable a service member's ACE-recommended JST credit to count toward core credits as well as electives. As mentioned earlier, for traditional schooling there are three different types of credits that must be earned in order to achieve a degree: general education, core, and elective. SOC schools will look at a service member's JST (https://jst.doded.mil) and possibly award prior learning credit based on experience, typically in the elective category. SOC schools with MOS-related degrees can often harness a service member's JST for core credit as well, which helps to lower the credit demands that are placed on the student even further. More information on the JST can be found in the "Prior Learning Credit" section above.

SOC is currently in a cycle of change. The SOC Consortium of schools was dissolved at the end of 2014. Many SOC Consortium schools previously offered degree programs related to the different service branches, for example SOCAD for the Army and SOCNAV for the Navy. Depending upon the institution and your branch of service, you might have been able to participate in one of these options. With the new changes, members from each branch will now be able to participate in any of the available options, widening their potential for degree completion. The degree pathways are referred to as Degree Network System (DNS)-2 and DNS-4. DNS-2 is for students seeking an associate's degree, and DNS-4 is for students seeking a bachelor's degree.

Along with the dissolution of the "consortium" of schools and a new focus on the DNS, or the degree itself, the Army has created specific partnerships with schools to help create these degrees. While it cannot be assumed these degrees will give you the most amount of credit among all degrees, these partnerships attempt to provide you an edge in knowing which degrees to target to increase your chances of taking advantage of your military training as college credit.

The Army Career Degrees are specific degrees that match specific MOSs. Go to http://www.soc.aascu.org/socad/ACD.html to find your MOS under each Career Management Field (CMF). Click your MOS and it will provide a list of specific schools and degrees within the partnership for that MOS. Clicking the degree will present a very lengthy document that explains how your credits may fit into this degree. The first two to three pages of the document will provide an overview of the degree, point-of-contact information for the degree, and a chart that shows the different potential sources of credit that may fulfill that degree requirement. Scrolling through the entire document explains each degree section requirement and how it may be fulfilled.

The primary six sources of credit include many of the topics already mentioned here, but take note of the SOCAD as a source of credit. This features a SOC Code that many courses are assigned and if two courses from two different schools share the same code, then each school can use each other's courses interchangeably. For example, the course English Composition I with Research Paper has the SOC Code of EN202B. If another school has the same code in that section of the degree you know they will accept that course if taken at another institution that shares that same code. Check this website for a full list of SOC Codes: http://www.soc.aascu.org/dnstools/GrntdTransfCrs.html. The guide on the website is commonly called an "articulation guide," and it can be a powerful tool in planning which schools and degrees will accept the majority of your credits.

Having an articulation guide available means that you are not waiting for an institution to give you an answer as to whether you will receive credit. You will also have a better way of gauging if the school is the best bet in terms of accepting your previous credit. This allows you to compare the credits you may receive from a variety of different schools without having to approach each one and obtain an answer, which might take months.

The College of the American Soldier allowed the Army to strengthen these existing partnerships to make degrees more tailored to the military training soldiers receive. Under the program there are two separate programs targeting a specific type of soldier—the Career NCO Degrees and the Enlisted Education Program (EEP). The Career NCO Degrees option, as the name implies, is for career NCOs, and many of the degrees are in subjects such as business, management, and leadership in order to specifically take advantage of NCO management training. Check https://www.goarmyed.com/public/public_cas.aspx for a full list of schools and the specific degrees within this program.

The EEP targets combat MOSs because many soldiers in combat MOSs were not receiving college credit for a significant amount of their training to put toward a degree. This program is geared toward the MOSs of 11 Infantry, 13 Field Artillery, 14 Air Defense Artillery, and 19 Armor. These degrees attempt to bring soldiers as close to associate degree completion during their first enlistment as possible. To maximize this possibility the degrees focus on giving credit for Basic Combat Training, Advanced Individual Training, Structured Self-Development I, and Warrior Leader Course. Visit https://www.goarmyed.com/public/public_eep.aspx for the full list of schools and degrees.

Conduct research on the schools and the degrees that are part of the College of the American Soldier, then ask the institutions to see the amount of credit you may have already earned and how it will apply toward a degree.

If you want to maximize your military training as college credit, these programs can tip the odds in your favor by helping you find the right degree and advancing your education.

Even though the SOC consortium has dissolved, the Degree Network System, which features the particular pathways, has not. The SOC changes are not complete as of yet and more information regarding these topics and any future changes can be found on the SOC Consortium's website (http://www.soc.aascu.org).

SUBJECT MATTER PROFICIENCY EXAMS

Subject matter proficiency exams allow students to earn college credit by taking tests as opposed to sitting through the traditional class. The exams enable students to save money and time, prepare on their own timeline, and fast-track their degrees. All of these reasons are incredibly important for veterans who have to maintain a class load specified by the VA if they want to continue with full benefits.

The testing center at your education center offers the College Level Examination Program (CLEP) and the DANTES Subject Standardized Tests (DSST). The first exam in every subject is free for active-duty personnel. If a service member fails and would like to test again, he or she will need to wait three months and pay a fee to retest. Verify with your base what the retest fee is for that particular location. At most locations in the continental United States and outside the continental United States, tests are run by schools and at many locations they are administered by the education center, so fees can vary. Retirees, dependents, and separated soldiers can test for the same fee as well (be aware that test costs can increase in the future).

The first thing students should do prior to taking CLEP or DSST exams is to verify with their school that the institution accepts these exams, which version, and in which subjects. There is no point in taking exams for no reason. Many colleges and universities do accept subject matter proficiency exams, but they limit the amount of credit awarded through this pathway, and sometimes they limit which subjects they accept. CLEP exams are more widely accepted than DSST exams.

After verifying exam acceptance through your school, look at http://www.petersons.com/dod. The Peterson's website maintains free study material for all of the CLEP and DSST exams offered on the bases. Now it is time to study, study, study! After all, who wants to pay to test again?

Once you have determined you are ready to test, contact the education center at the base and book an appointment. If the local center offers computerized testing, you will receive instant results for all exams except for the English essay component.

CLEP has thirty-three tests available in six different subject areas: English composition, humanities, mathematics, natural science, social sciences, and history. The exams cover material typically learned during the first two years of college. The College Composition exam is 120 minutes, but all other exams are ninety minutes. Most exams are multiple choice, although some, including the College Composition, have essays or other varieties of questions. CLEP essays are scored by CLEP or the institution giving the exam. If CLEP holds responsibility for scoring, essays are reviewed and scored by two different English composition professors. The scores are combined and then weighted with the multiple-choice section. Exams usually match college classes that are one semester in duration.

The DSST exam program has thirty-eight available tests. DSST exams cover lower- and upper-division classes. This is beneficial for students who have deep knowledge of certain subjects, as it will enable them to test further along the degree pathway. Testing further into a specific subject area may also enable a student to participate in classes that can usually only be accessed after prerequisites are completed. Two tests include optional essays, "Ethics in America" and "Technical Writing." Essays are not scored by DSST; they are forwarded to the institution that the test taker designates on his or her application and graded by the college or university. DSST exams are offered only for three-credit courses.

As I (Jillian) stated earlier, you will benefit greatly as a veteran using your GI Bill if you take and pass CLEP or DSST exams while still on active duty, because during that time you can test for free. Veterans should still consider paying for the exams; the result can get you into the workforce faster. Veterans who take and pass subject matter proficiency exams may reap two major benefits: build a buffer to the required semester credit load and graduate early.

The VA demands that students maintain a minimum of twelve credit hours per semester in order to rate the full housing and book stipend. Twelve credits equals four classes. Maintaining four classes per semester is not a difficult course load; however, if your goal is a bachelor's degree and you have no previous college credit, you will need to take five classes (which typically equal fifteen credit hours) every semester. Most bachelor's degrees demand 120 credit hours of predetermined courses (found on your degree plan) in order to graduate. Twelve credit hours each semester will total ninety-six credit hours, which are not sufficient to graduate, and you will be out of monthly benefits. If you can add some CLEP or DSST scores into each semester, you will have reduced your required course load.

Reaching graduation early can be a boost to many veterans, especially those with families. Veterans who have completed CLEP or DSST credit may be able to combine those exams with their JST credit and finish their degrees in less than the four years normally required. This enables students to get into the workforce faster or save GI Bill benefit for graduate school, certificate programs, and so on.

ACE also recommends credit for Defense Language Proficiency Tests (DLPTs). The Defense Language Institute Foreign Language Center (DLIFLC) is a school that select soldiers may attend to become proficient in foreign languages. The DLIFLC produces the DLPTs that the DoD uses for military and other select personnel. These exams might be taken while on active duty if you speak a second language. DLPTs score the test takers' reading, listening, and real-life proficiency in a foreign language. In some cases, sailors can receive extra pay on a monthly basis depending upon their scores, the language tested, their current assignment, and possibly the test taker's MOS. If you took a DLPT while on active duty but cannot remember your score, you can check your JST (https://jst.doded.mil). The ACE policy on DLPT credit can be found online (http://www.dliflc.edu/academiccredit-fo2.html). Ask your school if the institution awards credit for DLPT exams. If you speak a second language and you are still on active duty, contact the local education center for more guidance regarding DLPT testing policies. For study materials, visit the DLIFLC website (http://www.dliflc.edu).

Soldiers with families are always looking for ways to pursue higher education at a faster pace, ways that offer the least interruption to their working careers while they complete their degrees. This is a reasonable desire: They have families and need to maximize their income-earning potential. Passing CLEP, DSST, or DLPT exams while on active duty can have a major impact on the amount of time these soldiers must spend in the classroom later. Often, they take several CLEPs on active duty even if they do not elect to take classes until after they separate from the service. Both planning for long-term goals and accomplishing what is possible at the moment give soldiers good insight into their future academic pathways and help with time management.

Chapter Eight

Troops to Teachers

Troops to Teachers (TTT) is a US Department of Defense (DoD) program that may help eligible service members pursue a career as a teacher in the public K–12 school system.

The TTT program has two pathways:

1. Counseling pertaining to credentialing pathways and resources to help the service member or veteran achieve success, or
2. Financial support to help obtain a credential. Note that this pathway incurs a three-year payback commitment.

The thought process behind TTT is to empower service members and veterans to pursue secondary careers as public school teachers while filling teacher shortage needs, especially in subjects such as math and science. The program aims to service schools that maintain populations of low-income families with highly qualified teachers.

Although TTT does not train veterans to be teachers, the counselors give guidance and direct eligible personnel toward appropriate credentialing programs. I (Jillian) am a credentialed English teacher and have a few ideas that I will go into in more depth in this chapter.

At this time, education in this country is taking a beating. Many states have experienced massive teacher furloughs and big pay cuts. Very few areas are facing teacher shortages. Hopefully, this will change in the future, but there are no guarantees. Look into all possible options to protect your future—for example, private schools, community colleges (maybe a different education pathway!), teaching abroad (sounds like fun, right?), online teaching, and charter schools, just to name a few.

Look into all the available resources, including TTT. Check with your state's chapter (http://troopstoteachers.net/Portals/1/National%20Home%20 Page/stateoffices.pdf) to determine what it can offer you. Almost every state has a chapter. If your state does not, check with the national TTT department at (850) 452-1242 or (800) 231-6242 or via email at ttt@navy.mil.

TTT can be used by eligible personnel while still on active duty; however, you must be within one year of retirement. The program does not participate in job placement, but the website offers links to each state's teacher job bank for self-directed searching. If you are a veteran and have already exhausted your GI Bill, TTT may give you the money you need to pursue a teacher credential.

Before you follow through on your decision to be a teacher, read below and check the TTT website (http://www.dantes.doded.mil/service-members/ troops-to-teachers/index.html) for some good advice.

THOUGHTS FOR TEACHER CREDENTIALING

Teacher-credentialing programs are next to impossible to do while on active duty. They always require some form of student teaching, ranging from six weeks to a full semester. If you are on active duty, would like to be a teacher, and do not have a bachelor's degree in an applicable subject, that should be your first goal.

Always contact the state credentialing authority first. You need to determine an appropriate pathway based on the information the state gives you. Some third party sites, such as www.teach.com, can be used as resources to give you an idea of what is required to become credentialed in your particular state, but you should always verify this information before proceeding. Usually, state governments maintain this information on their websites. A quick Google search should lead to that site. Second, research the schools in that particular state, to determine the academic pathways they follow to obtain a teaching credential and/or bachelor's degree that leads in that direction. Check the Department of Defense Memorandum of Understanding website (http://www.dodmou.com) to see if your school is eligible for Tuition Assistance.

If you are unable to attend a school in your desired state, make an appointment at your local education center to find an available equivalent pathway in your current location, or complete your own search on the College Navigator website. You can always consider the time you have left while on active duty. Maybe a better pathway for you if you are just getting started would be to attend a local community college and begin working toward the credit you will need in order to finish at a school back home. You cannot go wrong by starting with general education classes: math, English, arts and humanities, social and behavioral sciences, and sciences.

If this is the case, contact the four-year university you are interested in attending and obtain a degree plan for its recommended academic pathway, then bring that plan with you to meet the education counselor. He or she will help you find a college you can attend while on active duty that will enable you to fulfill the prescribed parameters. Typically, a state community college will provide you with the safest transfer credit. After you find a local school to attend, you will need to contact the future school and ask about transfer-ability of the credits. Many schools have strict transfer guidelines you must abide by.

Many teacher-credentialing programs take more time than just a bache-lor's degree, but some do not. Check with the schools in the state where you want to earn a credential to determine the proper pathway. You might prefer to complete a master's degree with an attached credentialing program. Typi-cally, a master's degree will earn you more money as a teacher. You may get an extra yearly stipend, it may push you up the pay scale because it is college credit beyond a bachelor's degree, or you may receive a combination of both.

Both GI Bills only afford you thirty-six months of benefit, so you may not have enough to finish a full bachelor's degree and a credentialing program. Think ahead! Whatever you accomplish while you are still on active duty leaves less to do after you separate. This pathway will save you time, money, and potentially some GI Bill benefit to use toward a master's degree later. Many of the clients I (Jillian) have worked with prefer to finish their bache-lor's degree while on active duty (if possible), then, use their GI Bill for a master's degree and/or a credentialing program after separation.

If you are a veteran and have already exhausted your GI Bill, TTT may give you the money you need to pursue a teacher credential.

Chapter Nine

Vocational Programs

Not all soldiers want to pursue traditional education. Some prefer vocational training that might include an apprenticeship or on-the-job training pathway. The GI Bills offer great flexibility in the different types of programs that the benefits can be applied toward. Some service members want to pursue career fields similar to the job they have been holding while in the military, but civilian sector credentials or training are needed. Many of these same individuals are surprised to find out that their benefits can cover these pathways as well. More information on both pathways can be found on the GI Bill website: http://www.benefits.va.gov/gibill/onthejob_apprenticeship.asp. This chapter includes information on the following topics:

- On-the-Job Training/Apprenticeship Programs
- GI Bills and Training

ON-THE-JOB TRAINING AND APPRENTICESHIP PROGRAMS

On-the-Job Training

Some companies use on-the-job training (OJT) to tailor their workforce needs and others use it to enhance an individual's preexisting skill set. Typically, a combination of tactics is used to train employees to operate functionally in their new or changing environment. OJT is one strategy that is used in almost all instances, for blue-collar and white-collar job positions, and is designed to help hire and train employees who might not already possess the required knowledge for the position.

Think about your time in the military. You were trained to do a specific task, then sent to your duty station. Did your new duty station operate exactly like the school where you learned your new skill, or did you need to have OJT to learn how to function properly within your new unit? The same strategy is often used in the civilian workforce. For example, you might already know how to install and maintain cable systems, but if you take that skill set to a civilian company, they will want to train you to their standards.

Employers and employees reap numerous benefits from participating in OJT. OJT allows companies to use their preexisting environment to train new employees while instilling performance expectations at the same time. It is cost-effective, increases productivity, and produces employees that are taught to company-driven standards. Employers training employees using OJT promote a good public image through their commitment to the community, help create a more skilled workforce, and see immediate return on their investment. The skills, knowledge, and competencies that are needed to perform a specific job within a specific workplace are delivered from day one, typically by another employee or mentor (mandatory for the GI Bills) who can already perform his or her duties competently. Sometimes, special training rooms or equipment are used to demonstrate performance parameters. OJT is not like an apprenticeship program, because it does not have an instructional portion that requires you to attend classes. Many apprenticeship programs are covered by the GI Bills and will be discussed in the next section.

Employees also benefit from OJT. They begin earning wages as they learn a new skill, gain job experience, and develop a new marketable skill set often by earning certifications or journeyman standing. Productivity is increased on both sides as training progresses, as does trust as relationships develop through teamwork.

Some potential fields of employment for OJT are heating and air-conditioning, law enforcement, welding, electrical work, machinist, tool and die maker, construction, and auto mechanics. If you are looking for a program that is VA approved, contact the state approving agency at http://www.nasaa-vetseducation.com/Contacts.aspx, or search participating employers on the US Department of Veterans Affairs site (http://department-of-veterans-affairs.github.io/gi-bill-comparison-tool/).

If you were recently hired at a new job, and your employer does not currently participate in OJT programs with the VA, contact the State Approving Agency (http://www.nasaa-vetseducation.com/Contacts.aspx) to determine if it is possible to facilitate your OJT with the GI Bill. The State Approving Authority within each state approves OJT programs within its borders.

Apprenticeship Programs

The US Department of Labor (DOL) oversees registered apprenticeship programs through its Employment and Training section. According to the DOL:

Registered Apprenticeship programs meet the skilled workforce needs of American industry, training millions of qualified individuals for lifelong careers since 1937. Registered Apprenticeship helps mobilize America's workforce with structured, on-the-job training in traditional industries such as construction and manufacturing, as well as new high-growth industries such as health care, information technology, energy, telecommunications, advanced manufacturing and more. [1]

The DOL uses this department to connect potential employees to employers by working with a variety of different companies and organizations, such as community colleges, labor organizations, and state workforce agencies. The federal program has regional contacts in almost every state that can be found here: http://www.doleta.gov/oa/regdirlist.cfm. State-based apprenticeship searches on the DOL site can be conducted here: http://oa.doleta.gov/bat.cfm?start.

Like OJT, the GI Bills can be used toward apprenticeship training. Programs can last anywhere from one to six years, although most are geared toward four years, depending upon the technical field, and you work under a tradesman during that time before you earn the same status. Assessments throughout the program, mandatory testing, and work inspection conducted by a master tradesman are part of the apprenticeship process. Formal classroom training is part of an apprenticeship. Classes typically include general education, such as math and English, and classes pertaining to technical theory and applied skills. State-mandated licensing for many fields, such as plumbing, can demand numerous study hours and formal preparation prior to testing.

Apprenticeship programs are common in trades that are skill based, such as welding, construction, and electrical work. Often skilled trades require formal licensure, which is obtained partly by working under a journeyman within the field. This is only the starting point; journeyman and master tradesman are the following two steps. Apprentices are overseen by a journeyman or master tradesman, who ultimately is responsible for your work at that time. The goal, over time and with continuing education, is to reach journeyman or master tradesman status. High-level tradesman status leads to higher pay.

Registered apprenticeship participants receive pay starting from the first day of the program. This pay will grow over time as the apprentice learns more skill. Many programs have mandatory college classes, usually at the local community college, built into the program. Typically, these classes are paid for by the employer. Participants in apprenticeship programs often finish without any education debt. Completing a registered apprenticeship program earns participants certification that is recognized across the country, making them highly portable career fields.

Apprenticeable occupations come in all shapes and sizes, including airfield management, automobile mechanic, welder, and cabinetmaker. Major companies such as UPS, CVS, Simplex-Grinnell, Werner Enterprises, and CN (railways) provide apprenticeship opportunities. Green technology has a bright future for growth. Areas such as recycling in the green technology field have some of the fastest-growing apprenticeship programs. Wind turbine technicians, hydrologists, and toxic waste cleanup specialists are all in demand.

The American Apprenticeship Initiative launched in the fall of 2014. Through this initiative the DOL is making $100 million "available for American Apprenticeship Grants to reward partnerships that help more workers participate in apprenticeships. This competition will help more Americans access this proven path to employment and the middle class: 87 percent of apprentices are employed after completing their programs and the average starting wage for apprenticeship graduates is over $50,000."[2] The new American Apprenticeship Grants competition centers on organizations that create apprenticeships in new, high-growth fields, align them with possibilities for more learning and career progression, and create models that work. More information on the initiative can be found here: http://www.doleta.gov/oa/aag.cfm.

The DOL website has a wealth of information regarding apprenticeship programs (http://www.doleta.gov/oa/). The DOL site has links to search for state apprenticeship agencies, all approved apprenticeship programs, and state-based program sponsors. Contacts can also be found on the National Association of State Approving Agencies website (http://www.nasaa-vetseducation.com/).

Career One Stop, covered in chapter 3 (http://www.careeronestop.org/), is a free resource tool that can help apprentice-seekers find career-based information and training pathways. I (Jillian) often use this resource during my counseling sessions. On the main page there are six main search tabs:

- Explore Careers
- Education and Training
- Resumes and Interviews
- Salary and Benefits
- Job Search
- People and Places to Help

All six sections host valuable information for apprentice-seekers, but "Education and Training" is most informative regarding the topic at hand. After selecting "Education and Training" choose the "Apprenticeships" tab. This section allows for detailed exploration of apprenticeships including work option videos, a state-based search site, information from the DOL, and a local job center search. Users can even target specific states for their apprenticeship research.

GI BILLS AND TRAINING

Either the Montgomery GI Bill (MGIB) or Post-9/11 may be used for OJT. If you qualify for both, double-check with the institution within which you plan to work to determine the best pathway, or contact the VA directly (888-GIBILL-1).

The Post-9/11 GI Bill pays a scaled monthly housing allowance (MHA) if you are accepted into an eligible OJT or apprenticeship program. You will earn wages as well from the company training you, although normally wages are low while participating in OJT because both OJT and apprenticeship pay are usually not a percentage of (or related to) journeyman pay.

Post-9/11 payments for apprenticeship programs are:

- 100 percent of your applicable MHA for the first six months of training
- 80 percent of your applicable MHA for the second six months of training
- 60 percent of your applicable MHA for the third six months of training
- 40 percent of your applicable MHA for the fourth six months of training
- 20 percent of your applicable MHA for the remainder of the training

As your wages increase, the GI Bill payments decrease. A maximum of $83 per month for a book stipend can also be received during training.

MGIB payments as of October 1, 2014, were:

- First six months: $1,287.75
- Second six months: $944.35
- Remaining training time: $600.95

The VA maintains rules pertaining to how OJT must be run and whether a program is or can be eligible. For example, the length of the OJT program should be equivalent to what is normally required (for civilians), and the program must encompass the knowledge and skills demanded for the position. Participants should earn wages equal to a civilian partaking in the same program, and starting wages should be set with consideration of the previous experience of the participant. All records of the program need to be kept adequately and orderly to verify training with the VA.

Using the GI Bill for OJT purposes is not allowed while on active duty, nor can spouses who have had GI Bill benefits transferred to them participate.

Most states list the available OJT and apprenticeship programs for residents on the state government website. Look through the DOL section as well as the state VA website. You can also contact your VA Regional Office for help (http://www2.va.gov/directory/guide/map_flsh.asp). On the National Association of State Approving Agencies (NASAA) website (http://www.nasaa-vetseducation.com/), under the "Programs" tab, you can search approved education and training programs, which include universities, certificate programs, flight school, correspondence school, and OJT-approved programs. You can also access the approved license and certification programs and approved national exams lists.

Chapter Ten

VA Programs

The VA has several little-known programs available for veterans. Always check your eligibility because many stipulations apply, such as the disability rating for vocational rehabilitation. These programs may help you with academic preparation and support for school, funding sources for school, and part-time work. The following programs are discussed in this chapter:

- Veterans Upward Bound
- Vocational Rehabilitation and Employment
- VA Work-Study
- GI Bill Tutorial Assistance

VETERANS UPWARD BOUND

Veterans Upward Bound (VUB; http://www.navub.org/) is a US Department of Education program that assists and promotes veteran success within higher education. The free program aids veteran students who have not been to school for a long time, or simply need a refresher by assisting in academic preparation. The programs are conducted on college campuses. "The primary goal of the program is to increase the rate at which participants enroll in and complete postsecondary education programs."[1]

Participants in VUB may receive academic skills assessment and refresher courses to enhance their college-level skills. The courses consist of subjects such as math, science, English, computers, and foreign languages. Veteran education services may also be available—for example, assistance completing college admissions applications or GI Bill applications, academic advising, tutoring, or cultural field trips.

In order to qualify, veterans must:

- Have completed a minimum of 180 days of active service, or have been discharged prior to that point because of a service-connected disability *or* have been with a reserve component that served on active duty on or after September 11, 2001, for a contingency operation
- Have any discharge other than dishonorable
- Be low income (based upon family income and number of household dependents) *or* be a first-generation college student (parents do not have degrees)

If you feel that your school-based skills are rusty, VUB will help boost the deficient areas. Participating in a program will create a more solid foundation for you to begin your studies and achieve success.

Not every school hosts a VUB program, but you can attend a program at a school where you are not enrolled as a student. To find a VUB program in a specific state, check http://www.navub.org/VUB-Program-Information.html and contact the program director. Information about the program can also be found on the Department of Education's website, http://www2.ed.gov/programs/triovub/index.html.

VOCATIONAL REHABILITATION AND EMPLOYMENT

The VA Vocational Rehabilitation and Employment program (commonly referred to as "Voc Rehab"; http://www.benefits.va.gov/vocrehab/index.asp) may assist eligible service-connected veterans with job training, job skills, education, or employment accommodations. The ultimate goal of Voc Rehab is to make you as employable as possible considering any potential limitations of your disability. Voc Rehab counselors will work with individuals to determine career interests, skills, and existing abilities. They will help participants find jobs, on-the-job training, or apprenticeship programs. Formal education through an institution of higher learning might also be a necessary component to the retraining program.

Veterans with severe disabilities can seek assistance through Voc Rehab to find help for independent living. Voc Rehab often pays for new laptops for studying or equipment and uniforms needed for school. I (Paul) was working with a staff sergeant who suffered from memory loss due to traumatic brain injury. Voc Rehab paid for a $150 "smartpen" that captures both handwriting and audio during usage that can be converted into digital text on a computer. This allowed the veteran to organize and maintain his classroom notes more effectively, which assisted him in completing assignments for his classes and promoted long-term success.

Voc Rehab can be a very generous program, but remember that all benefits are meant to lead to successful employment in the field of your choice.

Sometimes, employment plans are not justifiable and must be modified. The Voc Rehab office has complete control over funding. You will not have the complete freedom to choose any school or program you wish to attend like you would with eligible institutions under the MGIB and Post-9/11 GI Bills.

Eligible service members must meet the following parameters:

- If still on active duty, must be expecting to receive an honorable discharge, becoming service connected at a minimum of 20 percent.
- Veterans must receive a discharge that is anything other than dishonorable, and receive a VA service-connected rating of 10 percent or higher or a memorandum rating of 20 percent or higher.

After a veteran receives a service-connected rating, he or she must apply for Voc Rehab and schedule an appointment with a counselor. The vocational rehabilitation counselors (VRCs) will complete an evaluation to determine final eligibility. If eligible, the VRC and the veteran will work together to determine the appropriate retraining pathway for the desired career outcome.

Potentially, Voc Rehab can cover far more than any of the current GI Bill benefits in regard to education. The program also comes with a subsistence rate that is similar to a traditional Basic Allowance for Housing (BAH), but this allowance is not particularly generous. Currently, the monthly amount is $594.47 plus $63.34 per dependent. If education is part of your Voc Rehab program you can opt to switch to the Post-9/11 GI Bill and borrow its Monthly Housing Allowance (MHA) to replace the Voc Rehab subsistence rate while attending school. Combining the two programs in this manner is very often the best way to maximize the total amount of money that can be made while attending school.

To apply for Voc Rehab, visit the VONAPP website (under the "Apply for Benefits" tab) on eBenefits (http://www.vba.va.gov/pubs/forms/VBA-28-1900-ARE.pdf) and fill out Vocational Rehabilitation Form 28-1900. .

VA WORK-STUDY

VA Work-Study is a part-time work program available to veterans who currently attend school at the three-quarter pursuit rate or higher. The program offers an opportunity for veteran students to earn money while pursuing education. Work-Study payments are tax free. Participants work within a community of peers and build skills for résumés. All services rendered within the program relate to work within the VA. Eligible participants may not exceed 750 hours of VA Work-Study per fiscal year and are paid based upon fifty-hour increments.

Selected participants receive the federal minimum wage or state minimum wage, depending on which is greater. Sometimes, positions at colleges or universities are paid an extra amount by the school to make up the difference in pay between the institution and the VA Work-Study program.

Students are placed in a variety of positions depending upon availability, institution of attendance, and local VA facilities, such as Department of Veterans Affairs (DVA) regional offices or DVA medical offices. Priority may be given to veterans who have disability ratings of 30 percent or higher. Selection depends on factors such as job availability and a student's ability to complete the contract prior to exhausting his or her education benefits. Positions can include processing VA documents, assisting in VA information dispersal at educational institutions, and working at a local VA facility.

Veterans must be using one of the following programs in order to be eligible:

- Post-9/11 (including dependents using transferred entitlement)
- Montgomery GI Bill (MGIB) active or reserve
- Raising the Educational Achievement of Paraprofessionals (REAP)
- Post–Vietnam Era Veterans' Educational Assistance Program
- Dependents' Educational Assistance Program
- Dependents who are eligible under Chapter 35 may use Work-Study only while training in a state.
- Vocational Rehabilitation

To apply for VA Work-Study, visit the VA link at http://www.vba.va.gov/pubs/forms/VBA-22-8691-ARE.pdf or check with your local processing center at http://www.gibill.va.gov/contact/regional_offices/index.html.

GI BILL TUTORIAL ASSISTANCE

If you are a veteran and you are having trouble in one of your classes, tutorial assistance is available under MGIB and Post-9/11. Veterans eligible for this assistance have a deficiency in a subject or prerequisite subject that is required for their degree plan. The assistance is a supplement to your selected GI Bill. To be eligible, you must be pursuing education at a 50 percent or greater rate, have a deficiency, and be enrolled in the class during the term in which you are pursuing tutoring.

The cost cannot exceed $100 per month or the cost of the tutoring if less than $100. If the eligible student is under MGIB, there is no charge to the entitlement for the first $600 of tutoring received. If the eligible student elected the Post-9/11 GI Bill, there is no entitlement charge.

VA Form 22-1990t, "Application and Enrollment Certification for Individualized Tutorial Assistance," must be completed by the eligible student, the tutor, and the VA certifying official to apply for the benefit. The form must be signed, dated, and filled out either monthly or after a combination of months.

More information can be found on the VA website, http://www.benefits.va.gov/gibill/tutorial_assistance.asp. For application and enrollment certification for individualized tutorial assistance, see http://www.vba.va.gov/pubs/forms/VBA-22-1990t-ARE.pdf.

Chapter Eleven

Other Service Member and Spousal-Based Programs/Organizations

Many programs are available for veterans and dependents to assist in education and career development. Some of the programs are volunteer-based, others are run on set schedules through institutions of higher learning. Several service members I know (Jillian) have gone through the programs listed in this chapter, and all speak highly of their experiences.

In this chapter, we will discuss:

- Programs available for active-duty personnel, veterans, and dependents
- Military Spouse Career Advancement Accounts
- General advice for spouses

PROGRAMS AVAILABLE FOR ACTIVE-DUTY PERSONNEL, VETERANS, AND DEPENDENTS

I (Jillian) have run across a few organizations and programs that service members have found especially beneficial over the past few years. I am sure many more wonderful programs are available, but these are the few I use almost daily. Usually, we discuss the organizations that have been around for a while, such as the Veterans of Foreign Wars, Disabled American Veterans, and American Veterans, mainly because the organizations have very established, credible programs.

Volunteering is a great way for veterans to continue to serve after they leave the service and build skills for their résumés. Staying active with others in the community can give veterans a sense of purpose. Many service members I counsel enjoy volunteering after separating from the service and sometimes while still on active duty.

Often younger service members prefer some of the newer organizations, such as the Iraq and Afghanistan Veterans of America (IAVA), which cater more specifically to Iraq and Afghanistan veterans. Team Rubicon and The Mission Continues are interesting possibilities for those interested in hands-on participation; those programs handle disaster relief and community building.

The first few organizations listed in this section offer services and programs for veterans. The last few are volunteer-based organizations.

Syracuse University Institute for Veterans and Military Families (IVMF)

http://vets.syr.edu/

Syracuse University, partnered with JPMorgan Chase & Co., has several programs available through the IVMF to assist transitioning Post-9/11 service members with future career plans depending upon their interests and pursuits. Many of the programs consist of free online courses that users can access from any location at any time to promote veteran preparedness and understanding of the civilian sector. Other courses are offered in a face-to-face format that lasts roughly two weeks, and they are now available in several different locations. IVMF offers courses for veterans, active-duty soldiers, active-duty spouses, and disabled veterans.

The programs currently offered by IVMF include the following:

- EBV: Entrepreneurship Bootcamp for Veterans with Disabilities
- EBV-F: Entrepreneurship Bootcamp for Veterans' Families (caregivers and family members)
- V-WISE: Veteran Women Igniting the Spirit of Entrepreneurship for veteran women, female active-duty service members, and female family members
- E&G: Operation Endure & Grow for Guard and reserve members and family
- B2B: Operation Boots to Business: From Service to Startup for transitioning service members
- Veterans' Career Transition Program: Great program for active-duty personnel to gain industry-level certificates in high-demand career fields.

Entrepreneurship Bootcamp for Veterans with Disabilities (EBV)

http://ebv.vets.syr.edu/

EBV is designed to help Post-9/11 veterans with service-connected disabilities in the entrepreneurship and small business management fields. Syracuse University, Texas A&M, Purdue University, UCLA, University of Connecticut, Louisiana State University, Florida State University, and Cornell

University currently participate. EBV promotes long-term success for qualified veterans by teaching them how to create and sustain their entrepreneurial ventures (http://whitman.syr.edu/ebv/). All costs associated with EBV are covered by the program, including travel and lodging.

Entrepreneurship Bootcamp for Veterans' Families (EBV-F)

http://vets.syr.edu/education/ebv-f/

EBV-F is offered through Syracuse University's Whitman School of Management and the Florida State University College of Business. The cost-free (including travel and lodging) one-week program assists family members in their pursuit to launch and maintain small businesses.

Eligible spouses include the following:

- A spouse, parent, sibling, or adult child who has a role supporting the veteran (health, education, work, etc.)
- A surviving spouse or adult child of a service member who died while serving after September 11, 2001
- An active-duty service member's spouse

Veteran Women Igniting the Spirit of Enterpriseship (V-Wise)

http://whitman.syr.edu/vwise/

V-Wise is a joint venture with the US Small Business Administration (SBA). The program helps female veterans along the entrepreneurship and small business pathway by arming them with savvy business skills that enable them to turn business ideas into growing ventures. Business planning, marketing, accounting, operations, and human resources are covered. The three-phase approach consists of a fifteen-day online course teaching basic entrepreneurial skills, a three-day conference with two tracks (for startups or those already in business), and delivery of a comprehensive listing packet that details the community-level resources available to participants.

Eligible participants are honorably separated female veterans from any branch of the military from any time. Female spouses or partners of veteran business owners are eligible as well. Hotel rooms and taxes are covered, but other fees apply, such as travel.

Endure & Grow

http://vets.syr.edu/education/endure-grow/

Operation Endure & Grow is a free online training program open to National Guard, reservists, and their family members. The program has two tracks, one for startups and the other for those who have been in business for more than three years. The tracks are designed to assist participants in creating a new business and all related fundamentals, or to help an operating business stimulate growth.

Operation Boots to Business: From Service to Startup (B2B)

http://boots2business.org/

B2B is a partnership with the Syracuse University Whitman School of Business and the SBA. The program goal is to train transitioning service members to be business owners through three phases. Phases 1 and 2 are taken while the service member is still on active duty, preparing to transition to the civilian world, and attending the Transition Readiness Seminar (TRS). The third phase is accessible if veterans elect to continue and consists of an intensive instructor-led eight-week online "mini"-MBA. Active-duty service members and their spouses or partners are eligible to participate in B2B during the separation process. The entire B2B program is free. Speak to your career planner about electing the Entrepreneurship Pathway during TRS.

Veterans' Career Transition Program (VCTP)

http://vets.syr.edu/education/employment-programs/

The VCTP offers numerous classes for career training and preparation. Many of the courses lead to high-demand industry-level certifications. This free online program is available to eligible Post-9/11 veterans. The program is geared to help veterans understand corporate culture in the civilian business world. VCTP is a three-track program that includes professional skills, tech, and independent study tracks.

The professional skills track aims at training veterans in "soft" skills—mainly how to prepare for and implement job searches by conducting company research and creating cover letters and résumés. Foundations for advanced-level courses in Microsoft Office Word, Excel, PowerPoint, and Outlook can be achieved within this track. If a veteran participates in this track, he or she becomes an official Syracuse University student and receives a non-credit-based certificate upon completion.

The tech track is geared to prepare participants for careers in operations or information technology (IT). Industry-level certifications are offered in this level, and, where applicable, VCTP will cover exam fees. Participants also become Syracuse University students and receive non-credit-awarding certificates upon completion. Certificates include proficiency in subject areas such as Comp TIA (Server+, Network+, and A+), Oracle Database 11G, CCNA with CCENT certification, and Lean Six Sigma Green Belt.

The independent study track hosts a large library of online coursework. Coursework includes subject matter pertaining to professional and personal development, leadership, IT, and accounting and finance. Coursework is determined by veterans' demands and learning needs. Students will not be considered Syracuse University students. Veterans must be within eighteen months of their date of separation (front or back) to be eligible. Active-duty spouses and spouses of eligible veterans are now eligible as well.

American Corporate Partners (ACP)

http://www.acp-usa.org/
http://www.acp-advisornet.org

American Corporate Partners is a New York City–based national non-profit organization founded in 2008 to help veterans transition from active duty into the civilian workforce by enlisting the help of business professionals nationwide. Through mentoring, career counseling, and networking possibilities, ACP's goal is to build greater connections between corporate America and veteran communities. ACP has two available programs: ACP AdvisorNet, which is open to service members and their immediate family members; and a one-on-one mentoring program for Post-9/11 veterans. ACP AdvisorNet is an online business community that offers veterans and immediate family members online career advice through Q&A discussions. The mentoring program connects employees from ACP's participating institutions with veterans or their spouses for mentoring options, networking assistance, and career development. More than fifty major companies are participating in ACP's mentoring program, and success stories and videos are available on ACP's website.

Hiring Our Heroes

http://www.uschamber.com/hiringourheroes

The US Chamber of Commerce Foundation launched Hiring Our Heroes in 2011 to help veterans and spouses of active-duty service members find employment. The program works with state and local chambers as well as partners in the public, private, and nonprofit sectors. Hiring Our Heroes hosts career fairs at military bases. The program offers transition assistance, personal branding, and résumé workshops.

Google for Veterans and Families

http://www.googleforveterans.com/

Google offers a wide range of help for active-duty and veteran military members. It has tools to help families stay in touch during deployments, record military deployments, explore life after service (including résumé-building opportunities), and connect with other veterans.

VetNet on Google+

https://plus.google.com/+VetNetHQ

VetNet was launched by the US Chamber of Commerce's Hiring Our Heroes program, the IVMF, and Hire Heroes USA as a partnership program. The program is set up similar to the TRS with different pathways designed to help transitioning service members find a more tailored approach to their specific needs. VetNet has three different pathways depending upon your goals: basic training, career connections, and entrepreneur. The site hosts live events and video seminars designed to provide information from those who have gone before them and to generate group discussions about civilian career and entrepreneur challenges. You can find many VetNet videos on YouTube.

Iraq and Afghanistan Veterans of America (IAVA)

http://iava.org/

IAVA offers service members another way to maintain the brotherhood while actively participating in an organization that promotes veteran well-being. The nonprofit, nonpartisan organization is strictly for veterans of the Iraq and Afghanistan campaigns. IAVA actively generates support for veteran-based policies at the local and federal levels while assisting members through programs related to health, employment, education, and community resources. Its aim is to empower veterans who will be future leaders in our communities.

IAVA sponsors several academic and career-related programs for its members. Many of the Marines I work with have sought out IAVA for assistance. One active-duty E-7 I worked with was accepted to the Culinary Command program offered through IAVA's Rucksack. Culinary Command is a six-week, intensive, top-tier culinary arts program in New York with all costs covered, including travel and accommodations. Many other interesting programs are available for participation, including the War Writer's Campaign (http://www.warwriterscampaign.org/), my personal favorite. Programs are offered for online or on-the-ground participation depending upon members' needs.

The Mission Continues

http://missioncontinues.org/

The Mission Continues promotes community service and brotherhood through fellowships with local nonprofit organizations. The program empowers veterans to achieve post-fellowship full-time employment or pursue higher education while continuing a relationship with public service. Fellowships last for six months at twenty hours per week, and fellows receive a living stipend. The program also aims to bridge the military-civilian divide and allow veterans to connect with the community to feel a sense of belonging.

Team Rubicon

http://teamrubiconusa.org/

Team Rubicon unites veterans in a shared sense of purpose through disaster relief assistance by using the skills they have learned in the military. Volunteering veterans reintegrate into society and give back to communities in desperate need. Veterans are the perfect group of trained individuals to cope with the destruction seen in many places hit by natural disasters because many of the circumstances are similar to the conditions that service members were trained to handle while on active duty. Team Rubicon uses the combat skills that many veterans have already cultivated to facilitate greater momentum during disaster relief operations.

The Veterans Posse Foundation

http://www.possefoundation.org/veterans-posse-program

The Veterans Posse Program aims to support veterans who are interested in attending bachelor's degree programs at prestigious institutions across the country. The program creates cohorts of veterans and prepares them to matriculate into select schools. The Veterans Posse Program is currently working with Vassar College, Dartmouth College, and Wesleyan University. Selectees will attend a month-long, all-inclusive, precollege summer training program designed to foster leadership and academic excellence. The schools then guarantee that selectees' full tuition will be covered even after GI Bill and the Yellow Ribbon Program funding run out.

Warrior-Scholar Project

http://www.warrior-scholar.org

The Warrior-Scholar Project is a two-week intensive program designed to promote veteran academic success. Through classes, workshops, discussions, and one-on-one tutoring sessions, veterans are taught how to transition into higher education, challenged to become leaders in their classes at their institutions, and prepared to overcome challenges and embrace new learning experiences. Yale, Harvard, and the University of Michigan host the program. Be aware that some cost is involved with this program.

Student Veterans of America (SVA)

http://www.studentveterans.org/

The SVA organization is a nonprofit designed to help veterans succeed in higher education. Groups of student veterans on school campuses across the country have gotten together to create member chapters. The goal of these chapters is to help veterans acculturate to college life by offering peer-to-peer support. Chapters organize activities and offer networking opportunities.

SVA develops partnerships with other organizations that also aim to promote veteran academic success. Through these partnerships, the SVA has helped to create several new scholarship opportunities. In late 2014 the organization created its one thousandth chapter on a college campus in the United States. According to the Council for Higher Education Accreditation, there are about 8,300 campuses in the United States, so there is a one-in-eight chance that your future school will have a chapter.[1] Even if it does not, you can always organize and start your own. Check the website for more information.

MILITARY SPOUSE CAREER ADVANCEMENT ACCOUNTS (MYCAA)

https://aiportal.acc.af.mil/mycaa

Military One Source facilitates the MyCAA program. The program offers $4,000 to eligible spouses of active-duty military members to be used for education, either traditional or nontraditional. MyCAA is good for an associate degree, a certification, or a license. The program cannot be used toward a bachelor's degree, but it can be used for programs after a spouse receives a bachelor's degree. For example, I (Jillian) used the program for a supplementary teaching credential offered through the University of California, San Diego, after completing a master's degree in education when I qualified through my husband's rank.

MyCAA aims to increase the portable career skills of active-duty service members' spouses by developing their professional credentials to help them find and maintain work. Military One Source counselors can help eligible spouses find specific programs or schools that participate in the program. Counselors can also help spouses identify local sources of assistance, such as state and local financial assistance, transportation, and child care. They can also help with employment referrals.

Eligible spouses must be married to active-duty service members in the following ranks:

- E1–E5
- O1–O2
- WO1–CWO2

MyCAA will *not* cover the following:

- Prior courses
- Books, supplies, student activities, and the like
- Prepayment deposits
- Audited courses or internships
- Nonacademic or ungraded courses
- Courses taken more than one time
- College-Level Examination Program or DSST exams
- Associate of arts degrees in general studies or liberal arts
- Personal enrichment courses
- Transportation, lodging, and child care
- Course extensions
- Study abroad

To apply, visit https://aiportal.acc.af.mil/mycaa or call (800) 342-9647 to speak with a Military One Source Counselor.

GENERAL ADVICE FOR SPOUSES

Unfortunately, besides MyCAA, no other direct financial assistance is available for spouses to pursue their education. If spouses are just beginning their education and willing to attend the local community college, MyCAA will typically cover an associate degree, depending upon the cost of the school. Many community colleges offer associate degrees fully online, which may also offer spouses with children more flexibility.

Past the associate degree, scholarship options (see the "Scholarships" section in chapter 6) and in a few cases transferring GI Bill benefits from the active-duty spouse are the best bets. Many universities and colleges offer tuition discounts to spouses of active-duty service members but usually not enough to fully alleviate the financial burden.

Spouses should also apply for Federal Student Aid through the Free Application for Federal Student Aid. More information on Federal Student Aid can be found in chapter 6. Many spouses receive all or a portion of the Pell Grant money (see the "Federal Student Aid" section in chapter 6), which does not need to be paid back.

Spouses are entitled to receive in-state tuition rates at state schools in whatever state they are stationed with their active-duty service member. The

Higher Education Opportunity Act (H.R. 4137) signed into law on August 14, 2008, guarantees this benefit. This law eliminates all out-of-state tuition fees and at least eases the financial burden of pursuing higher education. Be aware that many schools will want to see a copy of the service members' orders to verify in-state tuition.

Some states offer low-income tuition waivers to residents, usually through the state-based community colleges. Because spouses are eligible for in-state tuition (as are active-duty service members), they may be eligible for this type of waiver as well.

For example, California offers the Board of Governor's Fee Waiver (see http://home.cccapply.org/money/bog-fee-waiver) through the state community colleges. Many spouses stationed in California with their active-duty service member are attending community colleges in California and receiving this waiver, and they do not pay to attend school. In fact, many soldiers receive this waiver as well and are not bound by the rules of Tuition Assistance.

Always check with the local community colleges first if you are a spouse and are just getting started. In most cases, it is hard to beat their low tuition rates and the flexible class offerings. Community colleges typically also offer vocational programs at drastically reduced prices when compared to private institutions. They should be your number one starting point!

The Officers' Spouses' Clubs on the different bases offer scholarships for the dependents of soldiers. If you can write an essay and watch the deadline dates, that is usually a decent option for a funding source. As a last resort, you may want to discuss GI Bill transferability with an education counselor at your base. Just remember, if you go that route, your active-duty spouse will not have those benefits later. For more information regarding eligibility and the process to transfer the GI Bill, see chapter 6.

Transferring the GI Bill to a spouse so that he or she can use it while the service member is on active duty is not the best option in most cases. Spouses are not eligible for the housing stipend while the soldier is still actively serving, but children are eligible. For example, consider the following case:

A soldier transfers his GI Bill to his spouse while still active duty. She uses the benefit to attend California State University, San Marcos. Although she will receive the book stipend, she will not receive the housing allowance. Her school is paid for, and she has some extra money for books. Another soldier transfers his GI Bill to his daughter. His daughter attends the same institution and receives the book stipend as well as the housing stipend, which is currently $2,052 per month. At the end of a nine-month school year, the monthly stipend totals $18,468. That is the amount of money the spouse did *not* get while using the benefit. Now consider the same monthly amount (even though it receives cost-of-living adjustments) over a four-year bachelor's degree: $73,872.

For this reason, only in very few circumstances do I recommend spouses using transferred GI Bill benefits while the soldier is still on active duty. Obviously, this does not take into account different variables. For example, did the soldier attain the degree through the use of Tuition Assistance funds while on active duty or do they need GI Bill benefits to reach degree completion upon transition out of the service? Remember, any benefits that a soldier transfers to a spouse or child are benefits that they do not have for their own education after separation from the service. Maybe the couple does not plan to have children, maybe the soldier has attained the maximum level of education he or she is interested in pursuing, or maybe the children are very young and the spouse has no other funding resources. In the end, the decision is personal and all outlets should be pursued.

Appendix A
Commonly Used Acronyms

AAS: Associate of Applied Science
ACE: American Council on Education
ACF: Army College Fund
AECP: AMEDD Enlisted Commissioning Program
AKO: Army Knowledge Online
AMEDD: Army Medical Department
AMVETS: American Veterans
APFT: Army Physical Fitness Test
ATRRS: Army Training Requirements and Resources System Transcript
BOG Waiver: Board of Governors Waiver
BSN: Bachelor of Science in Nursing
CAC: Common Access Card
CC: Community College
CE: Certified Enrollment
COA: Cost of Attendance
COE: Certificate of Eligibility
COOL: Credentialing Opportunities On-Line
CRM: Customer Relationship Management
DEERS: Defense Enrollment Eligibility Reporting System
DFAS: Defense Finance and Accounting Service
DNS: Degree Network System
DOE: Department of Education
DOL: Department of Labor
EFC: Expected Family Contribution
FAFSA: Free Application for Federal Student Aid
FSA: Federal Student Aid

FTA: Federal Tuition Assistance
G2G: Green to Gold
GPA: Grade Point Average
IAVA: Iraq and Afghanistan Veterans of America
IPAP: Interservice Physician Assistance Program
JST: Joint Services Transcript
LOI: Letter of Instruction
MGIB: Montgomery GI Bill (Chapter 30)
MGIB-SR: Montgomery GI BILL Selected Reserve (Chapter 1606)
MHA: Monthly Housing Allowance
MOS: Military Occupational Specialty
MSEP: Midwest Student Exchange Program
MSW: Master of Social Work
OCS: Officer Candidate School
OJT: On-the-Job Training
PCS: Permanent Change of Station
REAP: Reserve Education Assistance Program (Chapter 1607)
S1: Personnel Office
SH: Semester Hours
SME: Subject Matter Expert
SOC: Servicemembers Opportunity Colleges
SOCAD: Servicemembers Opportunity Colleges Army Degrees
STA: State Tuition Assistance
SVA: Student Veterans of America
TA: Tuition Assistance
USMA: United States Military Academy (West Point)
USUHS: Uniform Services University of Health Science
VA: Veterans Administration
VFW: Veterans of Foreign Wars
VONAPP: Veterans Online Application
VOTECH: Vocational Technical
VUB: Veterans Upward Bound
YRP: Yellow Ribbon Program

Appendix B
Resources

REGIONAL ACCREDITING BODIES

Middle States Association of Colleges and Schools: http://www.msche.org/

New England Association of School and Colleges: http://cihe.neasc.org/

North Central Association of Colleges and Schools: http://www.ncahlc.org/

Northwest Commission on Colleges and Universities: http://www.nwccu.org

Southern Association of Colleges and Schools: http://www.sacscoc.org/

Western Association of Schools and Colleges, Accrediting Commission for Community and Junior Colleges: http://www.accjc.org

Western Association of Schools and Colleges, Accrediting Commission for Senior Colleges and Universities: http://www.wascweb.org/

NOTABLE NATIONALLY ACCREDITING BODIES

Accrediting Commission of Career Schools and Colleges: http://www.accsc.org

Council on Occupational and Education: http://www.council.org

Distance Education Accrediting Commission: http://www.deac.org

OTHER RESOURCES

American Apprenticeship Grants: http://www.doleta.gov/oa/aag.cfm

American College Testing (ACT): http://www.act.org

American Corporate Partners (ACP): http://www.acp-usa.org/, www.acpadvisornet.org

American Council on Education: http://www.acenet.edu

American Legion: http://www.legion.org/

American Medical College: www.amcas.org

American Psychological Association (APA): http://www.apa.org

American Veterans (AmVets): http://www.amvets.org/

Army COOL: http://www.cool.army.mil

Army Knowledge online: https://www.us.army.mil/

Army OCS: http://www.goarmy.com/ocs.html

Army Recruiters: http://www.goarmy.com/locate-a-recruiter.html

Army ROTC: http://www.goarmy.com/rotc.html

Bureau of Labor Statistics Occupational Outlook Handbook: http://www.bls.gov/ooh/

California Board of Governors (BOG) Waiver: http://home.cccapply.org/money/bog-fee-waiver

Career One Stop: http://www.careeronestop.org/credentialing/CredentialingHomeReadMore.asp

Career Scope®: http://benefits.va.gov/gibill/careerscope.asp

Cash for College: http://www.calgrants.org/index.cfm?navid=16

College Board College Search: https://bigfuture.collegeboard.org/college-search

College Navigator: http://nces.ed.gov/collegenavigator/

College ScoreCard: http://collegecost.ed.gov/scorecard/index.aspx

Council for Higher Education Accreditation (CHEA): http://www.chea.org/search/default.asp

DANTES Kuder: http://www.dantes.kuder.com/

Defense Language Institute Foreign Language Center (DLIFLC): http://www.dliflc.edu

Department of Labor: http://www.dol.gov /

Direct Commissioning Course (DCC): http://www.benning.army.mil/infantry/199th/dcc

Disabled American Veterans (DAV): http://www.dav.org/

Edvisors, Filing the FAFSA, 2015-2016 Edition Free eBook: https://www.edvisors.com/fafsa/book/direct/

eKnowledge Corporation & NFL Players: http://www.eknowledge.com/military

Federal Student Aid: http://www.fafsa.ed.gov/

Federal Student Aid Pin Site: http://www.pin.ed.gov

GI Bill apprenticeship and OJT: http://www.benefits.va.gov/gibill/onthe-job_apprenticeship.asp

GI Bill Comparison Tool: http://www.benefits.va.gov/gibill/comparison

GI Bill information: http://www.benefits.va.gov/gibill/

GI Bill tutorial assistance: http://www.benefits.va.gov/gibill/tutorial_assistance.asp

GoArmyEd: www.goarmyed.com

Google for Veterans and Families: http://www.googleforveterans.com/

Graduate Management Admission Test (GMAT): http://www.mba.com/us/the-gmat-exam.aspx

Graduate Record Examination (GRE): http://www.ets.org/gre

Grammar Book: http://www.grammarbook.com

Grammar Bytes: http://www.chompchomp.com

Guide to Grammar Writing: http://grammar.ccc.commnet.edu/grammar/

Hiring Our Heroes: http://www.uschamber.com/hiringourheroes

Illinois Veterans Grant: https://www2.illinois.gov/veterans/benefits/Pages/education.aspx

Institutional Accreditation Search: http://ope.ed.gov/accreditation/, http://www.chea.org/search/default.asp, http://nces.ed.gov/collegenavigator/

Iraq and Afghanistan Veterans of America (IAVA): http://iava.org/

Joint Services Transcript: https://jst.doded.mil/

Khan Academy: http://www.khanacademy.org

Know Before You Enroll: http://www.knowbeforeyouenroll.org

Make the Connection: http://maketheconnection.net/

Midwest Student Exchange Program: http://msep.mhec.org/

MilConnect: https://www.dmdc.osd.mil/milconnect/

Military Spouse Career Advancement Accounts (MyCAA): https://aiportal.acc.af.mil/mycaa/Default.aspx

Mission Continues: http://missioncontinues.org/

MOS-related degrees: http://www.soc.aascu.org/socad/ACD.html

My Next Move for Veterans: http://www.mynextmove.org/vets/

National Association of Credential Evaluation Services: http://www.naces.org/

National Association of State Approving Agencies: http://www.nasaa-vetseducation.com/Contacts.aspx

National Student Loan Data System: https://www.nslds.ed.gov

O*NET OnLine: http://www.onetonline.org/

Peterson's: http://www.petersons.com/dantes

Principles of Excellence: http://www.benefits.va.gov/gibill/principles_of_excellence.asp

Purdue Owl: http://owl.english.purdue.edu/owl/

Purple Math: http://www.purplemath.com

Scholastic Aptitude Test (SAT): http://www.collegeboard.org

Servicemembers Opportunity Colleges: http://www.soc.aascu.org/

Servicemembers Civil Relief Act 2014: https://www.dmdc.osd.mil/appj/scra/

States' Departments of Veterans Affairs Offices: http://www.va.gov/statedva.htm

State workforce agencies: http://www.servicelocator.org/OWSLinks.asp

Student Veterans of America: http://www.studentveterans.org

Syracuse University Institute for Veterans and Military Families (IVMF): http://vets.syr.edu/

Team Rubicon: http://teamrubiconusa.org/

Troops to Teachers: http://www.dantes.doded.mil/service-members/troops-to-teachers/index.html

University of San Diego's Veterans' Legal Clinic: http://www.sandiego.edu/veteransclinic/

US Army Medical Department (AMEDD): http://www.cs.amedd.army.mil/

US Department of Defense Memorandum of Understanding: http://www.dodmou.com

US Department of Education—national accrediting agencies: http://ope.ed.gov/accreditation/

US Department of Education College Affordability and Transparency Center: http://collegecost.ed.gov/

US Department of Labor apprenticeship information: http://www.doleta.gov/oa/

US Department of Labor's career search tool: http://www.mynextmove.org/

US Department of Labor unemployment information: http://workforcesecurity.doleta.gov/unemploy/uifactsheet.asp

US Department of Veterans Affairs (VA): http://www.va.gov

VA Education and Career Counseling Program (Chapter 36): http://www.benefits.va.gov/vocrehab/edu_voc_counseling.asp

VA GI Bill Feedback System: http://www.benefits.va.gov/GIBILL/Feedback.asp

VA Regional Centers: http://www.va.gov/directory/guide/map_flsh.asp

VA Vet Centers: http://www.vetcenter.va.gov/index.asp

VA Vocational Rehabilitation: http://www.benefits.va.gov/vocrehab/index.asp

VA Work Study Local Office Search: http://www.gibill.va.gov/contact/regional_offices/index.html

VA Yellow Ribbon Program: http://www.benefits.va.gov/gibill/yellow_ribbon.asp

Veterans Access, Choice, and Accountability Act of 2014: https://veterans.house.gov/the-veterans-access-choice-and-accountability-act-of-2014-highlights

Veterans of Foreign Wars: http://www.vfw.org/

Veterans On-Line Application (VONAPP): http://vabenefits.vba.va.gov/vonapp/

Veterans Posse Foundation: http://www.possefoundation.org/veterans-posse-program

Veterans Upward Bound: http://www.navub.org/

Vet Net on Google+: http://www.vetnethq.com/

Warrior-Scholar Project: http://www.warrior-scholar.org

Wyakin Warrior Foundation: http://www.wyakin.org

APA FORMAT GUIDANCE

American Psychological Association: http://www.apastyle.org

Purdue Owl: https://owl.english.purdue.edu/owl/resourcc/560/01/

CITATION FORMATTING

Citation Machine: http://citationmachine.net/index2.php

KnightCite: https://www.calvin.edu/library/knightcite/

MLA FORMAT GUIDANCE

California State University, Los Angeles: http://web.calstatela.edu/library/guides/3mla.pdf

Cornell University Library: http://www.library.cornell.edu/resrch/citmanage/mla

Purdue Owl: https://owl.english.purdue.edu/owl/resource/747/01/

STATES CURRENTLY WITH IN-STATE TUITION LEGISLATION

Alabama: https://legiscan.com/AL/research/HB424/2014

Arizona: https://dvs.az.gov/services/education

California: https://www.calvet.ca.gov/veteran-services-benefits/education

Colorado: http://highered.colorado.gov/Finance/Residency/requirements.html

Florida: http://www.flsenate.gov/Session/Bill/2014/7015/BillText/er/PDF

Idaho: http://www.legislature.idaho.gov/legislation/2010/S1367.pdf

Illinois: http://www.ilga.gov/legislation/fulltext.asp?DocName=&SessionId=85&GA=98&DocTypeId=HB&DocNum=2353&GAID=12&LegID=74133&SpecSess=&Session=

Indiana: http://www.ilga.gov/legislation/fulltext.asp?DocName=&SessionId=85&GA=98&DocTypeId=HB&DocNum=2353&GAID=12&LegID=74133&SpecSess=&Session=

Kentucky: http://cpe.ky.gov/policies/academicpolicies/residency.htm

Louisiana: http://legiscan.com/LA/text/HB435/id/649958

Maine: http://www.mainelegislature.org/legis/bills/getDoc.asp?id=39934

Maryland: http://www.mhec.state.md.us/highered/acadaff/veterans benefits/MDVAEducationInfo2013.asp

Minnesota: https://www.revisor.mn.gov/statutes/?id=197.775&format= pdf

Missouri: http://www.senate.mo.gov/13info/BTS_Web/Bill.aspx?Session Type=R&BillID=17138567

Nevada: http://leg.state.nv.us/Session/77th2013/Bills/AB/AB260_EN.pdf

New Mexico: http://www.nmlegis.gov/Sessions/09%20Regular/final/ SB0136.pdf

North Dakota: http://www.legis.nd.gov/cencode/t15c10.pdf?2013110615 2541

Ohio: http://veteransaffairs.ohio.gov/

Oregon: https://olis.leg.state.or.us/liz/2013R1/Measures/Text/HB2158/ Enrolled

South Dakota: http://legis.sd.gov/Statutes/Codified_Laws/DisplayStatute. aspx?Type=Statute&Statute=13-53-29.1&cookieCheck=true

Tennessee: http://www.capitol.tn.gov/Bills/108/Bill/SB1433.pdf

Texas: http://www.statutes.legis.state.tx.us/Docs/ED/htm/ED.54.htm#54. 241

Utah: http://le.utah.gov/code/TITLE53B/pdf/53B08_010200.pdf

Virginia: http://lis.virginia.gov/cgi-bin/legp604.exe?000+cod+23-7.4

Washington: http://apps.leg.wa.gov/documents/billdocs/2013-14/Pdf/ Bills/Senate%20Passed%20Legislature/5318.PL.pdf

STATES CURRENTLY WITH STATE-BASED EDUCATION BENEFITS

Alabama: http://www.va.state.al.us/gi_dep_scholarship.aspx

California: https://www.calvet.ca.gov/veteran-services-benefits/education

Connecticut: http://www.ct.gov/ctva/cwp/view.asp?A=2014&Q=290874

Florida: http://floridavets.org/?page_id=60

Illinois: http://www2.illinois.gov/veterans/benefits/Pages/education.aspx

Indiana: http://www.in.gov/dva/2378.htm

Maryland: http://www.mdva.state.md.us/state/scholarships.html

Massachusetts: http://www.mass.gov/veterans/education/financial-assistance/tuition-waivers.html

Minnesota: http://mn.gov/mdva/resources/education/minnesotagibill.jsp

Missouri: http://www.dhe.mo.gov/files/moretheroesact.pdf

Montana: http://wsd.dli.mt.gov/veterans/vetedu.asp

New York: http://www.hesc.ny.gov/pay-for-college/financial-aid/types-of-financial-aid/nys-grants-scholarships-awards/msrs-scholarship.html

North Carolina: http://www.doa.state.nc.us/vets/scholarshipclasses.aspx

Oregon: http://www.oregon.gov/odva/BENEFITS/Pages/OregonEducationBenefit.aspx

South Carolina: http://va.sc.gov/benefits.html

South Dakota: http://vetaffairs.sd.gov/benefits/State/State%20Education%20Programs.aspx

Tennessee: http://www.tn.gov/sos/rules/1640/1640-01-22.20090529.pdf

Texas: http://veterans.portal.texas.gov/en/Pages/education.aspx

Utah: http://veterans.utah.gov/state-benefits/

Virgin Islands: http://www.militaryvi.org/benefits/

Washington: http://apps.leg.wa.gov/RCW/default.aspx?cite=28B.15.621

West Virginia: http://www.veterans.wv.gov/Pages/default.aspx

Wisconsin: http://www.wisvets.com/wisgibill

Wyoming: http://www.communitycolleges.wy.edu/Data/Sites/1/commissionFiles/Programs/Veteran/_doc/statue-19-14-106.pdf

ACTIVE DUTY EDUCATION CENTERS

Aberdeen Proving Ground, Maryland
  DSN: 312-458-2042
  Commercial: (410) 306-2042
  Baumholder, Germany
  DSN: 314-485-8893
  Commercial: 011-49-678-36-6484 / 8893
  Brussels, Belgium
  DSN: 368-9704
  Commercial: 011-32-27-17-9704
  Camp Arifjan, Kuwait
  DSN: 318-430-1322
  Camp As-Sayliyah, Qatar
  DSN: 318-432-2104
  Commercial: 011-974-460-9869 Ext 2974
  Camp Buehring, Kuwait
  DSN: 318-824-3389
  Camp Caroll, Korea
  DSN: 315-765-7730

Commercial: 011-82-54-970-7702
Camp Casey, Korea
DSN: 315-730-1826
Commercial: 011-82-31-869-1826
Camp Henry, Korea
DSN: 315-768-7919
Commercial: 011-82-53-470-6693
Camp Hovey, Korea
DSN 315-730-5161
Commercial: 011-82-31-869-5161
Camp Humphreys, Korea
DSN: 315-753-8901
Commercial: 011-82-31-690-8901 / 04
Camp Red Cloud, Korea
DSN: 315- 732-6329
Commercial: 011-82-31-870-6329
Camp Shelby, Mississippi
DSN: 312-286-2029
Commercial: (601) 558-2029
Camp Stanley, Korea
DSN: 315-732-4603
Commercial: 011-82-31-870-5731 / 5025
Camp Zama, Japan
DSN: 315-263-3015 Commercial: 011-81-46-407-3015
Carlisle Barracks, Pennsylvania
DSN 314-688-5389
Commercial: (845) 938-5389
Detroit Arsenal, Michigan
DSN: 314-786-5791
Commercial: (586) 282-5791
Djibouti, Africa
DSN: 311-824-4250
Dugway Proving Ground, Utah
Commercial: (435) 831-2905
Eglin Air Base, Florida
Commercial: (850) 883-1250
Elmendorf-Richardson, Alaska
Commercial: (907) 384-0970
Fort Belvoir, Virginia
Commercial: (703) 805-9264
Fort Benning, Georgia
Commercial: (706) 545-7397
Fort Bliss, Texas

Commercial: (915) 744-1333
Fort Bragg, North Carolina
Commercial: (910) 396-6721
Fort Buchanan, Puerto Rico
DSN: 312-740-4354 / 4352 / 2409
Commercial: (787) 707-4354 / 4352 / 2409
Fort Campbell, Kentucky
Commercial: (270) 798-3201
Fort Carson, Colorado
DSN: 312-691-2124
Commercial: (719) 526-2124
Fort Detrick, Maryland
DSN: 312-343-2854
Commercial: (301) 619-2854
Email: usarmy.detrick.usag.mbx.dhr-aces@mail.mil
Fort Drum, New York
Commercial: (315) 772-6878
Email: drum.edcounselor@us.army.mil
Fort Meade, Maryland
Commercial: (301) 677-6421
Fort Gordon, Georgia
DSN: 312-780-2000 / 3622
Commercial: 312-791-2000 / 3622
Email: usarmy.gordon.imcom.list.education-counselors@mail.mil
Fort Hamilton, New York
DSN: 312-232-4715
Commercial: (718) 630-4715
Fort Hood, Texas
Commercial: (254) 287-4432 / 4824
Fort Huachuca, Arizona
DSN: 312-821-3010
Commercial (520) 533-3010 / 2255
Fort Irwin, California
Commercial: (760) 380-4218
Fort Jackson, South Carolina
Commercial: (803) 751-5341
Fort Knox, Kentucky
Commercial: (502) 624-2427 / 4136
Fort Leavenworth, Kansas
Commercial: (913) 684-2496
Fort Lee, Virginia
DSN: 312-539-3570 / 1
Commercial: (804) 765-3570 / 1

Fort Leonard Wood, Missouri
Commercial: (573) 596-0172
Fort Polk, Louisiana
Commercial: (337) 531-1993
Fort Riley, Kansas
DSN: 312-856-6481
Commercial: (785) 239-6481
Email: usarmy.riley.imcom.mbx.education-service@mail.mil
Fort Rucker, Alabama
DSN: 312-558-2378
Commercial: (334) 255-2378
Fort Sam Houston, Texas
DSN: 312-471-1738
Commercial: (210) 221-1738
Fort Sill, Oklahoma
Commercial: (580) 442-3201
Fort Stewart, Georgia
DSN: 312-870-8331
Commercial: (912) 767-8331
Email: usarmy.stewart.usag.list.dhr-education-counselor@mail.mil
Fort Story, Virginia
Commercial: (757) 422-7151
Fort Wainwright, Alaska
Commercial: (907) 361-7486
Garmisch, Germany
DSN: 314-440-3560
Commercial: 011-49-8821-750-3560
Hohenfels, Germany
DSN: 314-466-2259
Commercial: 011-49-9472-83-2668 / 2882
Email: usarmy.bavaria.imcom-europe.list.hohenfels-aces@mail.mil and
usaghohenfels.edcenter.counseling@us.army.mil
Hunter Army Airfield, Georgia
DSN: 312-971-6130
Commercial: (912) 315-6130
Email: usarmy.stewart.usag.list.dhr-education-counselor@mail.mil
Illesheim, Germany
DSN: 314-467-4750
Commercial: 011-49-9841-83-750
Joint Task Force Bravo, Soto Cano, Honduras
DSN: 312-449-4999 / 4495
Commercial: 011-504-2713-5123 Ext 4495
Katterbach, Germany

DSN: 314-467-2817
Commercial: 011-49-9802-83-2817
Kleber Kaserne, Germany
DSN: 314-483-8125 / 7427
Landstuhl, Germany
DSN: 314-486-6797
Commercial: 011-49-637-186-6822 / 5331
Langley-Eustis, Virginia
DSN: 312-826-20823
Commercial: (757) 878-2083
Lewis-McChord, Washington
DSN: 312-357-7174
Commercial: (253) 967-7174
Email: usarmy.jblm.imcom.list.dhr-aces-education-office@mail.mil
Livorno, Italy
DSN: 314-633-7073
Email: livorno.edcenter@us.army.mil
MacDill Air Base, Florida
DSN: 312-968-3795
Commercial: (813) 828-3795
Miami Joint, Florida
DSN: 312-567-2287
Commercial: (305) 437-2287
Miesau, Germany
DSN: 314-481 3863
Commercial: 011-49-637-2842-3863
Myer-Henderson, Virginia
DSN: 312-426-3070
Commercial: (703) 696-3070
Email: usarmy.jbmhh.asa.mbx.education-center@mail.mil
North Camp MFO, Egypt
Commercial: 011-972-86-281-801-3404
Email: eso@mfo.org
Presidio of Monterey, California
DSN: 312-768-5325
Commercial: (831) 242-5325
Email: USARMY.PoM.106-Sig-Bde.List.PRES-EDCTR@mail.mil
Redstone Arsenal, Alabama
Commercial: (256) 876-9761
Email: redstone.edcenter@us.army.mil
Rhine Ordinance Barracks, Germany
DSN: 314-493-2588 / 2590
Commercial: 011-49-0631-3406-2588 / 2590

Rock Island Arsenal, Illinois
DSN: 312-793-2065
Commercial: (309) 782-2065
Schinnen, Netherlands
DSN: 314-360-7641 / 7651 / 7613
Commercial: 0031-046-443-7641 / 7651 / 7613
Email: usarmy.schinnen.imcom-europe.mbx.usag-schinnen-education
@mail.mil
Schofield Barracks, Hawaii
Commercial: (808) 655-0800 / 0805
Seoul Air Base, Korea
DSN: 315-723-7194 / 8098
Commercial: 011-822-7913 / 7194 / 8098
SHAPE, Belgium
DSN: 314-423-3466
Commercial: 011-32-65-44-3466
Email: usarmy.benelux.imcom-europe.mbx.dhr-education-center@mail
.mil
South Camp MFO, Egypt
Commercial: 011-972-86-281-801-4515
Email: sclpm@mfo.org
Stuttgart, Germany
DSN: 314-431-2506
Commercial: 011-49-7031-15-2506
Email: usarmy.stuttgart.usag.mbx.stuttgart-ed-center@mail.mil
Suwan Air Base, Korea
DSN: 315-788-5026
Torii Station, Okinawa, Japan
DSN: (315) 644-4463
Commercial: (719) 567-1110 Ext 315-644-4463
Tripler/Fort Shafter, Hawaii
Commercial: (808) 433-4184
Vicenza, Italy
DSN: 314-634-8925
Email: vicenza.edcenter@us.army.mil
Vilseck, Germany
DSN: 314- 476-2753
Commercial: 011-49-9662-83-2753
Email: usarmy.grafenwoehr.imcom.mbx.usag-grafenwoehr-aces@mail
.mil
Walter Reed, Washington DC
DSN: 314-295-2014
Commercial: (301) 295-2014

West Point, New York
DSN: 314-688-3762 / 3464
Commercial: (845) 938-3762 / 3464
White Sands, New Mexico
DSN: 314-258-4222
Commercial: (575) 678-4222 / 4211
Wiesbaden, Germany
DSN: 314-548-1302Commercial: 011-49-611-143-548-1302
Email: usarmy.wiesbaden.imcom-europe.list.education-center@mail.mil
Yongsan, Korea
DSN: 315-723-7194 / 4298 / 7783
Commercial: 011-822-7913-7194 / 4298 / 7783
Yuma Proving Ground, Arizona
DSN: 314-899-3926
Commercial: (928) 328-3926
Email: usarmy.ypg.imcom.mbx.education-center@mail.mil

NATIONAL GUARD EDUCATION CENTERS

Guard Support Center, Professional Education Center
DSN: 312-962-4940
Commercial: (866) 628-5999
Email: arng.gsc@mail.mil
Alabama
Commercial: (866) 456-2764 (Pin: 7528)
Alaska
Commercial: (907) 428-6228 / 6477 / 6674
Arizona
Commercial: (602) 267-2113
Email: usarmy.az.azarng.list.g1-education@mail.mil
Arkansas
Commercial: (501) 212-4022
Email: ng.ar.ararng.list.education-office@mail.mil
California, Northern
Commercial: (866) 338-2863
California, Southern
Commercial: (866) 338-2826
Colorado
Commercial: (719) 524-0997
Connecticut
Commercial: (401) 275-4143
Delaware

Commercial: (302) 326-7044
Email: usarmy.de.dearng.list.ngde-j1-eso@mail.mil
District of Columbia
Commercial: (202) 685-9908
Florida
DSN: 312-822-0398
Commercial: (904) 823-0398
Georgia
Commercial: (678) 569-5067
Guam
Commercial: (671) 735-0454
Hawaii
Commercial: (808) 672-1019
Email: hiarng.education@us.army.mil
Idaho
Commercial: (208) 272-3761
Illinois
Commercial: (217) 761-3698
Email: NGILG1incentives@ng.army.mil
Indiana
Commercial: (317) 964-7027
Email: ng.in.inarng.list.j1arp-eds@mail.mil
Iowa
Commercial: (515) 252-4468
Email: educationia@ng.army.mil
Kansas
Commercial: (785) 274-1814
Kentucky
Commercial: (502) 607-1550
Email: ng.ky.kyarng.mbx.education-services-office-mailbox@mail.mil
Louisiana
Commercial: (504) 278-8356 / 8314
Maine
Commercial: (207) 430-6220
Email: ng.me.arng.list.j1-esos@mail.mil
Maryland
Commercial: (410) 576-1499 / 6093 / 6025
Email: MDNG_Education@md.ngb.army.mil
Massachusetts
Commercial: (339) 202-3183
Michigan
Commercial: (517) 481-9839 / 9841
Email: ngmirrbta@ng.army.mil

Minnesota
Commercial: (651) 282-4589
Email: ng.mn.mnarng.mbx.assets-education@mail.mil
Mississippi
Commercial: (866) 403-1289
Missouri
Commercial: (573) 638-9500 Ext 7645
Montana
Commercial: (406) 324-3236
Email: ngmtmilitaryed@ng.army.mil
Nebraska
Commercial: (402) 309-8169
Email: ng.ne.nearng.list.ngne-education@mail.mil
Nevada
Email: ng.nv.nvarng.mbx.ngnv-eso@mail.mil
New Hampshire
Commercial: (603) 225-1312
New Jersey
Commercial: (609) 562-0797
Email: ng.nj.njarng.list.nj-education@mail.mil
New Mexico
Commercial: (505) 474-1746
Email: ng.nm.nmarng.list.education@mail.mil
New York
Commercial: (518) 272 6831
Email: ng.ny.nyarng.list.education-ny@mail.mil
North Carolina
Commercial: (919) 664-6272Email: nceso@ng.army.mil
North Dakota
Commercial: (701) 333-3071
Email: mailto:ng.nd.ndarng.list.j1-esos2@mail.mil
Ohio
Commercial: (614) 336-7275
Oklahoma
Commercial: (405) 228-5676
Email: ng.ok.okarng.mbx.education-incentives@mail.mil
Oregon
Commercial: (503) 584-3434
Pennsylvania
Commercial: (866) 920-7902
Email: ng.pa.paarng.list.jfhq-g1-education@mail.mil
Puerto Rico
Commercial: (787) 289-1126

Rhode Island
Commercial: (401) 275-4143
South Carolina
Commercial: (803) 299-4213
South Dakota
Commercial: (605) 737-6087
Tennessee
Commercial: (615) 313-0592
Email: ng.tn.tnarng.list.ngtn-j1-education@mail.mil
Texas
Commercial: (512) 782-5515
Email: ng.tx.txarng.list.education-office@mail.mil
Utah
Commercial: (801) 432-4345
Email: utng.education@us.army.mil
Vermont
DSN: 312-636-3378
Commercial: (802) 338-3378
Virgin Islands
Commercial: (340) 712-7734
Virginia
DSN: 312-441-6222
Commercial: (434) 298-3020
Email: ng.va.vaarng.mbx.ngva-education@mail.mil
Washington
Commercial: (253) 512-8435
Email: usarmy.wa.waarng.list.per-education@mail.mil
West Virginia
Commercial: (304) 561-6366
Wisconsin
Commercial: (608) 242-3454
Wyoming
Commercial: (307) 772-5069

RESERVE EDUCATION CENTERS

1st MSC, Fort Buchanan, Puerto Rico
    DSN: 312-740-4354 / 4352 / 2409
    Commercial: (787) 707-4354 / 4352 / 2409
9th MSC, Honolulu, Hawaii
    DSN: 315-438-1600 Ext 3298
    Commercial: (808) 438-1600 Ext 3298

Email: Education@9rsc.army.mil
63rd RSC East, North Little Rock, Arkansas
Commercial: (501) 771-7340
63rd RSC West, Los Alamitos, California
Commercial: (562) 795-1231
7th Civil Support Command, Wiesbaden, Germany
DSN: 314-337-7435
Commercial: 011-49-611-705-7435
81st RSC, Birmingham, Alabama
Commercial: (205) 795-1538
88th RSC, Fort Snelling, Minnesota
Commercial: (612) 713-3081
88th RSC, Fort McCoy, Wisconsin
Commercial: (608) 388-7311
88th RSC North, Salt Lake City, Utah
Commercial: (801) 656-4244
88th RSC South, Wichita, Kansas
Commercial: (316) 681-1759 Ext 1352 / 1367 / 1279 / 1376
88th RSC West, Washington
Commercial: (253) 671-6324
99th RSC East, Fort Devens, Massachusetts
Commercial: (978) 796-2331
99th RSC North, Fort Belvior Belvoir, Virginia
Commercial: (800) 845-3362
99th RSC West, Coraopolis, Pennsylvania
Commercial: (800) 567-9518
Email: usarmy.usarc.99-rsc.mbx.education-services1@mail.mil
HQ USACAPOC, Fort Bragg, North Carolina
Commercial: (910) 432-5745

Notes

2. EDUCATIONAL CONCERNS FOR ACTIVE-DUTY PERSONNEL AND VETERANS

1. Kimberly Griffin and Claire Gilbert, Center for American Progress, "Easing the Transition from Combat to Classroom," last modified April 2012, accessed June 2, 2013, http://www.americanprogress.org/wp-content/uploads/issues/2012/04/pdf/student_veterans.pdf.

2. Nisha Money, Monique Moore, David Brown, Kathleen Kasper, Jessica Roeder, Paul Bartone, and Mark Bates, "Best Practices Identified for Peer Support Programs," Defense Centers of Excellence, January 1, 2011, accessed October 10, 2014, http://www.dcoe.mil/content/Navigation/Documents./
Best_Practices_Identified_for_Peer_Support_Programs Jan 2011.pdf.

3. The University of Alabama Student Affairs, "Veteran and Military Affairs," accessed January 7, 2015, http://vets.ua.edu/.

4. WHAT SHOULD I LOOK FOR IN A SCHOOL?

1. Sandy Baum and Jennifer Ma, "Trends in Higher Education 2014," College Board, http://trends.collegeboard.org/sites/default/files/2014-trends-college-pricing-final-web.pdf (accessed October 21, 2014).

2. Health, Education, Labor, and Pensions Committee, "For Profit Higher Education: The Failure to Safeguard the Federal Investment and Ensure Student Success," last modified July 30, 2012, http://www.help.senate.gov/imo/media/for_profit_report/PartI.pdf.

3. National Association of Independent Colleges and Universities, "Independent Colleges and Universities: A National Profile," last modified Marchy 8, 2011, http://www.naicu.edu/docLib/20110317_NatProfile-Final4.pdf.

4. Judith Eaton, "An Overview of U.S. Accreditation," Council for Higher Education Accreditation, http://www.chea.org/odf/Overview%20of%20US%20Accreditation%202012.pdf (last modified August 2012).

5. Barbara Brittingham, et al. "The Value of Accreditation," Council for Higher Education Accreditation, June 1, 2010, accessed October 25, 2014, http://www.chea.org/odf/Value of US Accreditation 06.29.2010_buttons.pdf.

5. UNIQUE ARMY-BASED PROGRAMS

1. *U.S. News and World Report*, January 1, 2015, accessed January 5, 2015, http://colleges.usnews.rankingsandreviews.com/best-colleges/search?name=United States Military Academy&state=).

2. "America's Medical School What You Need To Know," Uniformed Services University, May 1, 2014, accessed December 5, 2014, http://www.usuhs.edu/medschool/pdf/What-YouNeedtoKnow.pdf.

6. COST AND PAYMENT RESOURCES

1. Federal Student Aid, "School Costs and Net Price," accessed November 5, 2014, https://studentaid.ed.gov/prepare-for-college/choosing-schools/consider#school-costs-and-net-price.

2. Federal Student Aid, "How Aid Is Calculated," accessed November 5, 2014, https://studentaid.ed.gov/fafsa/next-steps/how-calculated.

3. Ibid.

9. VOCATIONAL PROGRAMS

1. "Registered Apprenticeship," US Department of Labor Employment and Training Administration, January 10, 2010, accessed November 1, 2014, http://www.doleta.gov/oa/aboutus.cfm#admin.

2. "American Apprenticeship Initiative," US Department of Labor Employment and Training Administration, December 11, 2014, accessed December 15, 2014, http://www.doleta.gov/oa/aboutus.cfm#admin.

10. VA PROGRAMS

1. "Veterans Upward Bound Program," US Department of Education, http://www2.ed.gov/programs/triovub/index.html (last modified June 30, 2014).

11. OTHER SERVICE MEMBER AND SPOUSAL-BASED PROGRAMS/ORGANIZATIONS

1. Council for Higher Education Accreditation, "Database of Institutions and Programs Accredited by Recognized United States Accrediting Organizations," January 1, 2015, accessed January 5, 2015, http://chea.org/search/default.asp.

Bibliography

American Council on Education, "Military Guide Frequently Asked Questions," accessed December 13, 2013, http://www.acenet.edu/news-room/Pages/Military-Guide-Frequently-Asked-Questions.aspx.

"America's Medical School What You Need To Know," Uniformed Services University, May 1, 2014, accessed December 5, 2014, http://www.usuhs.edu/medschool/pdf/WhatYouNeed-toKnow.pdf.

Army Credentialing, Opportunities OnLine, December 3, 2014, accessed October 19, 2014, https://www.cool.army.mil/.

"Army Knowledge Online," January 1, 2013, accessed December 5, 2014, https://www.us.army.mil.

Baum, Sandy, and Jennifer Ma, College Board, "Trends in Higher Education 2013," accessed July 12, 2013, http://trends.collegeboard.org/sites/default/files/college pricing-2013-full-report.pdf.

Brittingham, Barbara, Mary Jane Harris, Michael Lambert, Frank Murray, George Peterson, Jerry Trapnell, Peter Vlasses, et al., "The Value of Accreditation," Council for Higher Education Accreditation, June 1, 2010, accessed October 25, 2014, http://www.chea.org/pdf/Value%20of%20US%20Accreditation%2006.29.2010_buttons.pdf.

Career One Stop, "Get Credentials," January 1, 2015, accessed November 13, 2014, http://www.careeronestop.org/EducationTraining/KeepLearning/GetCredentials.aspx.

College Board, "Veterans and College Admissions: FAQs," accessed December 5, 2014, https://bigfuture.collegeboard.org/get-in/applying-101/veterans-college-admission-faqs.

College Board, "Why Community College," accessed October 17, 2014, http://professionals.collegeboard.com/guidance/college/community-college.

The Council for Higher Education Accreditation, "Database of Institutions and Programs Accredited by Recognized United States Accrediting Organizations," January 1, 2015, accessed January 5, 2015, http://chea.org/search/default.asp.

The Council for Higher Education Accreditation, "The Fundamentals of Accreditation," last modified September 2002, accessed October 29, 2014, http://www.chea.org/pdf/fund_accred_20ques_02.pdf.

Council of Regional Accrediting Commissions, "Regional Accreditation and Student Learning: Principles for Good Practice," last modified May 2003, http://www.msche.org/publications/Regnlsl050208135331.pdf.

Defense Activity for Non-Traditional Education Support, "Troops to Teachers," last modified July 2, 2013, http://www.dantes.doded.mil/Programs/TTT.html.

Eaton, Judith, The Council for Higher Education Accreditation, "An Overview of U.S. Accreditation," last modified August 2012, http://www.chea.org/pdf/Overview%20of%20US%20Accreditation%202012.pdf.

Federal Student Aid, "For Members of the U.S. Armed Forces," February 1, 2013, accessed December 2, 2014, https://studentaid.ed.gov/sites/default/files/military-student-loan-benefits.pdf.

Federal Student Aid, "How Aid Is Calculated," accessed November 5, 2014, https://studentaid.ed.gov/fafsa/next-steps/how-calculated.

Federal Student Aid, "School Costs and Net Price," accessed November 5, 2014, https://studentaid.ed.gov/prepare-for-college/choosing-schools/consider#school-costs-and-net-price.

Federal Trade Commission, "Choosing a Vocational School," last modified August 2012, http://www.consumer.ftc.gov/articles/0241-choosing-vocational-school.

Griffin, Kimberly, and Claire Gilbert. The Center for American Progress, "Easy the Transition from Combat to Classroom," last modified April 2012, accessed June 2, 2013, http://www.americanprogress.org/wp-content/uploads/issues/2012/04/pdf/student_veterans.pdf.

Health, Education, Labor, and Pensions Committee, "For Profit Higher Education: The Failure to Safeguard the Federal Investment and Ensure Student Success," last modified July 30, 2012, http://www.help.senate.gov/imo/media/for_profit_report/PartI.pdf.

Kleinman, Rebecca, Annalisa Mastri, Davin Reed, Debbie Reed, Samina Sattar, Albert Yung-Hsu Liu, and Jessica Ziegler, Mathematica Policy Research, "An Effectiveness Assessment and Cost-Benefit Analysis of Registered Apprenticeship in 10 States," last modified July 25, 2012, http://wdr.doleta.gov/research/FullText_Documents/ETAOP_2012_10.pdf.

Kurtzleben, Danielle, "Apprenticeships a Little-Traveled Path to Jobs," *U.S. News and World Report*, January 13, 2013, http://www.usnews.com/news/articles/2013/01/13/apprenticeships-a-little-traveled-path-to-jobs (accessed March 4, 2013).

Maryland Higher Education Commission, "The Importance of Accreditation," accessed October 29, 2014, http://www.mhec.state.md.us/highered/colleges_universities/accreditation.asp.

Money, Nisha, Monique Moore, David Brown, Kathleen Kasper, Jessica Roeder, Paul Bartone, and Mark Bates, "Best Practices Identified for Peer Support Programs," Defense Centers of Excellence, last modified January 1, 2011, http://www.dcoe.mil/content/Navigation/Documents/Best_Practices_Identified_for_Peer_Support_Programs_Jan_2011.pdf.

National Association of Independent Colleges and Universities, "Independent Colleges and Universities: a National Profile," last modified March 8, 2011, http://www.naicu.edu/docLib/20110317_NatProfile-Final4.pdf

National Skills Coalition, "On-the-Job Training Recommendations for Inclusion in a Federal Jobs Bill," last modified January 2010, http://www.nationalskillscoalition.org/resources/publications/file/issue-brief-cte.pdf.

Peterson's, "Colleges and Universities: Choosing the Right Fit," accessed October 29, 2014, http://www.petersons.com/college-search/colleges-universities-choosing-fit.aspx.

State of California Employment Development Department, "Workforce Investment Act," accessed December 1, 2014, http://www.edd.ca.gov/jobs_and_Training/Workforce_Investment_Act.htm.

University of Alabama, "Veteran and Military Affairs," January 1, 2009, accessed January 5, 2015, http://vets.ua.edu/.

US Department of Education, "Accreditation in the United States," last modified December 1, 2014, http://www2.ed.gov/admins/finaid/accred/accreditation_pg2.html.

US Department of Education, "Career Colleges and Technical Schools—Choosing a School," last modified June 18, 2013, http://www2.ed.gov/students/prep/college/consumerinfo/choosing.html.

US Department of Education, "Federal Versus Private Loans," accessed November 15, 2014, http://studentaid.ed.gov/types/loans/federal-vs-private.

US Department of Education, "Learn About Your College and Career School Options," accessed October 29, 2014, http://studentaid.ed.gov/prepare-for-college/choosing-schools/types.

US Department of Education, "Veterans Upward Bound Program," last modified December 31, 2014, http://www2.ed.gov/programs/triovub/index.html.

US Department of Labor, "Unemployment Compensation for Ex-Servicemembers," accessed November 20, 2014, http://workforcesecurity.doleta.gov/unemploy/ucx.asp.

US Department of Labor, "Unemployment Insurance," accessed November 20, 2014, http://www.dol.gov/dol/topic/unemployment-insurance/.

US Department of Labor Employment and Training Administration, "American Apprenticeship Initiative," December 11, 2014, accessed December 15, 2014, http://www.doleta.gov/oa/aboutus.cfm#admin.

US Department of Labor Employment and Training Administration, "Registered Apprenticeship," January 10, 2010, accessed November 1, 2014, http://www.doleta.gov/oa/aboutus.cfm#admin.

US Department of Labor Employment and Training Administration, "Registered Apprenticeship: A Solution to the Skills Shortage," accessed February 2, 2014, http://www.doleta.gov/oa/pdf/fsfront.pdf.

US Department of Veterans Affairs, "On-the-Job Training and Apprenticeship," last modified November 4, 2014, accessed November 20, 2014, http://www.benefits.va.gov/gibill/onthejob_apprenticeship.asp.

US Department of Veterans Affairs, "Tuition Assistance Top Up," last modified December 2, 2014, http://www.benefits.va.gov/gibill/tuition_assistance.asp.

US Senate: Health, Education, Labor, and Pensions Committee, "For Profit Higher Education: The Failure to Safeguard the Federal Investment and Ensure Student Success," last modified July 30, 2012, http://www.help.senate.gov/imo/media/for_profit_report/PartI.pdf

Index

Index

About the Authors

JillianVentrone's family's service background extends from World War I through the current war in Afghanistan, from Air Force pilots to the Marine Corps Infantry, including two Purple Heart recipients. Her job as a service members' higher education counselor aboard a federal installation has her working with combat veterans who aspire to pursue higher education. She has a passion for veterans and their higher education benefits, and writing this book enabled her to disseminate much needed information.

Paul Karczewski has lived in Army communities for the majority of his life. After growing up the son of an Army career NCO he chose to give back to the same community that had helped shape the person he is today. He jumped at the opportunity to work with service members in a variety of downrange locations as an education counselor and instantly knew he wanted to continue to serve soldiers in this capacity. Once coming back home he now guides transitioning service members in navigating the often complex and confusing world of higher education.